Hidden Holiness

Hidden Holiness

Michael Plekon

FOREWORD BY ROWAN WILLIAMS

University of Notre Dame Press
Notre Dame, Indiana

Library of Congress Cataloging-in-Publication Data

Plekon, Michael, 1948–
Hidden holiness / Michael Plekon ; foreword by Rowan Williams.
    p.   cm.
Includes bibliographical references and index.
ISBN-13: 978-0-268-03893-9 (pbk. : alk. paper)
ISBN-10: 0-268-03893-7 (pbk. : alk. paper)
1. Holiness.   I. Title.
BT767.P73   2009
234'.8—dc22

                                        2009001153

Contents

Contents
vi

Foreword

"The patriarch Enoch was a shoemaker; with every stitch by which he joined the lower leather of a shoe to the upper leather, he united the Glory that is below with the Glory that is above." This ancient rabbinical Jewish saying represents a vision in which holiness is a matter of connecting the ordinary matter of earth with its depths in the life of God. The saint is not primarily the high achiever of the moral life, the honours graduate in discipleship, but the person in whom the depths of the ordinary become visible. The face of the saint is just as the tradition of Orthodox icon painting conceives it—a face that is unmistakably distinctive and human, yet "thinned out" so as to let the light through, the light that is found in the deep background of the picture.

It is a model of holiness that makes specially clear sense in the context of the basic belief of Christians that humanity is, in the life of Jesus Christ, taken up into the active energy of God, so that the plain elements of a human body and a human psychology are made carriers of God's infinite gift—burning but not consumed. So we should expect a holy life to be one that shed light around it, and (to pick up what is still a requirement for the recognition of sanctity in the Western Church) that was a cause of joy to those who encountered it.

But, given the shape and character of what Christians acknowledge about the unique holiness of Jesus Christ, we shouldn't be surprised if the light and the joy were manifest in the middle of profound loss, trauma, and human failure. Holiness is nothing to do with measurable success, not even with an unbroken record of triumphantly negotiating temptation and avoiding error and hurt. Saints can hurt and be hurt; they can exhibit wildly fluctuating behaviour and chaotic judgement. Yet, in the light of the Gospel, what matters is their fidelity to the source of light and energy, their freedom to let their fractured humanity be upheld and saturated in that infinite gift that is God in Christ at work in the Spirit.

Father Michael Plekon has written before about holiness in the modern Orthodox world, and has done so with learning, profound sympathy, and imagination. Here he extends his reach, boldly, to discern the marks of Christ-like holiness in figures both inside and outside the Orthodox Christian family, not to say at the edges of any sort of explicit Christian faith. He does so not to minimise the absolute centrality of confessing that faith gratefully and joyfully as the truth delivered once and for all, but to remind us of the liberty of our God to work with even the most obscure and deeply buried turnings of the human heart towards God. He challenges us to accept the fact that the light of the infinite gift shines in unlikely and unrespectable places, and by doing so he deepens our sense of what that gift is and means for the human race. These portraits of surprising sanctity, transformed faces where we had not thought to look for them, transparent lives in which confusion and failure are overcome through an unceasing awareness of the gift of Jesus Christ, will speak powerfully to our society. The world around us does not look for high achievers or religious celebrities, but for the saving glimpse of what is quite Other to us, made known in a humanity we recognise as really human. Only the saint—not the hero or the success story—can meet this hunger for light and truth and transformation. In these vivid pages, this is what is offered for our challenge and our joy.

Rowan Williams, Archbishop of Canterbury
Lambeth Palace, Pentecost 2008

Introduction

The manifest just are themselves sustained by these hidden ones. Moreover that within them which serves to sustain men belongs to their
hidden and not to their manifest nature. All that sustains belongs to
the realm of the hidden.[1]

There has been an explosion of interest in saints in recent years. The
cries and banners with the message *subito santo*—"a saint very soon"—
during the funeral of Pope John Paul II come to mind. This same John
Paul II was responsible during his tenure for creating more saints in the
Roman Catholic Church than any other pope. Perhaps too the death of
Mother Teresa of Calcutta tells us a great deal. The almost immediate emer-
gence of her veneration and a very swift start of the process for her canonization are signs of this fascination. For years she was before us as a kind of
"living saint," there on our television screens and in media photos, like John
Paul II. And (as we shall see) the publication of letters documenting her
spiritual struggles have caused a sensation, provoking suspicion but also
massive interest in what holiness looks and sounds like in a person's life.

I will mention quite a few books that have done well, all of them about
saints. This tells me that we remain intrigued by holy women and men,
whether officially recognized as saints or not. Jesuit James Martin is an

author who comes to mind quickly. In his volumes are many great holy women and men from the past whose lives (and escapades) are nothing short of extraordinary—the martyr Joan of Arc, contemplative Carmelite nun and mystic Thérèse of Lisieux, Peter the apostle, as well as Mother Teresa. But Martin also chooses to look at some very complicated, yes, even flawed individuals from our own time, people such as social activist Dorothy Day, monk and writer Thomas Merton, and the priest and author Henri Nouwen. And what makes Martin's books so appealing is the way in which he shares how the saints and other persons of faith have been important to him, caught up in the journey of his own life. I hope to do some of that here, although with much less of my own biographical baggage imposed on the reader.

We are much taken with saints but also put off by their feats and their seemingly unattainable virtues. But are we wrong in thinking this way? Could it be that we have missed some very important truths about saints? Orthodox lay theologian Paul Evdokimov reminds us that becoming a saint has little to do with virtue and a great deal to do with goodness, being like God. And everyone can become like God![2]

This book stems directly from my earlier ones about holy people.[3] In them, my focus was on the lives and writings of a number of figures from the Eastern Church tradition in the modern era. My aim was to examine both their diverse incarnations of holiness as well as their often provocative ideas about this. In particular I was interested in their ideas about the shape of holiness in our time, something to which each of them gave expression in their own actions. What follows here also flows from teaching religious studies and about persons of faith in our time at a very large, public university. With over a hundred language groups represented in the students and faculty, Baruch College of the City University of New York has been a kind of laboratory for me, not only for assessing what students of very diverse ethnic and religious traditions think about holiness but for listening to their responses to what holy people themselves have said and done. A great many of the accounts of both holy people and holiness in our time conveyed here have been tested with my students, as well as with groups at retreats and conferences, and with excellent response everywhere.

I have also "tested" my thinking about holiness and its shape with a number of very generous colleagues who were good enough to take time

out of their very full schedules to read what I had written and respond criti-
cally. I especially want to thank his eminence, Archbishop of Canterbury
Rowan Williams, for his encouragement and positive assessment of what
I will put forward here. Likewise, I am grateful to Brother Patrick Hart,
Brother Christopher Mark, Antoine Arjakovsky, Robert Thompson, Sophia
Compton, Jerry Ryan, Carol Zaleski, and Frs. John Bostwick, William Mills,
and John Garvey for their careful reading, criticism, suggestions, and enthusiasm for the project. I want to thank both Fr. Alexis Vinogradov, my
colleague at our parish and a friend, and Bishop Seraphim Sigrist, also a
friend and colleague, for many conversations that they will recognize here.
I especially want to thank Sara Miles, whose own remarkable account of her
conversion I read while writing, for her insightful suggestions and strong
support. This book would not have been completed without the sabbati-
cal I was given in the 2007–2008 academic year, and for it I am grateful
to my chair, Glenn Petersen, the members of my department, the person-
nel and budget committee, and dean Jeffrey Peck of the Weissman School
of Arts and Science of Baruch College of the City University of New York.
I also thank those from the University of Notre Dame Press who contributed to the publication process, especially Barbara Hanrahan and Matthew
Dowd. Finally I want to thank all those who helped provide the photos
for the gallery in this volume. I believe it is crucial to have a face to connect with the words and voices heard in the text. While it isn't possible for
the gallery of images to be exhaustive, I have tried to provide images of
many to whom we listen throughout the book.

All of the people mentioned above were most generous with their time
and were especially encouraging about my striving for an ecumenical perspective in this look at holiness. The diversity of Christians from the Anglican, Catholic, Orthodox, and other churches—both the writers and figures in this book as well as those who "tested" the text—witness, I hope, to
my aim to be truly catholic in listening to the saints and following after them
in everyday life. To them and others too many to be named, my thanks.

In this book there are a number of things about saints and sanctity
upon which I want to reflect. One is that there is a crisis of holiness in our
time. Is it possible, as a colleague has asked, to exhaustively define a "saint,"
to specify what constitutes "sanctity," over against the life and actions
of a good person, say a remarkable humanitarian who is an atheist or an

agnostic? Can we call such a person a saint?[4] I want to say at the outset that the "official," that is, the ecclesiastical process of recognizing saints, either in the East or the West, is not my focus. The canonizing, or glorifying, as the Eastern Church also terms it, was there in the earliest days of the church, albeit it in a very local and less formal way. Kenneth Woodward and others have examined the history as well as the development of the ecclesiastical process, as well as some of its problems.

I will begin by arguing that despite the rather remarkable number of canonizations by John Paul II, many formally recognized saints, even well-known ones, have become distant from our experience and sensibilities. For example, one admires from afar, say, Mother Teresa or Padre Pio the stigmatic, marveling at their sufferings, witness, and wonders. Yet there is little if any immediate connection between them and ourselves. They are truly "larger than life," sometimes superhuman and not really capable of imitation. The crisis is due, in part, to the increasing gulf between us and the time and culture in which these holy persons lived. It may also stem from the fact that it is not easy to find saints whose lives were ordinary. There seems to remain a penchant for what I will call the "cult of celebrity."

Yet, as some of the persons of faith I profiled themselves describe it, there is always need for the tradition of the church to be *living*, that is, to be expressed and enacted anew in different historical and social contexts. In the Eastern churches there are those for whom tradition may appear "timeless." The teachings of the fathers and mothers of the church, the canons or rulings of the church councils, even the words of the liturgical services are considered "unchangeable," despite the historical record, which says that clearly this is not the case. The history of the church reveals that the very lives of holy women and men and their words are diverse, constantly open to new situations and possibilities, places and times where the Holy Spirit will blow as she wills. Paul Evdokimov has eloquently argued this.[5]

Drawing upon Evdokimov's work and that of a number of those profiled in my earlier book, *Living Icons,* such as the newly canonized martyr, nun, and social activist Mother Maria Skobtsova, I want to explore the shapes of a *universal* and more *ordinary,* and thus less noticeable or *hidden* holiness, one founded on the baptismal calling of all to be prophets and priests, witnesses to the Gospel. I also want to explore further Rowan

Williams's insistence that people of faith find God's work in *their* culture, *their* daily lives. I want to listen to poet Kathleen Norris's ideas about a "holy realism" and Etty Hillesum's learning how to pray. Likewise the prior of Bose monastery Enzo Bianchi's thoughts about people of faith making a difference in our culture and world, Sara Miles's beautiful experience of a eucharistic conversion and subsequent messy adventure of becoming part of the church, along with Darcey Steinke's ruthless yet tenderly honest memoir of growing up the daughter of a Lutheran pastor and falling out of and back into faith. While I am leery of "how-to-do-it" literature on sanctity, we could benefit from listening to Alexander Schmemann's very practical thoughts about the spiritual life. He was dean of St. Vladimir's Orthodox Theological Seminary for almost thirty years and became a kind of spokesman for Eastern Orthodoxy in America. I will look at some of the equipment for such sanctity, as well as the lives of several who lived a relatively unnoticed holiness.

There are many others whom I hope the reader will listen to: Thomas Merton, Dorothy Day, Simone Weil, Charles de Foucauld, Mother Maria Skobtsova, Paul Evdokimov, Mother Teresa, and some saints of hidden holiness I myself have met. I will look and listen at greater length to the lay theologian Elisabeth Behr-Sigel; nun and iconographer Joanna Reitlinger; a Yup'ik Alaskan woman of whom I am confident most will never have heard, Olga Michael; and Paul Anderson, the YMCA staffer whose name is hardly a household item either. Please do not panic at all these names! I am myself very bad at remembering names at first meeting at a coffee hour or reception or conference. Don't worry. You will be more properly introduced to all these and more and learn from their own experience in living in and with God and one's neighbors. At times I have allowed some to speak at greater length, in quotations, precisely because there is no replacement, in any commentary or analysis I could offer, for the power as well as the beauty of the firsthand expression of people struggling to live a holy life. I do not attempt to be exhaustive, but I provide a substantial bibliography within the endnotes, so a particular writer or figure can be followed up directly.

Who will want to read this book and why? I hope not just specialists in hagiography and the history of saint-making, and certainly not just readers interested only in Eastern Orthodoxy. This is most definitely not a "recipe" book about holiness, but I will talk a bit about the tools that many have used in leading such a life. I will also reflect on what the tradition says about holiness, the theological background, in accessible terms. As so many in the "emergent church" movement insist, the first theology was in terms of stories and proverbs, parables and sayings accessible to all.[6] I am among those who also believe, as do theologians Alexander Schmemann and David Fagerberg, that the most basic or "primary theology" is to be found in our prayers and rituals. Theology consists of words, thoughts, ideas about God. But these flow in singing and praying, in the reading of the scriptures and the commentary on them heard in our liturgical assemblies. But it is never just words that express who God is and our response, but very much actions such as washing and eating and drinking. And these require some very ordinary material things such as water, bread, wine, and oil, as well as sound, light, and color, as well as human gestures of thanksgiving, intercession, affection, and respect.[7]

I have been turning over and over, for the past few years, Paul Evdokimov's observation that the holiness of our time is at once quite simple and thus not so noticeable, most diverse and not limited to certain shapes with which we have become familiar. A succinct statement, but the questions that Evdokimov raises are most complex. Has it not always been the case that the churches have recognized heroic, that is, highly visible and extraordinary people (and their lives) as saintly? How does one begin to describe, to identify really anonymous, even "invisible" saints? And what are the implications for all of us in our own lives? It is just these strands I hope to follow here with clarity.

I should also say that while I did not intend this to be a reflection on holiness only within the boundaries of the Eastern Church, some of my natural reference points are there. I have tried to think beyond East-West confines, but I have also tried to allow some distinctive angles and perspectives from *both* the Eastern and Western churches to occupy center stage. My impression, as I have looked carefully at the burgeoning literature on saints, classic and contemporary, well known and obscure, is that most of the authors and figures examined are from the Roman Catholic or Protestant churches. While some of these will come into play and significantly here, nowhere else will one find the lives and words of Olga Michael, as well as several others.

Finally, I will admit at the outset that I raise more questions here than I answer. Scanning the recent flood of books in religion, one could conclude that there is a crisis of faith, with journalists and scientists, not to mention intellectuals, attacking belief in God and the actions of religious institutions in an unprecedented manner. Is this the reaction to the violence produced by religious extremists internationally? Is it a response to the demands of fundamentalists here in our own political system in recent years? Are we finally experiencing Europe's allegedly corrosive secularism here in "God's own country"?

Looking from a different vantage point, I would rather say that criticism and questioning reveal our concern for the sacred, our realization that we touch other worlds but most often pay scant attention to these other realities. I would agree with those who feel there is an authentic hunger for God, for the spiritual life, and for those who have lived this holiness well who have gone before us. So we also ask, how can this holiness be ours, how can we be saints?

CHAPTER ONE

Holiness and Holy People

SAINTS

It is the glory
of the Church
that it cannot
name
all the saints.

It is the glory
of the Church
that it cannot
remember
all the saints.

It is the glory
of Christ
that we cannot
count
all the saints.

Saints are found
behind all the rocks

of the
mountain.

Saints are found
among the trees
of the wood.

Saints hide in
blossoms,
ride birds, top clouds;
follow passages
under the
earth.

They sweep the floors
of the universe.

They take out the garbage
of the cosmos.

The seeds they scatter
soften and green the hillsides;
leaves open
their hands;
joyful beasts
wander among trees,
cling to grassy
slopes.

The faithful
cling to the roots
of the saints,
growing up
from the ground.
—Matthew R. Brown

HOLY CARDS, HOLY PEOPLE

It well may be the glory of the church that all of the saints cannot be named or numbered, but this otherwise beautiful fact hides some confusing and frustrating attitudes. In the past few years, "holiness," which sounds a great deal like and is intimately related to "wholeness," doesn't sound so bad. Some of the overgrowth has been scratched away from "holiness" so that we can again glimpse its roots, the deeper meaning behind plaster statues and stained glass windows. As Evdokimov points out, whatever linguistic path one chooses, Hebrew, Greek, or Latin, for the word "holiness," the trail leads to "perfection," "the sacred," "sanctity," "blessedness," "completeness," and all of these lead in turn to the One who is their source, God.

Rudolph Otto likewise directed attention toward the holy as "wholly Other," *das ganz Andere.* Holiness was for him the *mysterium tremendum,* the reality whose numinous character makes one shudder in fear. Yet the very same awesome otherness attracted with a power greater than any eros, any desire or passion of human knowing. For the "whole" and "holy" Other was the pinnacle of beauty, goodness, and truth.

Outside of a course in philosophy of religion or comparative traditions, and even in regular preaching, I am afraid, such talk, although it is technical and historically employed, has become empty. It is "pious" language of another age, riddled with stereotypes. There is little to which we can connect the everyday details of our lives, our sorrows and joys. Even if we respect its historical character, we nevertheless quickly dismiss this theological talk, abandoning it to dusty library shelves. All that it evokes is dead, museum pieces of piety, the old fashioned and so often tasteless "holy cards" Romans Catholics and some other Christians know.

Part of the problem here is allowing a tradition to stagnate out of exaggerated reverence. In our everyday language, the very ways we talk about "saints" reveal this. They are impossibly virtuous and pure, hopelessly out of contact with everyday life and feelings and concerns. They perform unbelievable miracles, pray for impossible numbers of hours, eat next to nothing, go without sleep, and appear in more than one place at the same time. Some are able to hover in the air, others fly. Perhaps they have other, more unusual, even repulsive physical characteristics like bleeding wounds, the "odor of sanctity" despite never bathing or changing clothes. Like the saints on so many "holy cards," they are surrounded by cotton-candy-like clouds, seem lost in some kind of trance before the altar or an icon. They clutch the crucifix or a chalice or, on the more colorful side, the gruesome instruments of their torture and death. Many, if not most, are bishops and priests, monks and nuns, great ascetics or martyrs. In short they are very different from us ordinary people with jobs and debts, houses and spouses, children and careers. Although they are our brothers and sisters in the faith, very often they come across as beyond human. We would never want to look, act, or sound like they did, and we probably could not, even if we tried very hard. Remote from us both in time and in identity, the distance between the saints and ourselves is increased by the events that surround them after their deaths. I mean here miracles, apparitions, the kinds of supernatural happenings and powers and deeds that are even required in some processes of saint-making.

It wasn't always like this. The earliest Christians to be revered as holy people may indeed have suffered under persecutions and given their lives in witness of their Lord, yet they were members of the local church community. Early martyrs whose accounts of sufferings remain, such as the bishops Polycarp of Smyrna and Ignatius of Antioch and the North Africans Perpetua and Felicity, are still recognizable, beloved brothers and sisters, despite the formal shape of these documents. The great love for a figure such as Nicholas of Myra remains evident in hymns as well as in all the stories of his generosity and miraculous abilities to save people (from being sold into prostitution, from drowning at sea, from murder and mutilation). Small details of real humanity can be found in the genuine fears of Ignatius, Perpetua's experience of imprisonment, Augustine's personal difficulties rearranging his life, Mother Maria Skobtsova's periodic frustrations, Dorothy Day's regular discouragements. Within our own time we have not only photographs but film and tape footage of Thomas Merton, Simone Weil, Flannery O'Connor, Alexander Schmemann, and Alexander Men. We also have numerous pages they left behind, revealing their prayers, their frustrations, their insights, and their humanity. One confesses his enduring love for a cold beer, another irritation with Catholic piety, particularly the cult of saints. Some are afflicted with all kinds of conditions, including multiple sclerosis and eating disorders, not to mention depression. Still another records the idiocy of self-proclaimed ascetic masters and the joy of and importance of playing with children, while another laughs and acknowledges he has lost his place in the baptism and confirmation of a large number of new Christians. Quite a collection of personalities and idiosyncrasies, but are they saints? Is this holiness incarnate?

SAINTS AS REAL PEOPLE, REAL PEOPLE AS SAINTS

Only very recently have we begun to recognize the authentic holiness of ordinary people: married women and men, parents, teachers and lawyers, medical professionals and social activists, and even clergy and religious who did not perch on pillars or subsist only on the eucharistic elements. Can saints be political radicals, poets and writers, professors and resistance fighters, ordinary married couples and parents? Or should the question be reversed?

There are indeed holy individuals who listened to the radio, watched television, went to the movies, and enjoyed a good bottle of wine and a steak. Schmemann was one, Merton another. Pierre Toussaint as a barber-surgeon of his day both cut hair and treated the sick. Others wrote novels and poetry, newspaper columns and essays for journals, while caring for the homeless and lost. Some liked jazz and Bob Dylan and beer. A few smoked and still others told jokes and were deeply in love with their fiancée or wife, like Lutheran pastor and theologian Dietrich Bonhoeffer and the Russian Orthodox priest Alexander Men, both of whom died as martyrs.

In one of the episodes of the documentary series "The Long Search," from awhile back, the host, director Ronald Eyre, was trying to put together quite diverse strands of Christian spirituality. He was following the Little Brothers of Jesus in their urban residences and desert retreats, recording their attitudes toward faith and the authority of the church, in particular that of the pope. He profiled an articulate, critical Catholic mother and wife. And he also looked at folk religion, in particular, the popular exuberance of pilgrims at the Benedictine abbey of Monserrat in Spain. In his inimitable manner, Eyre peppered the abbey's guest master, Fr. Miguel, with questions about authentic faith and prayer in contrast to what appeared to be mere religious entertainment, people enjoying the good weather and some religious activity on a beautiful spring day, the abbey as "theme park." The camera captured long lines of the faithful waiting to kiss the foot of an ancient statue of the Virgin, lighting candles, walking in procession after the cross, attending service in the abbey church, but also laughing, eating, and drinking at their own picnic tables. They appear to be as much tourists on a vacation day trip as pilgrims.

Father Miguel's quiet insight left Eyre with thoughts that we will our-selves pursue throughout this book. "Faith, prayer," he said, "these do not really exist in the abstract. There are only *people* who believe, *people* who pray." Holiness can be analyzed as the essential character of God, but even here we depart from the personalism of the Bible. We do not find theologi-cal definitions or philosophical concepts of God in the scriptures, either the Hebrew Bible or the New Testament. Rather we find God and the human beings of his creation in every kind of action imaginable, from the most wonderful and creative to the depths of ugliness and cruelty.

When we encounter evil, it is rarely as a political institution or eco-nomic system. Evil is perpetrated by people against each other, against God. Likewise, goodness is observed primarily in personal ways: in the heal-ing of a widow's child, the feeding of hungry people, compassion for a leper or crippled soul, the love of a spouse for a spouse, a child for a parent. In fact, there seems to be less of the religious or "spiritual" in the Bible than on the racks at Borders or Barnes & Noble. Temples are built and torn down and rebuilt. King after king parades by, among the chosen people of God, and the majority did not walk in the way of the Lord. Prostitutes save people from death. Tax collectors, who are corrupt civil servants, traitors to their own religious tradition and political community, are called to be disciples and numbered among those who would force their way into the kingdom of God. Priests and teachers walk as far as they can on the other side of the road from a traveler beaten, robbed, and left to die. Second-class citizens, heretics by the standard of the established tradition, show mercy, ask the right religious questions. Prophets cowardly try to run from their callings, make excuses for why they cannot bring the awesome word of the Lord. Widows give generously, even using up all their resources to show hospitality to a holy man. Aged couples bear children who lead the people back to God. Mothers witness the torture and killing of their children, all the while encouraging them to stand up for God before their killers. On and on stretches the biblical gallery of the "righteous," of holy women and men—down-to-earth, scandalous, full of life, even libido.

Perhaps the problem with holiness is not so much the problem of a concept but rather some confusion or disillusion in our time with people who are said to be . . . holy. As a child I was a great collector of things, but I suspect baseball cards and holy cards were my favorites. No explanation of the former is necessary, for I am one who believes the game is one of our culture's greatest mysteries. But the sentimental, cheesy cards of saints given out at parish events, by well-intentioned religious, arranged in so many rows at religious good stores and monastery gift shops! It is closed now, but the old Pilgrim's Bookstore not far from where I live at Graymoor, the Friars of the Atonement motherhouse in Garrison, New York, was major league in their holy card holdings.

Surely my enjoyment of them was not for esthetic reasons except rarely when the cards were reproductions of masters like Fra Angelico, Cimabue, Rembrandt, Russian and Byzantine icons, or the rare contemporary artist like the Dominican Sister Mary of the Compassion. More often than not the depiction of the saints was maudlin and even silly. Yet for me, it was the sheer diversity of the saints that first drew me to their cards and later to their lives in Butler's and the Bollandists' collections, and most recently to Robert Ellsberg's wonderful book.

There was a saint for everything and from everywhere: Dymphna, the intercessor for the emotionally ill; Anthony of Padua, the finder of lost objects; the apostle Jude Thaddeus, the last-ditch helper for impossible causes. Somehow, there was less distance from the saints back then, a kind of easy familiarity, almost as if we came from the same neighborhood. Growing up, I went to a church with early-twentieth-century stained glass windows produced in Germany and a grove of life-size statues of saints. The saints there surrounded us. People went up and lit their candles, occasionally grasping the foot of St. Joseph or the Virgin Mary. In my grandmother's Ukrainian Catholic church the saints in the icon screen and in the wall frescoes also formed a familial gathering. We went up and kissed them, leaving candles as our prayers. Churches were named for many of them: Peter and Paul, John the Baptist, Michael the Archangel, Francis of Assisi. In Orthodox churches where I have served as a priest I have seen people lean their heads against the icons, carrying on whispered conversations of prayer, others holding onto the edges while making their confession. And not only in the churches but in so many homes, domestic shrines were filled with the images of the Lord, his mother, and the saints. The saints, although different and distant, were nevertheless closer to us. Perhaps it was the culture in which we lived, not yet secularized, not punctured by rebellion and questions.

SOME SAINTS OF OUR TIME

That was then. Now, things are different. But, despite the difficulty in dealing with "holiness" and with the saints of the past, are there not saints of the present?

My earlier book, *Living Icons*, mostly the reading and reflection that led up to it, also led me here. For a good decade I have been making acquaintance with a number of men and women of the Eastern Church. Most are not well known in the West, or for that matter, even in the Eastern Church. With one exception, the nineteenth-century monk and mystic Seraphim of Sarov, all lived the better part of their lives in the twentieth century. Quite a few had rejected the faith of their childhood homes and parishes. In one case, the revolt was especially wrenching, since there were blurred borders between home and church, Sergius Bulgakov being the son of a priest. Seminary cured him of his first faith, and of faith altogether, until he came back to the church, "the house of the Father."

Some of these had to flee the Russian revolution, making the unexpected journey through various cities and eventually reaching Paris. Nicolas Afanasiev set out to study history but also became an expert in canon law, in the worship life of the church, and in her path through the centuries. In the middle of World War II he was ordained a priest, served an isolated parish in Tunisia, and came home to resume his position as a professor at the St. Sergius Theological Institute in Paris. He would train a generation of clergy and scholars and his vision of the church as a eucharistic community would shape the thinking of the Roman Catholic and many other Western churches. Two of his students, John Meyendorff and Alexander Schmemann, would bring to the United States the importance of the *ressourcement*, the "return to the sources" they learned in post–World War II Paris, not only from Orthodox teachers but from a diverse collection of theologians drawn together by the common experience of the war.

Schmemann, in turn, became the leading voice of a liturgically rooted theology and Meyendorff, though a specialist in medieval Byzantine thought, became a bridge between American Christians and the Eastern Church. Trapped in Soviet Russia in the same postwar years, Fr. Alexander Men would launch a single-handed effort to restore education about the world religions, and Christianity in particular, to the consciousness of an officially atheistic culture. As a priest, he became informal chaplain to the young intellectuals who experienced the opening of doors in the Gorbachev *glasnost* and *perestroika* policies and finally freedom after the demise of the Party. He would be assassinated in 1990 for his prominent role as educator and lecturer in Moscow and on Russian television and radio. Paul Evdokimov worked in the Paris Renault factory and the maintenance shops of the French Railway while he studied at St. Sergius Institute under Fr. Sergius Bulgakov. He married, cared for his children while his wife supported the family by her teaching, wrote his doctoral dissertation between feedings and baths, and then worked with the Resistance during World War II. Afterwards, rather than accept an academic position, he led ecumenical hostels for the poor and marginalized for a decade before taking a faculty post at his alma mater. While he lectured and published prolifically, he contributed to Vatican II, became one of the major figures linking the churches of the East and West, and all along he never lost the everyday ministry of service to the suffering.

Elisabeth Pilenko packed several lives into one: a protégé of the poet Alexander Blok, one of the first women enrolled in the St. Petersburg Theological Institute, mayor of her hometown in the Crimea. She was almost executed both by the Bolsheviks and the White Army, married twice, and saw both marriages disintegrate. The mother of three, she entered religious life as Mother Maria, only to reject the forms of traditional monasticism. The world became her monastery. She ran hostels for the elderly, the unemployed, the homeless and despairing in Paris. She begged food as well as prepared it. She counseled the residents while continuing to write for the Russian periodicals of the city. Turned in by a resident for hiding Jews from the Nazi sweep of occupied Paris, she endured almost three years in Ravensbrück concentration camp, going to the gas chambers only days before the camp's liberation, taking the place of another assigned to death there.

The talented but tormented artist George Krug worked in the ateliers of the leading émigré Russian painters in Paris. Outstanding in several media, he suddenly devoted himself to not just the painting of icons but, with colleagues Leonid Ouspensky and Sister Joanna Reitlinger, to nothing less than the rediscovery of traditional iconographic style and its creative renaissance in the twentieth century. A nervous breakdown and depression almost cost him his life in the psychiatric hospital of St. Anne. During the Nazi occupation, the patients of that hospital were deemed "unworthy of life," and their food rations were withdrawn. Reduced to eating grass, plants, and other vegetation, the patients faced starvation and death. Ill as he was, George would make pencil and charcoal drawings—of landscapes or portraits of fellow patients—and his sister would sell them in Paris, buying food for him. This he shared with his fellow inmates, keeping them alive until liberation. When released into the care of his spiritual father, Fr. Sergius Shevitch, his health was slowly restored and he resumed painting. At first he refused to paint icons, feeling unworthy to do so because of his emotional illness and hospitalization. However, Fr. Sergius gently but firmly urged him to again work on icons, and after the war's end Fr. Sergius received him into monastic life with the name of Gregory, one of the great sainted icon painters. Father Gregory would live at a small monastic house outside Paris, close to Versailles. The chapel remains, the interior of which he loving covered with fresco icons. He then spent another two decades producing quite likely the most beautiful corpus of icons in history, occasionally travelling to other locations where he would create larger scale icons such as at Montgeron and Moisenay.

Lev Gillet started out to be a psychiatrist, producing the first French translation of Freud's *On the Interpretation of Dreams*. But military service in World War I somehow led him toward profession in the Benedictine order and graduate work in liturgical theology. One of the first ecumenical leaders in Europe, he helped found the monastery of Chevetogne, composed of both Eastern and Western monks. Intense and often hypersensitive to those around him, he nevertheless became a monk without a monastery, a priest without a parish, a spiritual guide to many through his retreats and books and constant traveling across Europe and to the Near East. In his heart a Christian of the undivided church, he connected the divided churches of the East and West in his ministry first as a Catholic and then as an Orthodox monastic priest.

Looking back on lives like these, we are able to recognize the extraordinary holiness in such individuals, men and women whose holiness was not necessarily noticed as such in their own time or even now. As I worked on the profiles of their lives, more than once my choices of these persons of faith from the Eastern Church were seriously challenged and criticized. Since then, Mother Maria and her companions Fr. Dimitri Klepinine, Ilya Fundaminsky, and her son Yuri have been canonized. This action itself has not gone without criticism in some church circles. The others . . . well it may be years till any of them receive "official" recognition. My guess is that they will not.

For the most part their lives were quite ordinary, and in some cases the openness they demonstrated and the freedom and energy that marked their actions were not appreciated by all around them. Evdokimov was more valued and respected outside the Orthodox churches, by both Catholics and Protestants in France and other parts of Europe. Vladimir Lossky, not without some sarcasm, referred to him as a "Protestant among the Orthodox." Mother Maria's association with the marginal and the suffering earned her ridicule within her own Russian community. A figure as renowned as Metropolitan Anthony Bloom has regretted the distance, even the disdain, with which he regarded her in the years before World War II.

The realization common to these and others I studied was that the call to holiness was universal, not the gift to a special few. The cult of what I will call "celebrity saints" has been around for a long time in the church. Authentic holy people of our time, though, tell us, not only by their words but even more so by their lives, that there is really no limit to the ways in which holiness can be lived.

In what follows, I do not want so much to dwell on the images of holiness in the past. These, I think, we know rather well. Evdokimov affirms
that some will always be able to respect and venerate the great saints of the
tradition, those who populated the walls of our churches and our homes
with their images.[1] However, such is not the case for all of us.

> In our time when we speak of "holiness," a kind of psychological
> barrier goes up. Immediately one thinks of the former giants, hermits
> and stylites (pillar-dwellers), those hidden away in their cave-cells or
> perched upon their columns, so that such "illuminated ones," those
> "equal to the angels," seem no longer to be connected to this world.
> Holiness appears to be out of date, from an age that has long since
> passed and now seems alien to the discontinuous forms and synco-
> pated rhythms of modern life. A stylite today would not arouse cu-
> riosity but would provoke the question of the very purpose of such
> a feat. Today a saint seems to be nothing more than a kind of yogi,
> or put more crassly, one who is sick, maladjusted, in any case no use
> to us.[2]

Yet this will not define the kind of saints we are to become. Although we
honor the past, we must not become trapped by it. God calls people of
every time and every place to be the signs of his kingdom.

Evdokimov thinks the life of a modern saint, Seraphim of Sarov, may
give some insight to this. Beloved among Russian Orthodox, Seraphim's
life is, on first view, thorough in conforming to the traditional criteria,
events, and even stages of development of sainthood. He is cured of a life-
threatening illness not once but twice through the intervention of the
Mother of God. He enters monastic life and progresses through the various levels from the novitiate to full monastic profession, even priestly ordination. But, upon closer inspection, Seraphim seems incapable of being
held by any of the statuses and roles he inhabits. From an important member of the Sarov community, he abruptly moves into the hermit life. He
hides from all visitors except children at his forest hermitage. When or-
dered back to the monastery, he becomes a recluse, leaving his cell only
for the most important liturgical services, breaking contact with virtually

everyone. Suddenly, one day, he throws open the doors of his cell, tells his assistant to go open the monastery gates, and until his death he greets, meets, and prays with thousands of pilgrims daily. He also launches into a one-man campaign of founding not one but two monastic houses—for women! And this, he affirms, is upon direct request of the Mother of God, who appears to him on several occasions. He even selects candidates, based on their personalities, for one or another of these two monasteries and is roundly criticized for meddling in the lives of women monastics. After his death, local ecclesiatical authorities prey upon the monasteries Seraphim founded. There is no happy ending for his nuns, they did not "live happily ever after." And the great stature of his holiness did not protect his monastery and the other monastic houses from the Russian revolution. They were closed, the monastics scattered or imprisoned, many of the buildings, including the church into which his tomb had been moved, were demolished. Even his relics were thought to have been destroyed, only to be found at the end of the Soviet regime. What was left of his sayings and writings after his death were substantially edited by the scholarly metropolitan of Moscow, Filaret (Drozdov), later canonized himself. Only the Diveyevo Chronicles, firsthand accounts and reminiscences of Seraphim, capture something of the great singularity, even eccentricity, of his personality and life. It took pressure from the Romanovs to convince the synod of the Russian Orthodox Church to finally canonize Seraphim in 1903, his cult having flourished since his death in 1833.

Try as many have to fit Seraphim neatly back into the traditional mold of holiness, the reality of his life, personality, and fate resist such efforts. Is Seraphim an example of the bizarre, even pathological sanctity to which Evdokimov referred? Hardly, for in the many changes in his life, in the shedding of one status and work after another, Evdokimov believes we see the freedom and creativity that holiness displays in our time, what Simone Weil claimed was demanded in our era. In the lives of other holy people we will examine in this book, we will see that traditional expectations of sanctity are not always fulfilled, the usual profiles of holiness often discarded, the boundary lines of churches often crossed or irrelevant. Persons of faith such as Simone Weil, Etty Hillesum, Thomas Merton, Maria Skobtsova, Dorothy Day, and others like them cannot be easily placed in the older categories of saints, for they journeyed through many changes in their lives.

There is a long procession of people from our time, who though not officially recognized or canonized nevertheless witness to the universality, diversity, and ordinary qualities of sanctity in our time. Some are relatively well known and others not at all. What we will examine are the problems posed, as well as the possibilities that emerge, when we look at holiness in our time, holiness that Evdokimov called "hidden" because of its universal, everyday, and ordinary features.

CHAPTER TWO
Celebrities as Saints
The Canonization of the Extraordinary

Syriac scholar Susan Ashbrook Harvey has written a great deal about holy women. As she observes, in the case of Mary the Younger, an early figure, everyday goodness, the ordinary following after Christ, did not seem to be enough to qualify for sainthood.

> [S]aints by their nature are as disturbing as they are inspiring. They inspire by their glorious witness and achievements: they are the promise than we can truly live as God intended, in God's own image. But they disturb, for they are the constant reminder of how much we fall short of the life to which we are called. We are given our true model and challenged to conform to it. Hagiography, like the saints who are its subjects, also inspires and disturbs, for it too, contains an ever-present critique of our failings as a church. When the relics of Mary the Younger began performing miracles, the archbishop would not believe it. He said, "We know this woman to have been good, and her life to have been virtuous; but we cannot believe that she has been found worthy of such grace [to perform miracles]. God has granted the ability to perform miracles to chaste men, holy monks, and martyrs. She, on the other hand, lived with a man [her husband], and did not change her mode of life [i.e., become a nun], nor did she ever do any great or extraordinary things. Whence her power to perform miracles?"[1]

Fascination with saints has been a constant in Christian history, but it is not an exaggeration to say that there has been a recent surge in interest that has led to a whole new literature on the making of saints, the kinds of people being canonized, and our relationship to the saints and the life of holiness. Kenneth Woodward's study of the history of the canonization process was an important breakthrough in understanding the history of the process of making saints, one that has dramatically changed and become more institutionalized as well as centralized over the centuries.[2] More recently Lawrence Cunningham has pursued the bureaucratization of sainthood.[3] So too has Michael Higgins.[4] Elizabeth Johnson has looked at saints from a feminist perspective.[5] Robert Ellsberg has been indefatigable. As editor-in-chief at Orbis, he directs an ongoing series of almost forty anthologies of writings from modern spiritual masters. These have included Thomas Merton, Mother Maria, Gandhi, and many more. He has also focused on women saints and even more so on the life and work of Dorothy Day, now editing her papers.[6] Ellsberg not only looked at a year's collection of very diverse holy people but in doing so stretched some of the ecclesiastical boundaries to sainthood. He went beyond the church or denominational borders to include outsider persons of holiness who would never qualify for official recognition. Several other collections have followed this path, one of the most notable being the martyrology compiled by the ecumenical monastic community of Bose.[7] Sophia Compton has assembled a year of women saints from diverse backgrounds, one to ponder each day.[8] Paul Elie won praise for his look at four American Catholics writers who might be seen as saintly: Dorothy Day, Thomas Merton, Flannery O'Connor, and Walker Percy.[9] Carol Lee Flinders has focused on a number of women mystics and activists, from Etty Hillesum and Jane Goodall to Thérèse of Lisieux, Teresa of Avila, Julian of Norwich, Clare of Assisi, and two Catherines, of Siena and Genoa.[10] James Martin's recent very personal and stimulating books have won awards and have attracted significant readership.[11] Martin stresses the humanity of the saints but also elaborates his own relationship with them—the effects of their presence and witness on his own life. Kate Fodor, who previously did a play about philosophers Hannah Arendt and Martin Heidegger, has written one on everyday holy people, *100 Saints You Should Know,* which opened in New York City in September 2007.[12]

Despite all this interest, the universal vocation to holiness has become a problem in our time, for we, no less than those before us, still tend to identify as saints only extraordinary individuals such as Mother Teresa. Recent canonizations and the urge to enter individuals in the official process of saint-making seem to bear this out. One thinks here of such figures recently sainted such as the mystic and stigmatic Padre Pio; the controversial founder of Opus Dei, Josémaria Escrivá; and the physician, wife, and mother Gianna Beretta Molla.[13] Even with the unprecedented number of canonizations done by Pope John Paul II—480 new saints, 1300 beatifications, 1000 more in other stages of the canonization process—as well as by the Moscow Patriarchate, the individuals selected are overwhelmingly members of the episcopate, the clergy, or the monastic and religious communities.[14] Conspicuously absent are laypeople in general, married women and men in particular.

Some cases are more problematic and for reasons that are telling. I have in mind here Thomas Merton, Dorothy Day, Oscar Romero, and John Henry Newman. Each is well known, not only for writings but for lives at once eventful and in conflict with church and culture. Merton's criticism of American domestic and foreign policies in the 1960s; his outspoken views on nuclear proliferation, civil rights, and the Vietnam war; as well as his criticism of the state of monastic life make him controversial even today, an outsider to classical patterns of holiness. An article on him as an example of Christian witness in America was recently dropped from an officially endorsed Roman Catholic reference work, despite the hundreds of signatures on a petition opposing this move. While there is probably no modern Catholic author who could equal his stature—many of his books having remained in print for over half a century—at least one defense of the motion to exclude him questioned whether his life was "exemplary" and representative of Catholic faith. However, while sometimes in the Catholic Church "radical" personalities are canonized centuries later when distance has provided more perspective, in other cases fairly extreme personalities are made saints relatively quickly. One could expect this will be the case with Mother Teresa of Calcutta.

Official recognition of sainthood would be problematic to an even greater degree with Dorothy Day. Her life had far too many colorful turns (radical politics, an abortion, a child born out of marriage) to merit serious consideration as a saint in the Roman Catholic process—until the late Cardinal John O'Connor entered her into it. Moving from Catholicism, the same held true among Orthodox Christians with respect to Mother Maria Skobtsova until her canonization in May 2004, along with several of her associates from her Paris settlement house. Though the Lutheran Church in Germany has no canonization process, Dietrich Bonhoeffer's status remains problematic. Was he a martyr or one of the many destroyed by the Nazi Reich? Some do not see him as a "martyr" in the classic sense of one who died for the Gospel, choosing to see his actions as admirable, even heroic, but more political than religious.

Holiness does seem to have a kind of "celebrity" status clinging to it. The much more visible imperfections and peculiarities of persons of faith sometimes add to the aura, sometimes detract, leaving them, so to speak, on the sidelines of the official process of sainthood. The long struggle and debates that culminated in the recent canonization by the Moscow Patriarchate of the assassinated Czar Nicholas I, Alexandra Romanov, and other members of their family reveal something of the controversial notion of sainthood today. The Romanovs were not canonized as "martyrs" but in another category historically recognized by the Russian Orthodox Church, that of "passion-bearer" (*strastoterpets*), those who suffered with dignity but not necessarily because of their faith. The eleventh-century brother princes Boris and Gleb were the first to fill this category, further described by hagiographical scholar George Fedotov as "non-resistant sufferers," examples of the Russian "kenotic" spirituality, imitating Christ who "emptied himself" (*kenosis*) in suffering for the life of the world (Phil. 2:7).[15] That extreme nationalist groups in Russia are promoting the canonization of such notorious figures as Ivan the Terrible and Rasputin only add to the complexity. In my own church, the Orthodox Church in America, there are also some instances open to scrutiny. Was Alexis Toth, the Greek Catholic priest who converted to Orthodoxy, canonized for that action, for his own holiness of life, or for bringing dozens of Greek Catholic parishes into the Orthodox Church? Syrian Bishop Raphael Hawaweeney is called "defender of Orthodoxy in America." Why did it take so long for him to be canonized? And despite an ongoing local cult, why has Olga Arsumquq Michael, a priest's wife and grandmother, not entered the process of canonization? Has the very idea of "sainthood" certain limitations as to candidates? Has it, across the churches, been modified and used for other than theological reasons?

We live in a time of celebrity obsession. Yet we are quite fickle when it comes to those we consider notable. Often their notoriety is less than Andy Warhol's infamous statement of fame lasting fifteeen minutes. In the aftermath of September 11, the designation of "hero" has been extended to so many. Some say too many, others welcome the realization of numerous "everyday heroes," most of whom will never enjoy any recognition or notice for their deeds. While it is true that we experienced unusual heroism in the attacks and their aftermath, is it possible we have so stretched the category of the heroic that it too has become useless? As for those we say we admire, is this done at some distance? Is not their heroism, their goodness, therefore inaccessible to us and thus beyond us? Is it the case that we could not possibly imitate their actions, nor have the desire or courage to do so? Perhaps the merging of saints and celebrities is prompted not only by fascination with the famous but also by the need to keep such figures at an emotional distance from ourselves.

The history of the making of saints is a complicated story and not the aim here. Studies already mentioned, such as those of Woodward, Cunningham, and Higgins, thoroughly describe the development of the saint-making process, as well as some interesting differences between the Eastern and Western churches that persist today. Yet the further back we go, the closer becomes the bond—the very human ties, not just feats of heroism—between a holy person and the community to which they belonged. The remains or relics of martyrs were rescued and kept by the members of their local church community. On the anniversaries of their "heavenly" birthdays, their entrance into eternal life, the usual celebrations—*refrigeria,* originally "refreshments," picnic meals carried to the burial places and eaten there—became ecclesial or liturgical ones, the celebration of the Eucharist at their place of burial, on their tombs. Here is the origin of relics being placed in the altar or the altar stone, or in the Eastern Church sewn into the *antimension,* the altar cloth upon which the eucharistic vessels are placed, as well as within the actual altar table.

During the era of persecution the "witnesses" to the faith were those who suffered torture, imprisonment, even death. In time other kinds of "martyrs" were identified, those who were "confessors" of the faith in their preaching and teaching, their ascetical lives, or their generosity to those in need. It is no coincidence that in the Eastern Church the proper liturgical antiphon or troparion for St. Nicholas of Myra became the common text for all bishops. Nicholas's own well-known biographical details notwithstanding, every other chief pastor worthy of veneration was a "model of kindness and faith, a teacher of self-control," whose "lowliness has raised you to the heights of fame," and whose "poverty has filled your hands with riches."

Communities would add to the lists of those "red" martyrs, "white" ones as well, those who witnessed to Christ not by suffering or death but by the lives they led. Evdokimov, as many others, suggests that right after martyrs of blood came the monastic fathers and mothers who sought God alone in the deserts, in lives of prayer, work, hospitality, and healing. Monastic life began as a "resistance movement." Chief pastors of churches who competently led their communities or who intervened when important teachings were in question also were included. In his study of the history of the spiritual life, Evdokimov notes how many of the "marks" or insignia of holiness that were the vernacular of times past have become puzzling to us today.[16] We cannot see the inner meaning of say, sitting for years on a pillar, of walling oneself up in a cave as a recluse, of other extraordinary ascetical lifestyles characterized in the literature of saints by radical deprivations—of sleep, food, speech, even human contact. The signs of holiness of an early period appear to us now as anything from nonconformity to bohemianism, if not extreme pathology or deviance.

But the question of whether we are simply not able to understand the language of sainthood from another time is not the only issue. Whether in centuries past or today, are there not individuals of an authentic but very ordinary holiness, men and women who have none of the marks of the cult and status of celebrity, that is, some very ordinary saints? Clearly there were. The sayings of the desert fathers and mothers have their ascetical giants, figures larger than life. But these same texts do have shorter passages on a brother or sister who is much more ordinary. Such texts ask questions sometimes naïve, sometime obvious, but they reflect the reality of the ordinary Christian seeking God.

A New Hagiography: Different Stories, Different Saints

It would not be an exaggeration at all to say that starting in the twentieth century a new kind of writing about the saints appeared. The historian George Fedotov, who taught both at St. Sergius Theological Institute in Paris and St. Vladimir's Seminary in New York, was a major figure in this new "hagiography," a more historical look at the actual lives and writings of holy people.[17] Nadia Gorodetsky did not ignore the depression suffered by St. Tikhon of Zadonsk in her biography. Neither did other authors previously mentioned: Jim Forest and Michael Mott on Thomas Merton and Dorothy Day, Gillian Crow on Metropolitan Anthony Bloom, Elisabeth Behr-Sigel (herself a student of Fedotov) on Fr. Lev Gillet, Olga Lossky on Elisabeth Behr-Sigel.[18]

None of these felt the need to do the literary equivalent of Botox treatments or plastic surgery on the wrinkles and imperfections of their subjects. The great teacher of prayer Metropolitan Anthony Bloom said that in some ways he could be called a pig. He records this and several other disturbing aspects of his childhood and family life in memoir essays, and Gillian Crow does not omit these details from her biography of him.[19] Mott allows us to see Merton's neuroses, egoism, and impulsivity, while Forest reveals Dorothy Day's crankiness and the contradiction of her judgment of young people in the 1960s over against her own escapades in her twenties. Elisabeth Behr-Sigel is honestly depicted through her own letters and reminiscences by Olga Lossky as the victim of her friend's (Fr. Lev Gillet) neuroticism and her husband André's depression and alcoholism, not to mention her own dominant personality.

One can see more of this new hagiographical honesty in Thomas Craughwell's book, *Saints Behaving Badly,* playfully subtitled, "The Cutthroats, Crooks, Trollops, Con Men, and Devil-Worshippers Who Became Saints."[20] In it we meet a collection of men and women both well known and obscure. But what his subjects have in common is a less-than-apparently-holy style of life, a humanity at once flawed but by this very fact more accessible. In many cases, perhaps most of them, they changed their ways— but not always! Augustine, the great North African bishop and church teacher, had a child with his lover, whom he never married, and in book eight, chapter seven of his *Confessions* prayed, "Give me the gift of being chaste, Lord, but not yet." Francis of Assisi, *il Poverello,* the "little poor man," and founder of communities of brothers and sisters, was a high living court hanger-on, who dabbled in armed squabbles between Italian city-states and lived the good life of wine, women, and song. But his vision of Christ, calling him to leave everything and rebuild his church, led him to a life of extreme renunciation, to the preaching of the holiness of all creation, and even to the receiving of the marks of Christ's wounds, the stigmata. However, his idealism and radical spirit died with him, allowing all sorts of modifications to his demanding rule and forcing his friars to reform themselves many times over down the centuries. Ignatius of Loyola was in some ways quite similar, a mercenary soldier and *bon vivant,* who likewise experienced a conversion after being wounded in armed conflict. Then there are the Jesuits, his society, today.[21] Thomas à Becket was an arrogant aristocrat, wealthy enough to have his own naval fleet and insensitive enough to turn the chance to clothe a freezing homeless man into a battle of wit with Henry II. Later he was the victim of the monarch's desire to be "rid of that troublesome priest." Mary of Egypt was not just by trade a prostitute. In the account of her life still used in the Eastern Church she appears to have been a nymphomaniac. Moses the Black was a mugger whose armed robberies included homicides. Alipius, an associate of Augustine, was a fan and organizer of the Roman arena blood sports. Matt Talbot was an alcoholic who destroyed his health and his family before he stopped drinking. And the list goes on, to practitioners of the occult, emotionally unbalanced figures, active opponents of Christianity—the great apostle Paul coming to mind here.

Craughwell's point is clear. Saints are not always, and not necessarily, models of virtue. As he and Cunningham and other students of sainthood observe, only later in Christian history does the major theme in hagiography and the cult of saints become their heroic, very often extraordinary, even bizarre behavior. Thus we have those ascetics whom Paul Evdokimov describes perched in trees or on tall pillars, recluses virtually walled up as in the monastery of the caves in Kiev, others who subsisted only upon the communion bread they received or who never slept. *National Catholic Re-*

porter correspondent John Allen raises the issue of some individuals either canonized or beatified in the Roman Catholic Church processes having historically documented misdeeds. Augustinian priest Gabino Olaso Zabala, beatified as a martyr, along with more than four hundred others killed by Republican forces in 1936 in the Spanish Civil War, himself participated in the torture of another priest, Mariano Dacany during the revolt in the Philippines. On Oct. 29, 1896, Olaso and other Augustinians observed the torture, encouraged the perpetrators, and when the victim fell over from his bound squat position, Olaso kicked him into unconsciousness. The victim's account, naming Olaso, is not disputed even by the present day Augustinian who prepared and supported the cause for beatification. Allen notes several other examples, such as the opium addiction in the case of Boxer Rebellion martyr Mark Ji Tianxiang canonized in 2000 and membership in the Masonic Lodge of Laval by Fr. Jean-Marie Gallot, beatified with French Revolution martyrs in 1955.[22]

The recent and numerous canonizations in both the Roman Catholic and Russian Orthodox Churches seem to be changing tendencies in this direction. It would be fair to say that unusual, even bizarre behavior is not often lifted up any longer. Yet among the many new saints, the majority are members of the clergy or religious communities or are martyrs in various times of intense persecution such as the Russian revolution or the Spanish Civil War. Founders and members of religious communities and the clergy seem to still dominate the list of newer saints. The Moscow Patriarchate canonized a victorious naval commander, Fyodor Fyodorvich Ushakov (1744–1817).[23] But then the Patriarchate also glorified a surgeon, a married man and widower, Valentin Voino-Yasetsky (1877–1961), who became a priest and bishop and continued both medical and spiritual care of people during Soviet persecution. He was canonized under his monastic and episcopal name, Luke of Simferopol.[24] Also raised to sainthood by the Russian Church was missionary Makarey Glukharev (1792–1847), who among the Altai preserved culture and language and customs while preaching the Gospel and planting the church, much as missionaries in Alaska did. There is also an unofficial cult of a young soldier killed for his faith during the fighting in Chechnya, Evgeny Rodionov (1977–96), not yet canonized, including icons and prayers.[25] And there is an equally strong unofficial devotion to a handicapped woman, Matrona Nikonova (1885–1952), with liturgical texts in her honor, icons, and records of miracles.[26] Perhaps the most popular of modern Russian saints, the priest-monk Seraphim of Sarov (1759–1833) had to wait till 1903 and only with intense pressure from the Romanovs for canonization. His writings, though spare, were edited, that is, modified by St. Filaret of Moscow before publication, so unusual was his life and thinking.

While here and there a young lay leader of youth work or a mother and physician were canonized in the Catholic Church, both stood out from ordinary existence by unexpected medical conditions and early deaths. The Commission on Faith and Order of the World Council of Churches organized a conference at Bose in the fall of 2008 to reflect upon martyrs, canonized and not, across the churches; official ecclesiastical processes can identify more recent martyrs and witnesses of an extraordinary sort, but ordinary women and men still seem to have difficulties measuring up.

FROM HEROISM TO THE ORDINARY

> You cannot help us, but we must help You and defend Your dwelling place inside us to the last. There are, it is true, some who, even at this late stage, are putting their vacuum cleaners and silver forks and spoons in safekeeping instead of guarding You, dear God. And there are those who want to put their bodies in safekeeping but who are nothing more now than a shelter for a thousand fears and bitter feelings. And they say, "I shan't let them get me into their clutches." But they forget that no one is in their clutches who is in Your arms. I am beginning to feel a little more peaceful, God, thanks to this conversation with You. I shall have many more conversations with You. You are sure to go through lean times with me now and then, when my faith weakens a little, but believe me, I shall always labor for You and remain faithful to You, and I shall never drive You from my presence. (12 July 1942)[27]

I think it is helpful now to go directly to the last part of the complete and unabridged collection of Etty Hillesum's (1914–43) diaries and letters, the letters she wrote from the Westerbork internment camp for Dutch Jews. While the conditions there were much better than at the concentration camps where exterminations were carried out, Westerbork was a place of terror and despair. Anyone there had already been rounded up and deprived of freedom, and as the months progressed there was but one way out, the packed trains to Auschwitz, Bergen-Belsen, and other final destination camps with their gas chambers and crematoria.

In these letters, despite the surroundings, there is real life. Hillesum expresses tender and profound love for her mentor, and sometimes lover, psychologist Julius Spier, dying of cancer. She notes that recently arrived priests, monks, and nuns continued to pray at Westerbork in the wooden barracks and mud as much as in a stone monastery or "anywhere on this earth where God, in these troubled times, feels like casting his likeness."[28] This remarkable twenty-nine-year-old was staring into the face of indescribable human cruelty and death for the victims of this hatred. She had never been an observant Jew, and only in her later twenties, under Spier's direction, had she ever thought about God, read the scriptures and other texts, or considered praying.

> I think that I can bear everything life and these times have in store for me. And when the turmoil becomes too great and I am completely at my wits' end, then I still have my folded hands and bended knee. A posture that is not handed down from generation to generation with us Jews. I have had to learn it the hard way . . . What a strange story it really is, my story: the girl who could not kneel. Or its variation: the girl who learned to pray. That is my most intimate gesture, more intimate even than being with a man. After all, one can't pour out the whole of one's love over a single man, can one? (Saturday night, 10 October 1942)[29]

Like some of the others we are meeting and listening to, Etty Hillesum does not fit the pattern of ordinary religiosity much less sainthood. She is a volatile, passionate woman, torn by depression and career frustration but also ablaze with compassion for her friends and the desire to be in contact with . . . God. All of this in less than thirty years of life.

Rowan Williams has drawn upon Etty's letters and journals to drive home something of the concrete and specific character of the spiritual life.[30] Living with awareness, with discernment, striving for truth and the good—this is not merely a mental construct but a lived reality. Williams is direct:

> A religious life is a material life. Forget for a moment the arguments we might have about the definition of the "spiritual"; living religiously is a way of conducting a bodily life. It has to do with gesture, place, sound, habit; not first and foremost with what is supposed to be going on inside. The whole idea of an "inner life" is, properly, what we put together from a certain reading of visible lives; it is not a self-evident category, a cluster of intangible experiences or mental dispositions, but what comes to light as the sense, the intelligibility, of a certain pattern of acts. It's a point made more economically by the Apostle James in refusing to accept a smooth demarcation between belief and action.[31]

Williams uses Hillesum's journals and letters to illustrate the tangibility and specificity of the holy life. With precision, discernment, and passion, she talks about her own complicated life. She was a gifted student though her grades were not the highest. She completed both an undergraduate degree and a law degree but did not practice and her further Russian language studies were halted by the occupation and the war. Any conventional form of religiosity, such as the Judaism into which she was born, was distant to her, either in belief or observance. Yet she also chronicled a growing interest in God through her therapist and friend Julius Spier, reading in Augustine and the Bible, Rilke and Dostoevsky, just as she documents her own personal journey, her sexual experiences, her failures and achievements in therapy and in relationships, and most of all the consequences of the Nazi occupation of Holland and the rounding up and deportation of all Dutch Jews to the camps. Etty's Amsterdam was also that of Anne Frank. Etty actually mentions the recently canonized Carmelite nun and philosopher Edith Stein and her sister in her Westerbork letters. Etty Hillesum's diaries in large part were the outcome of Spier's advice to keep a journal of her intellectual and spiritual life. Not unlike Anne Frank, Etty's life was without any remarkable or unsual aspects externally. She was as good as hidden among the thousands of other Dutch Jews caught up in the Holocaust. But as someone slowly coming to live a reflective life and contemplating becoming a writer, her rich perceptions and expression, her volatile personality and sexuality, her distinctive voice and person come through in the journal entries and letters that were saved.[32] Of the many things covered in the diaries it was particularly important for her to describe minutely the process by which she tried to pray, learned to kneel, became aware of the reality and presence of God, and grew into an intimate relationship with him. She seems to be able, even in the Westerbork holding camp, to be able to see the humanity of the guards. She confesses that it is her duty to keep alive the reality of God in a place where all the violence and destruction aim to annihilate him and any belief in him. But as Rowan Williams points out, this is anything but theoretical or abstract. The very act of kneeling reveals this.

> Etty Hillesum learned to kneel. The physical position is part of a whole protracted story of how she "places" herself in the world in such a way as to become a symbol and an event, the witness to the fact that God lived during a certain epoch of terror, dehumanization and the apparent absence of God ... Etty Hillesum learns to kneel, and learns in due course to plot her location within the tumultuous spiritual geography of the Gestapo office and the camp at Westerbork. And those religious traditions that lay special emphasis on material disciplines would say that the planned engagement with the processes of your own body that constitute Sufi or Zen or hesychast contemplation is a training for a free engagement with an entire material and historical environment— for a liberated life. We begin to learn how to be a sign inhabited by God's meanings as we accept a shape for our physical practice that arises in response to the sort of pressure Etty Hillesum charts, the pressure of a passion for transparency to oneself and truthful feeling.[33]

To be sure, traditional hagiography does not disregard the mundane, particular, even physical details of a person's life when considering their holiness. Details such as kneeling—often for extended periods, eating little or nothing, sleeping little if at all—figure as very important indications of ascetical commitment and accomplishment, thus signs of one at the very least pursuing, if not achieving, holiness. But this is not Rowan Williams's point. Rather he wants us to perceive in Etty Hillesum, by all usual standards an irreligious person, that the search for God does not follow only traditional paths. Holiness is not just an intellectual pilgrimage but one with very ordinary consequences. Even the conventional devotional act of kneeling is for her first a discovery, then an immediate way of connecting not only with God but with those around her.

Williams has other issues on the table in this discussion. He takes aim at the convenient but not very well examined distinction between "religion" and "spirituality" in our time, one which sees the former as constricting and the latter as much more liberating. Likewise, we might reject the perennial opposition of belief and prayer versus action, the "Mary" versus "Martha" dichotomy. In the Gospel there is no such conflict, thus in the life led according to the Gospel there can be no valuation of prayer or doctrine or liturgical worship over doing the works of love, caring for those around us, standing up for what is right. When we see or hear a person of faith—we should in actuality say, a saint-in-the-making—whether a Teresa of Avila or an Etty Hillesum, we should understand that the abstract categories of sainthood must be discarded. One who is seeking God will always be a mix of weaknesses and strengths, failures and accomplisments. The notion of the holy person as perfect makes the rest of us fade by comparison and shrink from imitation. Likewise, distinctions such as those just mentioned begin to disappear when we confront a person, a set of experiences and written thoughts about them—in short an incarnate person of faith, a "living icon," rather than a stereotypic "holy picture."

For a woman of such depth and sensitivity as Etty Hillesum to grow into a relationship with God meant further growth in her own self, in her own awareness. And it meant as well a specific set of activities. Learning to kneel and to pray were only parts of a more comprehensive learning or conversion in her life. It meant she was discovering and reading the Psalms, the Gospel of Matthew, and Augustine, but also Rilke and Dostoevsky in a new way, with a transformed vision. And as she grew, we should say, in godliness, in holiness, was there anything extraordinary, or extreme? Well, extreme and extraordinary in that perhaps she became able to look at the camp guards, the disease and death there, and the certain future of her own death without hatred for the Germans, without rage against God (though that too would have been possible), and with the need "to give God shelter," room, a place even in hell. One thinks of the line in the Creed that is depicted in the Eastern Church icon of the Resurrection of Christ. "He descended into hell." Sometimes called the "harrowing of hell," Christ is shown blasting open the gates of Hades, the realm of the dead, with such force that bolts and the pieces of the lock are flying about. He takes by the hands Adam and Eve and behind them, those who died before he came, prophets, David the king, John the Baptist, the parents of his mother and of John the Baptist—and we are to see ourselves, daughters and sons of Adam and Eve, in the crowd that he leads in the holy dance into the heavenly kingdom. We think mostly of God as the one who protects, saves, gives shelter, but his friends the saints do the same for him and for each other. Christ is welcomed in the kingdom of death, Hell, by his cousin John the Baptists, other righteous figures—prophets, kings, martyrs, holy women and men—and truly he "rests in the saints." That we as creatures could do something for God is a reality often obscured by piety, but very much in line with what Sergius Bulgakov considered as the consequences of "God's becoming human" in the Incarnation.

Sanctity is always first a gift from God and of God himself. Sergius Bulgakov has God bending down over his creatures, his children, Adam and Eve, to explain to them why he made them—only out of love, only to have others with whom to share this love, himself. One is not just the possessor of holiness, one is living, breathing with Someone else, and then with many others. Thus the startling even disturbing idea that dominates Etty Hillesum's letters, that she is to give shelter, give a place to God in the camps, and that no matter the horror, God in turn holds her in his embrace of love.[34] Is this the reaction any rational person would expect to all the degradation and brutality, the inhumanity of one group of human beings to another? Perhaps in such a particular place and time, Rowan Williams wonders, the very reality of God and love had become homeless, thus in need of shelter. Thus he comes to see that such a life as Etty's ends up becoming a sign, becoming itself a sacred text, a "word."

> Remember that for Etty, the self's "safeguarding" of God is inseparable from that careful attention to what is given room in the self's encounter with itself: making space for sorrow, without its being crowded out

by anger or hate, is bound in with the self's hospitality to God. "God is in safe hands with us despite everything," she wrote, in September 1943. She died in November. To see that what matters is not that you are—in any easy sense—safe in the hands of God but that God is safe in your hands is to turn upside down any consolatory version of faith, to stake yourself indeed on an "eternal covenant". On this kind of inversion, we do not decide. Doors open, because of how life is in our times; through them something enters that we do not understand. A life is shaped, to the extent that we call it a home, a shelter, for something. And we argue for it or commend it not by dialectical nimbleness but by fidelity in some very prosaic things; perhaps we might even start by practising how to kneel.[35]

In considering Etty Hillesum with Rowan Williams, for all practical purposes we have left the ambit of the "cult of celebrity." True, Etty's writings have a minor cult status, but surely in this earthy young woman we are way beyond the pool of *santabili*—those capable of being recognized as saints. We have also gone beyond the usual boundaries and definitions of sainthood or sanctity. Perhaps difficult cases or candidates for canonization such as Thomas Merton, Oscar Romero, and Dorothy Day are also to be found here. Holiness knows no restrictions of ecclesiastical jurisdiction, position in life, miracles. In Etty, as well as others we are examining, we see someone whose personal life simply cannot fit within conventional moral or for that matter ecclesiastical frames. As women and men of intellect, they were also persons of passion. Their passion was revealed in their writings and concern for others, but also in their sexuality and in their relationships, whether happy or failed, whether ecclesiastically approvable or not. And in all of this, their "word" still can be listened to, we can see their witness and their connection to God. With the passage of time, their lives have taken on extraordinary, heroic colors. However, in their days they were easily lost in the crowd—of those swept up in the Great Depression, the wars, the Holocaust, the nuclear arms build-up, the civil rights movement, and beyond. They could easily have been forgotten, but their words and their lives remain with us. If we faced people like them today, would we be moved, edified? Merton was, in the words of a fellow monk I know, all his life a most restless being, constantly changing, moving away from where he had been earlier, now criticizing old comrades, ever finding new causes. His sheer interest in Eastern religions has made him suspect, like Bede Griffiths, Henri Le Saux, and others who were accused of promoting syncretism or even abandoning Christianity for Buddhism or Hinduism. The rumors and myths about Merton still continue to swirl, forty years after his death. Had he left monastic life or did he plan to do so? Was he assassinated by the CIA? Like Dorothy Day, Merton found himself in confrontation with the American Catholic hierarchy regarding the nuclear arms race, the civil rights movement and the war in Vietnam. After decades as a Catholic insider, a virtual icon revered for his best selling writings on the spiritual life, Merton wound up in his final years attacked, censored by his abbot general, criticized by conservative bishops and intellectuals.

One can also think of archbishop Oscar Romero here, whose process toward beatification and canonization is paused for further investigation of the social doctrine of the church in his homilies and writings.[36] Is it necessary that such as Merton, Day, or Romero be canonized at all? Clearly there are more saints than those canonized, as Thomas Rosica notes.

> Many think that sainthood is a privilege reserved only for the chosen few. Actually, to become a saint is the task of every Christian, and what's more, we could even say it's the task of everyone! How many times have we thought that the Saints are merely "eccentrics" that the Church exalts for our imitation; people who were so unrepresentative of and out of touch with the human scene? It is certainly true of all those men and women who were "eccentric" in its literal sense: they deviated from the centre, from usual practice, the ordinary ways of doing things, the established methods. Another way of looking at the saints is that they stood at the "radical centre."
>
> We need the example of these holy women and men who had no moderation but only exuberance! They were people with ordinary affections, who took God seriously and were therefore free to act with exuberance. Not measured or moderate, the Saint's response to God's extravagant love is equally immoderate, marked by fidelity and total commitment. G. K. Chesterton said: "[such] people have exaggerated what the world and the Church have forgotten."[37]

Yes, but with those we are thinking of here—Thomas Merton, Dorothy Day, Oscar Romero (among others)—their eccentricity was not accepted and officially approved by the church. Etty Hillesum and Simone Weil were not even in the Catholic Church. In their own time they had their critics, their detractors, and they still do. Maybe we can say that unlike a Padre Pio or a Mother Teresa or a Pope John Paul II, such persons of faith do not merit the cry, *subito santo!* As one reader of this study has wondered, perhaps there are good reasons for not quickly or even ever canonizing such people. Dorothy Day herself was adverse to ever being part of the process, and when it was inagurated there was at least one member of her family who protested it and vigorously.

The point was made earlier. Despite deliberate efforts to be more inclusive—and there are a number of examples to the contrary—those who are canonized overwhelmingly remain members of the clergy, founders and members of religious orders, martyrs, and individuals of heroic stature. Ordinary married people, professionals, and those who stand over against the culture, society, and the church remain unrepresented and to some extent marginalized. Almost thirty years after his assassination, Oscar Romero remains a conflicted, embattled figure in El Salvador and in the church in Latin America. The same holds for Fr. Alexander Men in Russia. A prophet *does* make enemies. Not just the writings but the lives of Dorothy Day and Thomas Merton and these others make it hard to incorporate them officially, at least, into the ranks of canonized saints, no matter Fr. Rosica's arguments for holy audacity.

But is their "exaggeration," their eccentricity, or better singularity, not somehow holy? I would like to think their lack of official recognition or their ecclesiastical marginality is significant, eschatologically so. They, like the prophets of the Hebrew Bible, like the first martyr, Stephen the deacon, stand in witness to God's holiness transcending assessment, evaluation, and institutional recognition. These people also point us in the direction we will head, in pursuit of the holiness of our time.

CHAPTER THREE

God's Humanity and Humanity's Becoming Godly

Eternal life consists in being continuously present before the face of God and continuously seeing oneself in God's light, from which one cannot hide. Does the dogma of the veneration of the saints and their canonization not exclude the notion of the relativity and compatibility of heaven and hell, even if in different forms and compoundings? This question can be answered by another question: Does human saintliness signify perfect sinlessness, and does canonization presuppose precisely such a conception of saintliness? We think that the testimony that canonization gives concerning saintliness has a somewhat different meaning, that of a sum total, in which sinful infirmities are submerged in a general saintliness. And this sum total is different in each individual case. It is not by chance that the Church distinguishes between major and minor saints . . . [T]his is what the prayer of the Church says about all human saintliness: "there is no one living who does not sin. You alone are without sin," . . . every human being has need of forgiveness and redemption by the Blood of the Lamb. In other words, the saintliness glorified by the Church signifies not sinlessness but righteousness as the sum total of pluses and minuses, experienced as a synthesis of bliss and suffering.[1]

This is the great Russian theologian of the twentieth century Sergius Bulgakov's (1871–1944) perceptive reflection on human holiness in the last book of his great trilogy, one of the last he completed in his remarkable life. Not surprisingly, it is called *The Bride of the Lamb,* from the vision of the seer John in the book of Revelation, and deals with the church as the communion of saints and the last things—life with God beyond this world and time. Despite questions about the orthodoxy or the conventionality of his theological writing, Bulgakov brings together tradition and modernity, Christianity and humanism, the divine and the human, as perhaps no other theologian of the modern era. Hans Urs von Balthasar is closest, and some of his thinking too has provoked controversy, and for the same reasons as Bulgakov's.

Typically, Bulgakov packs almost an entire book of ideas into a couple paragraphs, cited judiciously above. We will examine most of these themes as we move forward, such as the reality that holiness starts with God, is a gift of his life, is God's constant presence in a human life. Closely connected with this interpretation and emphasized by his student Paul Evdokimov, is the corollary, namely that holiness is not heroic feats of asceticism or virtue—exactly what the celebrity version of sanctity seems to insist. Rather, holiness has to do, is a relationship, with the Holy One and thus is connected to wholeness. Holiness, further, does not require the absence of sin and human qualities, eccentricities, phobias, sufferings—the substance of ordinary human life. Holiness is a struggle with the baggage of human existence, all the elements that make us who we are. Despite the claims of hagiography, the written lives of saints, and the characteristics deemed necessary for official church recognition or canonization, the personalities and lives of the saints remain truly human and particular, even imperfect. One can see in them the process of sanctification in progress. Every saint says, in the Eastern Church's prayer before communion, quoting St. Paul, "of sinners, I am the first." Likewise the funeral service notes "there is no one living who has not sinned," only God is without sin.

Holiness is diverse in shape because of the diversity of the saints. Bulgakov notes this in mentioning traditional categories, even "minor" and "major" saints. Icons of the assembly of saints often indicates this by grouping together, just as the preparatory rite of the Eastern liturgy (*proskome-*

dia), the prophets, apostles, martyrs, bishops, fathers and teachers, healers, holy women, and locally venerated saints of a country or region or monastery. Bulgakov observes too that there will always be saints never officially recognized by the churches. So, not only is sanctity diverse, never restricted to one set of categories, it is also universal. There are holy people of every century, every social class and country, every state in life, gender, age bracket.

Bulgakov featured the figure of Divine Wisdom or Sophia in much of his last twenty years of theological writing. He was accused, unjustly, of turning this figure from the Hebrew Bible into a fourth member of the Trinity, thus adding to the number of divine persons. Ecclesiastical divisions among the Russian Orthodox in Paris exacerbated these and other accusations that Bulgakov's work was a departure from a rigid idea of what theology should be, that is, merely commentary on the fathers.[2] In a still significant essay, published in the important collection *Zhivoe predanie* (*Living Tradition*) in 1937, Bulgakov argues that the fathers themselves provide the model for theological creativity, drawing from the biblical tradition but constantly pressing on to express the tradition in new concepts and to take on new issues.[3]

It was not just the omnipresent figure of Divine Wisdom in his writings that created problems for Bulgakov. Surely his effort, in this most biblical of figures, to say something about the consequences of the Incarnation, about the difference God becoming human made for us, would have been sufficiently provocative. Yet even more basic and challenging was Bulgakov's effort to show that the God—who made himself part of space, time, and the material world—nonetheless remains other than it and thus incapable of being reduced to acting as we do. In other words, while everything about God's becoming human is both anthropological and divine, there is the error of assuming that God thinks, feels, and acts just as we do. This is the reason why Bulgakov's reflections on the resurrection of all people (*apokatastasis*) has been so threatening.[4] The resurrection of all people has also been considered by, among others, Origen and Gregory of Nyssa, as well as Russian thinkers Vladimir Soloviev (1853–1900) and Nicolas Fedorov (1828–1903). How can God overlook the punishment of the guilty, seemingly making or allowing all, even those who have turned away, to return to him? Does God not seem to subvert the free wills of those who reject him? Is this not God's rejection of the greatest gift he has given humankind, namely freedom?

Bulgakov, like the noteworthy Christian thinkers before him, does not seek to turn the restoration or restitution of all the dead to God into a dogma or doctrine. Following Gregory of Nyssa, Origen, and the rest, he holds it as a hope, something for which we should pray, only a theological opinion (*theologumenon*). Yet he does wonder how the triumph of Christ's resurrection is absolute if the Evil One in the end can claim billions as his own. The tradition, voiced in the liturgy, seems to suggest this. The Paschal troparion of the Eastern Church states, "Christ is risen from the dead, trampling down death by death and upon those in the tombs bestowing life." The kontakion of the seventh tone reads, "The dominion of death can no longer hold men captive, for Christ descended, shattering and destroying its powers. Hell is bound, while the prophets rejoice and cry: The Savior has come to those in faith. Enter you faithful into the Resurrection." The homily of St. John Chrysostom read at the Eastern Church's Paschal vigil proclaims, "Christ is risen, and there are none left in the tombs."

These passages, however, demonstrate what Bulgakov understood: the opposite of evil is not virtue but the good. Father Sergius was remembered by his contemporaries for the uncommon radiance and joy he experienced in the liturgy particularly at Easter.[5] The source of this joy and of his optimism—despite so many heartbreaks and disappointments in his own life and in the world of the revolution, the Great Depression, and World War II, which he lived through—was his conviction that in the Resurrection, Christ once and for always was victorious over the Evil One and all evil. Holiness or human saintliness, as he calls it, is not perfection, not the absence of weaknesses or the obliteration of all failings, but rather the triumph of Christ, the presence of the Good One.

The source of all holiness is the Holy One. And this divine origin is the primary theological perspective for us as we examine holiness in our time. The holy life of God is given to men and women by God's work of creation, by his becoming human in the Incarnation, and by his death, rising, and sending of the Spirit. In the Hebrew Bible and Christian New Testament, all holiness is of God but comes to dwell, literally, "pitch its tent," in the human person. The very act of creation by God is also one of sanctification. We are made "in the image and likeness" of God, so holiness must mean remaining in that image and likeness, growing ever more "similar," ever like God.[6] Despite the fall from God, Adam and Eve, and thus all of humankind, retain the spark of divine life. Holiness is both divine and human. Women and men, as "friends of God," can be said to participate with him in his work. Thus they invent, create, a life of holiness not on their own, but in, with, and through him. As we shall see later, Simone Weil spoke of the need for such creativity and invention of holiness in our time.

Bulgakov had much to say about the Incarnation as God's humanization. The aim of his great trilogy of books, perhaps of all his writing the last two decades of his life, was to explore the meaning and the consequences of God becoming human in Christ. While the Council of Chalcedon had made a Christological statement, a dogma, it was a compromise among competing theological schools—Alexandria and Antioch, among others—and theologians. In the end the council confessed the divinity and humanity of Christ "in two natures, without confusion, without change, without division, without separation."[7] Stated in the negative, actually in Greek the a-privative, the dogma about the Incarnation, for Bulgakov, also needed a positive formulation.

Bulgakov chose to follow the formulation, "the humanity of God" (*Bogochelovechestvo*), a theological perception dear to the Russian tradition. First expressed by Soloviev, it insists on the material, historical, in short the *human* qualities of God's work.[8] God's humanization in the Incarnation has as its goal the corresponding divinization of humanity, our becoming "very similar," our becoming like God. The saying attributed to Athanasius the Great is: "God became human so that humans could become God-like." Turn it around, Bulgakov in effect said, and wonder what it might mean for God to become human. What would this mean for God? What would it mean for us human beings?

This bold claim is the theological foundation for any understanding of holiness. Much of the understanding of holiness of the past has dwelt either on the divine or on unusual, extraordinary characteristics and miracle. But if much of what God created is extraordinary only in its ordinary qualities, what then might this mean for the holiness of men and women today?

The Call to All: Prophets, Priest, Kings, and Friends of God

A second theological perspective is at once sacramental, ecclesial, and communal. This is the holiness of the whole people of God emphasized in the Hebrew Bible (Ex 19:5–6; Nm 16:1–35; Dt 14:2; Is 43:20–21), then presented anew in the First Letter of Peter in the New Testament. Those who believe in the living stone, Christ, become themselves "living stones making a spiritual house" (1 Pt 2:4–5). The apostle calls them "a chosen race, a royal priesthood, a consecrated nation, a people set apart to sing the praises of God" who called them out of darkness (1 Pt 2:9). This vision of the holiness of all was echoed by St. Paul, who calls the members of the church at Corinth, Rome, Thessalonika, and other locations "saints" (e.g., Col 1:2; Phil 1:1; 1 Cor 1:2; 2 Cor 1:1).[9]

A number of church fathers and teachers likewise saw holiness in the priestly service of all the baptized. This was championed in the Reformation, and rediscovered in the "return to the sources" by Catholic, Orthodox, and Protestant theologians after World War II. This is the universal priesthood of all the faithful, as opposed to those set apart by ordination, whether the levitical priesthood of the Hebrew Bible or the various offices of bishop, priest, and deacon in the early church. More recently an Orthodox theologian, at once a specialist in the New Testament, liturgy, church history, and canon law, Nicolas Afanasiev, had a profound effect on the theology of the church, or "ecclesiology," expressed in the documents of Vatican II.[10] For years before the 1960s, along with others in the Russian émigré intellectual community and with colleagues in the Western churches like Bernard Botte, Louis Bouyer, Henri de Lubac, and Jean Daniélou, among others, Afanasiev insisted on looking freshly at the early church, before it became a law-dominated, clerical, and officially recognized institution of the Roman empire.

> Authority is part of the life of the Church, which has this ministry of administration. But the ecclesial authority ought to conform to the nature of the Church and not be in conflict with it. If such authority claims to be superior to the Church then it must also be su-

perior to Christ. This is why neither the Church nor its authority can ever be founded upon a juridical principle, for the law is external to love. Such authority cannot belong to the vicars of Christ on earth, since God has not delegated his power to anyone but has put all people in submission to Christ, "put all things under his feet." In the Church, which is love, there is only the power of love. God gives the pastors not the charism of power but that of love and, through it, the power of love. The bishops who exercise the ministry of administration are the bearers of the power of love. The submission of all to the bishop takes place in love and it is by love that the bishop submits to the faithful. Every submission of one to another is realized through the mediation of the love we have for Christ. The submission of all to the bishop is actualized by the love he has for all and by the reciprocal love of the faithful for him. There can be no other foundation of power in the Church, for Christ is the only foundation of power in it. The pastors are able to have only that which Christ gives to the Church. Law as a foundation of authority in the Church is not sent down as a charismatic gift, for Christ does not possess any law. "Take my yoke upon you, and learn from me; for I am gentle and lowly in heart, and you will find rest for your souls" (Matt. 11:29). The power of Christ in the Church is the power of love, acquired by the love which he has for it.[11]

Following the lead of a procession of scholars, from Ignatius of Antioch, Tertullian, and Irenaeus of Lyons down to Rudolph Sohm, Afanasiev sketched out a still-radical, challenging view of the church as a community of baptized women and men, ruled by the Holy Spirit's power and the gift or charism of love. Every position or office, from that of the bishop, presbyter, deacon, and reader on down, was founded upon the relation of every Christian to each other in the love of Christ and the Spirit. Each office in the church was rooted in relationships of mutual love and legitimated by service to the community and the recognition of the assembly. Consecration or ordination by the laying on of hands conferred both the Spirit's grace and the community's election and assent to work for the church. Hence the exclamation still heard in the Eastern Church ordination rite: *axios, axios, axios;* "Worthy, worthy, worthy."[12]

This relationship of love is quite the opposite of the extreme clerical and hierarchical pyramid of power, heading from an elite downward to the mass of the faithful. Afanasiev returns us to a smaller and simpler church, and a much more local one. Yet careful historian that he is, this is not a romantic evocation of a golden moment, forever lost. Contrary to a critic who characterizes him as discovering or creating an "ecclesial paradise" in the first centuries, Afanasiev insists that the essential elements of church life come from Christ himself, echoed in the teaching of the apostles in the New Testament.[13] Each eucharistic community was the church fully, though in the bonds of communion it was linked to every other such community in love. The one who presided on a day-to-day basis in the life of the church community was also the one who presided at the celebration of the "sacrament of the church," the Eucharist. And the one who presided did so in love and in service of the others and in constant relationship to them.

The apostolic church did not know the separation of clerics from laics in our meaning of the words and it did not have the terms themselves in its usage. This is a basic fact of the ecclesial life in the primitive era, but it would be wrong to infer from this fact that ministry in the Church was exhausted by the notion of the priestly ministry, common for all. It was a ministry of the Church. Another fact of the life of the primitive Church was the diversity of ministries. The same Spirit by whom all were baptized into one body and of whom all were made to drink distributes particular gifts to each one "for the common good (*sympheron*)" (1 Cor 12.7), for action and service within the Church. "And the gifts were that some should be apostles, some prophets, some evangelists, some pastors and teachers, to equip the saints for the work of ministry, for building up the body of Christ (Eph 4.11–12)." The diversity of ministries stems from the "organic" nature of the Church. Each of its members occupies in it his own position and place, proper to him alone. "God arranged the organs in the body, each one of them, as he chose" (1 Cor 12.18). In a living organism, place and position of its members depends on the functions executed by them. So in Christ's body, diverse ministries are associated with the place and position of the members. The gifts of the Spirit are not given for their own sake as a reward of some sort, but for ministry in the Church, and they are given to those who already have drunk of the Spirit.[14]

This church of the first five centuries, however, passed into the later models of the imperial episcopacy, into the domination of the clerical order, the centralization of all local churches in both a diocesan episcopal authority or, in the West, the universal pastoral authority of the bishop of Rome, "first among equals," later simply "first." There are a number of dangers inherent in looking back to the church of an earlier period. We risk idealizing, even romanticizing the earlier time at the expense of the reality of that period, not to mention the real demands of our own era. Further, we entertain the notion that we can return to a primitive purity, escaping all the decadence that has piled up over the centuries. The nostalgia for the past, for the "church of the apostles," obscures the very pointed conflicts and difficulties of the early years—something Afanasiev himself sought to make clear. There is no ideal church or era to which to we can return, whether in the first century of the common era or some other allegedly "golden age" of ecclesial existence.

The priesthood of all the faithful, however, is not the stuff of nostalgia. Rather it is the most important identity for all Christians. As Afanasiev shows, it is rooted in the Hebrew Bible's understanding of the consecration of the whole community by God, though in the New Testament there is no longer a priestly tribe or caste set apart. Rather, there is only one high priest, as the Letter to the Hebrews proclaims. Yet by initiation, by baptism and chrismation/confirmation, each and every person is consecrated to offer the sacrifice of praise and thanksgiving, to proclaim the Gospel, and to do the works of love as a sign of the arrival of the kingdom of God. So each Christian is priest, prophet, and king, but in all of these each is a servant of God and of the rest of the people of God. In the early church anyone elected, called, and ordained to preside over the Eucharist and thus the community had to be called from among the members of that community. And such a presider, whether later called bishop or presbyter or deacon, was called not to an elite position to be honored by a corps of servants. These individuals were called to be preachers and leaders, to be sure, but first and foremost they were called to be servants of the servants of God.

We could find no better universal model for holiness than this, because the priesthood of all the baptized incorporates virtually every state in life and admits to every kind of occupation or status, from that of a patriarch or bishop to that of a parent, from a monastic to a student, a spouse to a scientist. As Paul Evdokimov's son, retired professor and priest Michel Evdokimov, related to me, many a Sunday afternoon after a joint family meal, his father and Afanasiev had the opportunity to share their thinking and writing. It is thus no surprise that the priesthood of all the faithful plays so central a role in their work. Sentences from Afanasiev's posthumously published *The Church of the Holy Spirit* (or the journal article versions of its contents) seem to be quoted or echoed by lines from Evdokimov's *The Ages of the Spiritual Life* or his essay on marriage and vocation, *The Sacrament of Love*. Evdokimov surely acknowledges the commonality of vision in the section on Afanasiev in his study of contemporary Russian theology.[15]

The significance of the priesthood of the baptized is neither to make a detour in church history nor to dismiss the place of the ordained. It is not a form of clergy bashing. Rather the universality of this priesthood emphasizes the *communal character of holiness* versus the often individualized interpretation of sanctity. The identity of priest/prophet/king is given to *all*. At the eucharistic assembly and everywhere else, every Christian shares in celebration as well as the ministry, that is, service. The enactment of this service is personal, according to the individual talents and training, the life and place of the person. The *baptismal character* of holiness is rooted in the death and rising of Christ. Holiness is never just about me—my yearnings, my vision, my plans—but first and foremost about God. And yet holiness is supremely personal, even idiosyncratic.

HOLINESS AND WHOLENESS

The personal quality of holiness is a third theological element.

> There is in all visible things an invisible fecundity, a dimmed light, a
> meek namelessness, a hidden wholeness. This mysterious Unity and

Integrity is Wisdom, the Mother of all, *Natura naturans.* There is in all things an inexhaustible sweetness and purity, a silence that is a fount of action and joy. It rises up in wordless gentleness and flows out to me from the unseen roots of all created being, welcoming me tenderly, saluting me with indescribable humility. This is at once my own being, my own nature, and the Gift of my Creator's Thought and Art within me, speaking as Hagia Sophia, speaking as my sister, Wisdom.[16]

In his prose poem Thomas Merton celebrates the figure of God's Wisdom, *Hagia Sophia,* "Holy Wisdom," and inherent in his experience of Wisdom is his conviction of her feminine gender and personality. The figure of Wisdom, as noted, permeated Sergius Bulgakov's writing and was the cause of his being charged with heresy, a charge of which he was exonerated.

It is not only the feminine that is of significance but also the intimacy of Wisdom, or, better, the sense Merton had that within each of us was an authentic, true self, the gift of God's creation, whose companion constantly was God's Wisdom.

Sophia, the feminine child, is playing in the world, obvious and unseen, playing at all times before the Creator. Her delights are to be with the children of men. She is their sister. The core of life that exists in all things is tenderness, mercy, virginity, the Light, the Life considered as passive, as received, as given, as taken, as inexhaustibly renewed by the Gift of God. Sophia is Gift, is Spirit, *Donum Dei.*[17]

Throughout Merton's writings run the themes of the true self as the goal of sanctity. As early as his *Seeds of Contemplation* he writes:

For me to be a saint means to be myself. Therefore the problem of sanctity and salvation is in fact the problem of finding out who I am and of discovering my true self.[18]

Not only does our surrounding culture offer all kinds of identities based on youth, beauty, or wealth, we are expert concoctors of a myriad of false or illusory selves. They are evanescent, imaginary, alienated from others and

from our true being and meaning. This is a major theme in Merton's thinking and tracking it is far beyond our purpose here. Yet it must be said that
Merton by no means rejects the diversity of roles we perform and statuses
we occupy in life. Further, he himself became painfully conscious of how
much we change, in fact need to change as we live. He looked back in dis-
gust at the self-assured and rigid piety of his first books, especially the best-
selling autobiography, *The Seven Storey Mountain*. Many Mertons, that is,
many versions or caricatures of the writer, the monk, and the man, had to
die on the road to integrity, to true selfhood, to wholeness, to holiness. His
letters and journals document this personal pilgrimage, down to the last
days before an accident took his life in Bangkok on December 10, 1968.

In his first published collections of journal entries, *The Sign of Jonas*,
Merton leads the reader on a guided daily round of services, work projects,
frustrations, and joys in the early years of his monastic life and priesthood.
Unlike the posthumously published journals, these are deliberately chosen passages rather than the daily flow of entries, and Merton himself
admitted to polishing them stylistically. In the epilogue, "Fire Watch, July 4,
1952," we follow him on a late night fire safety tour of the monastery buildings. After hearing the snoring of those asleep on this hot, humid night,
watching the shadows in the empty long nave of the church, feeling the
rush of the night air high above the monastery in the church tower, an intense dialogue concludes the book, between the figure of Jonas the prophet,
who represents the young monk—Thomas Merton—and the Lord. The
most beautiful lines are God's, and several of them appear on an icon of
Merton, flanking the Mother of God with the great saint of his order, Bernard of Clairvaux.[19]

More than any other passage in the enormous body of Merton's writings, this passage expresses the boundless compassion, the "absurd love"
of God, and the action of mercy that is the heart of holiness.

The Voice of God is heard in Paradise:
*What was vile has become precious. What is now precious was never
vile. I have always known the vile as precious: for what is vile I know not
at all. What was cruel has become merciful. What is now merciful was
never cruel. I have always overshadowed Jonas with my mercy, and my*

cruelty I know not at all. Have you had sight of me, Jonas, My child?
Mercy within mercy within mercy. I have forgiven the universe without
end, because I have never known sin.
    What was poor has become infinite. What is infinite was never poor.
I have always known poverty as infinite: riches I love not at all. Prisons
within prisons within prisons. Do not lay up for yourselves ecstasies upon
earth, where time and space corrupt, where the minutes break in and steal.
No more lay hold on time, Jonas, My son, lest the rivers bear you away.
    What was fragile has become powerful. I loved what was most frail.
I looked upon what was nothing. I touched what was without substance,
and within what was not, I am.[20]

Note that the overwhelming mercy of God does not loom over us, does
not stand alone for Merton. God who is "love without limits" (a phrase
from the work of Lev Gillet) is inextricably tied up with Jonas, with each
of his creatures, his children. The fragile becomes powerful, what was
cruel becomes merciful. God does not need his creature, but the abun-
dance of love propels God into creation, into relationship, Covenant then
Incarnation, Torah then the cross and resurrection. As much as Merton
dwells on life as the search for wholeness, for the true self, it is for him also
a search for God, seeking to dwell in and with God.

Merton's idea of holiness as being the self, the true self that God created me to be, is an important ingredient to the exploration we are making
of holiness in our time. It highlights the personal but also the interpersonal dimensions of holiness. No one can be a Christian alone. No one can
be holy by oneself.

Merton remains an imposing figure, not just because of his monastic life and his many personal controversies but mostly because of his voice
and his honesty. His books remain in print, his ideas continue to intrigue
and challenge, scholarship grows about him, his life, and his writings.[21] It
is neither possible nor necessary to go over the terrain of his own life. But
if one is interested in sources on holiness in our time, holiness in everyday life, holiness of varying shapes and forms, Merton is a treasure trove.
His writing in many genres reveals his own journey of recognition. From
what he later would characterize as a too rigid, formulaic, and sentimental

religious observance, he matured but also deepened. He became able to accept human weakness, his own; and then at the same time his awareness of the world, its beauty and suffering, also was enhanced.

Holiness is both God's gift and action—not the result of our striving. Yet strive and struggle we must, to put God's work into action in our own. St. Paul spoke of putting on the mind of Christ. It is also a matter of struggling to see as God sees. A remarkable writer we will meet and listen to later—Sara Miles—learned this in her own conversion and in her spiritual as well as professional life.[22] The hungry people who came to the food pantry she organized in her parish church were not always loveable. First it was the new Russian immigrant women who were hard to take with their aggressive, almost assaultive behavior, then the Chinese, then fellow—but very different—Episcopalians. Eventually, but of course, this also would include members of her own parish community, those with whom she shared the bread of life and the cup of salvation, her sisters and brothers—a tough lesson in the reality of Christianity and the church.[23] And there were so many others who were not attractive, deserving, or grateful. Every person, though, is a child of God, Sara learned. Each is loved and created beautiful in God's sight. For many of us, the next step of growth is even harder— to be able to see the same truth about ourselves, holiness as wholeness, holiness as truth.

CHAPTER FOUR

A Call to All,
But Can There Be Models?

I still worry that focusing on the saints in heaven can draw attention away from the God who alone is worthy of worship. It is one thing to call my brother-in-law Jim in Nebraska and ask him to pray for me. Jim is a farmer who typically has mud on his boots. I like him a lot, but I am not inclined to bow in his presence. Calling on St. Anthony or St. Jude, though—that's a different thing altogether. Their pictures show them with halos around their heads, and when you look into the eyes on their statues you get the sense—at least I do—that you are in the presence of a different sort of being. I worry about people having holy feelings about the saints that are better connected directly to Jesus.

Evangelical theologian and president of Fuller Theological Seminary Richard Mouw, like many Christians, found it hard to get close to "saints" like Anthony or Jude or Francis of Assisi the way Catholics and Eastern Orthodox do. The halos and most likely the candles and prayers offered were too much for the directness of his Evangelical upbringing and experience. There is God . . . and there is the rest of us, whether the apostles,

Augustine, or Luther, or for that matter Martin Luther King Jr. or Mother Teresa—we are all God's creatures, his children, and we are all sinners. To single out anyone, no matter how heroic a life, for special treatment or veneration simply did not resonate with what the Bible teaches. Yet as homely as the example Mouw gives us is, it was enough to shed light for him on the most fundamental connection we have to the saints. They are human beings. So are we. And we all need each other, just as we all need God. Despite the prejudices of his Protestant views of God's transcendence and our salvation by "faith alone," it took the very human way in which people approach the saints to lift the veil, as it were. Mouw continues:

> So, even though I was a bit chastened for having been so firmly opposed to praying to the saints, I stuck with my Protestant convictions on the subject. After the debate, however, a priest came up to me to tell me a lively story that weakened my resistance a little more. One of his parishioners came to him a while back, he said, concerned about how to make it through Thanksgiving Day with his wife's family. "We go there every year," he told the priest, "and every year I end up fighting with my mother-in-law. We simply do not get along!" The man had pleaded with his wife to let him stay home this time around, but she wouldn't hear of it. So in desperation he was coming to the priest for help. What could he possibly do to make it through the day without getting into the annual battle?
>
> The priest told him to pick a saint who might have some special understanding of this sort of case, and to pray daily to that saint for help. The man agreed to do that. A few days after Thanksgiving the man returned. "Great advice!" he told the priest. "I picked St. Francis," he reported, "and I said to him, 'Francis, you hung around with some pretty undesirable people, so I think you can understand my problem. Please help me with my mother-in-law.'" After a few prayers to the saint, the man reported, he got this response: "I once hugged a leper," Francis told him, "and if I could do that, you surely can hug your mother-in-law." When Thanksgiving Day came, the first thing the man did was to give his mother-in-law a warm hug. "She was so surprised she started to cry," he told the priest. "And we had a great day. St. Francis helped me to have a wonderful Thanksgiving!"

Again, I was almost persuaded. As I thought about the priest's story, I realized that rather than worrying that the man who prayed to St. Francis had flirted with idolatry, I ought to be grateful that he was reaching past *American Idol* for examples about how to treat people.

I am still not ready to start talking with Christians who have already gone on to heaven. But I am more aware of how many of us in the Protestant world operate with a too-small circle of Christian fellow travelers. I may not feel the need for actual conversations with people who have halos around their heads. But I do need to know more of the stories about what they were like before they earned their halos. The statue of St. Francis that I now have in our yard, near the bird feeder, isn't for me an object of religious devotion. But it does serve as a reminder that there are times when a hug can make a big difference in how my day goes.[1]

Mouw's story is in its own way both very humorous and very beautiful. It is another testimony about the amazing way that a simple Tuscan friar from the twelfth and thirteenth centuries somehow connects with so many: not just Protestants hesitant about saints but Buddhists, agnostics, Buckminster Fuller—anyone who can resonate with his love of the world and people. Holiness has this inclusive quality, this irresistible attraction. Assisi is the sacred circus it is because of the millions who have come to be where the little poor brother lived. I would dare to say that there is something of this same very deep affection in the way that pilgrims continue to flock to Graceland, leaving flowers for Elvis, more than thirty years after his death.

To be sure, Elvis is not Francis. But the blessed tie that binds hearts to each other is at the core of faith, is it not? We get attached to others though they are miles away from us. We get enraged watching the news. We weep for the nameless victims of disasters and terrorism we see there. And at the heart of our attraction to holy women and men is the tie to them as people like us, sisters and brothers who have laughed and cried, worried and planned—in short, shared the joys and the demands of living. Francis, little poor man that he was, looms very large over the centuries, as do so many others mentioned here. We are also attracted to the magnitude of their lives, the heroism of both their words and actions.

Yet as has been argued here too, the call to holiness is for all: men and women, single and married, old and young, wealthy and poor, educated or not. Christ shatters all the seemingly impenetrable boundaries of the ancient world: Gentile and Jew, master and slave, male and female, and every other wall that continues to divide today. The Spirit comes down upon all, enabling those who could not understand each other's language or culture to be brothers and sisters. Paul calls all the members of the communities "saints." This is clearly the understanding of holiness in the New Testament and in the earliest days of the church. Among the most revolutionary aspects of the Christians' identity was the radical universal character of God's kingdom.

> But now that faith has come we are no longer under a slave looking after us; for all of you are the children of God, through faith, in Christ Jesus, since every one of you that has been baptized has been clothed in Christ. There can be neither Jew nor Greek, there can be neither slave nor freeman, there can be neither male nor female—for you are all one in Christ Jesus. (Gal 3:26–29)

The Gospel's way is for all, and every mark of distinction is removed, whether of nationality, social class, or gender. In the Eastern Church liturgy, when the eucharistic bread is elevated, the celebrant proclaims: "Holy things, for the holy," that is, the eucharistic gifts are for the holy people of God, the communion of saints. And the people respond: "One is holy, one is Lord, Jesus Christ, to the glory of God the Father. Amen."

There is a unity in holiness, rooted in Christ, and therefore holiness is also universal—holiness is for all. However, Christian history has witnessed much deviation from this primitive simplicity, equality, and universal appeal. As Afanasiev argues, law came to protect and then replace love as the norm for life in the community. Ordained ministries of loving service within the community became detached and formed independent, authoritarian hierarchies. As for holiness, a restriction of models to the martyrs, to clergy and monastics, to one or another gender, class, or state in life emerged. It seems as if there are great "public" saints to be canonized, celebrated in liturgical prayer and iconography. And then there is the rest of the community, who at best can become "private," anonymous saints. Such narrowing cannot capture the fullness and diversity of sanctity and has led to the stereotyping of patterns for holiness.

Cases Clashing

Past profiles of holy people collide with the actual men and women of our time. Historical definitions of likeness to God clash with both contemporary culture and the Gospel's openness. Less unusual, that is, more ordinary, "hidden" ways of life have yet to be discovered.

From traditional perspectives, especially those of hagiography, the narrative of saints' lives, the essentially hidden character of holiness in our time may at first appear problematic. However, the lives of Christ as well as that of his Mother, those of such righteous figures as Zechariah and Elizabeth, Simeon and Anna, Joachim and Anna, of the apostles and other earliest disciples, were most ordinary and for the most part (a few instances excepted) hidden from historical scrutiny. To speak of holiness in our time as both ordinary and hidden, while challenging in itself, does not imply a total rejection of the church's past, of the models and examples of holiness of former centuries. More often than not an unexpected continuity with the past will be uncovered. The continuing significance of the monastic life is one example. Yet a problem remains. If, according to Paul Evdokimov, the very features that distinguish holiness in our day include diversity and an everyday, most ordinary quality, then we should not be looking only for models in the traditional, historical categories of saints. Are there not some women and men of "hidden holiness" that we could contemplate?

A Clergy Spouse and Mother: Olga Arsamquq Michael

The life of Olga Arsamquq Michael (1916–79) is important to consider here, as well as the story since her death. Olga, or Olinka, was the wife of Archpriest Nikolai O. Michael, from the village of Kwethluk, on the Kuskokwim River in Alaska. In some of the passages cited she is called "Matushka" Olga, the familiar form of endearment among Russian Orthodox

Christians for priest's spouses, literally meaning "little mother." Revered in Alaska, she has yet to be even proposed officially for canonization review, and given the rise of more traditionalist directions in her church, the Orthodox Church in America (OCA), I would say, sadly, that her case will most likely wait for a very long time, if not be bypassed completely. This, however, has not deterred people from venerating her locally. The website from which some of the accounts about her are taken, as well as the icons displayed on it, are indications of unofficial veneration. Her case is also instructive of what can occur when a particular person's life is exemplary but perhaps not striking enough.

That she was a priest's wife in Alaska already meant a very full, demanding, and rich life. She seems to have come from a troubled family herself. But she married, raised her own children, worked as a midwife, and cared for grandchildren and the young and old of the parish. The collection of roles she fulfilled in both the life of her parish and her family was diverse: cooking, sewing clothes, directing the choir, baking eucharistic bread, counseling those in distress. She is remembered as having all the music and texts of the great liturgical feasts memorized. Her own children gave her more than a dozen grandchildren. Of all the skills and activities that were still so much a part of Yup'ik life even in the post–World War II years in Alaska, she excelled in sewing, outfitting her husband in liturgical vestments and members of her family in parkas, boots, sweaters, and mittens. Gifts of her sewing found their way far beyond the circles of family and parish. The accounts of her life and work will attest to this.

Olga possessed many gifts and skills integral to the broader circles of parish, family, village, and culture. With her children grown, she accompanied her husband to church gatherings and became a kind of informal yet important teacher for younger priests' wives and women leaders. She was diagnosed with terminal cancer after prolonged loss of weight and weakness, and faced death with joy and acceptance. After her daughters made a pilgrimage to the relics of St. Herman of Alaska on her behalf, their prayers apparently brought a miraculous healing or at least more than a year's remission. But in the end Olga succumbed to cancer on November 8, 1979. So widespread was her renown, hundreds came to her funeral and burial liturgies. Michael Oleksa described the circumstances of her burial.

It appeared that the normal snow and river ice of that time of the
year would prevent many people from attending her funeral. But the
weather uncharacteristically changed and a southerly wind helped to
melt the ice and snow, allowing parishioners from the neighboring
village to make the journey to Kwethluk. Hundreds of friends . . . filled
the newly-consecrated church on the extraordinary spring-day of the
funeral. Upon exiting the church, the procession was joined by a flock
of birds, although by that time of year, all birds have long since flown
south. The birds circled overhead, and accompanied the coffin to the
grave site. The usually frozen snows had been easy to dig because of
the unprecedented thaw. That night after the memorial meal, the wind
began to blow again, the ground froze, ice covered the river, winter returned. It was as if the earth itself had opened to receive this woman.
The cosmos still cooperates and participates in worship the Real People
[i.e. the name the native people give to themselves] offer to God.[2]

In addition to the various extraordinary aspects of her later life and especially the events surrounding her death and burial, those devoted to her
have begun to collect accounts of persons in distress "seeing" Mother Olga
in dreams, very typical for the indigenous culture. A theme apparent in
such dreams characterizes her as listener and healer, not only of emotional
burdens and physical illness but of spiritual affliction. Her own life of hard
work and very possibly her own history of abuse as a child figure promi-
nently in these sightings or visions, and are linked closely to the compassion
and healing she brings through them to those who are suffering.

John Shimchick recounts a tale from a woman who had long suffered
from the consequences of sexual abuse experienced as a child.

I was deeply at prayer and awake. I had remembered an event that
was very scary. My prayer began with my asking the Holy Theotokos
(Mother of God) for help and mercy. Gradually I became aware of
standing in the woods feeling a little scared. Soon a gentle wave of tenderness began to sweep through the woods followed by a fresh gar-
den scent. I saw the Virgin Mary, dressed as she is in an icon, but more
natural looking and brighter, walking toward me. As she came closer

I was aware of someone walking behind her. She stepped aside and gestured to a short, wise looking woman. I asked her, "Who are you?" and the Virgin Mary answered, "St. Olga." St. Olga gestured for me to follow her. We walked a long way until there weren't many trees. We came to a little hill that had a door cut into the side. She gestured for me to sit and she went inside. After a little while some smoke came out of the top of the hill and from the open hole on the top of the hill. Everything around me felt gentle, especially Mother Olga.

The little hill house smelled like wild thyme and white pine in the sun with roses and violets mixed in. Mother Olga helped me up onto a kind of platform bed, resembling a driftwood box filled with moss and grasses. It was soft and smelled like the earth and the sea. I was exhausted and lay back. St. Olga went over to the lamp and warmed up something which she rubbed on my belly. I looked five months pregnant. (I was not pregnant for real at the time.) I started to labor. I was a little scared. Mother Olga climbed up beside me and gently holding my arm pretended to labor with me, showing me what to do and how to breathe. She still hadn't said anything. She helped me push out what seemed to be afterbirth, that soaked into the dried moss on the bed. I was very tired and crying a little from relief when it was over. Up until this she hadn't spoken, but her eyes spoke with great tenderness and understanding.

We both got up and had some tea. As we were drinking it, holy Mother Olga gradually became the light in the room. Her face appeared to have a strong light bulb or the sun shining under her skin. But I think the whole of her glowed. It was the kind of loving gaze from a mother to an infant that connects and welcomes a baby to life. She seemed to pour tenderness into me through her eyes. This wasn't scary even though, at the time, I didn't know about people who literally shone with the love of God. (It made more sense after I read about St. Seraphim). I know now that some very deep wounds were being healed at the time. She gave me back my own life which had been stolen, a life that is now defined by the beauty and love of God for me, the restored work of His Hands.

After some time I felt that I was filled with wellness and a sense of quiet entered my soul, as if my soul had been crying like a grief-stricken abandoned infant and had finally been comforted. Even now as I write . . . the miracle of peacefulness, and also the zest for life which wellness has brought, causes me to cry with joy and awe. Only after this did Holy Mother Olga speak. She spoke about God and people who choose to do evil things. She said that the people who hurt me thought they could make me carry their evil inside of me by rape. She was very firm when she said, "That's a lie. Only God can carry evil away. The only thing they could put inside of you was the seed of life which is a creation of God and cannot pollute anyone." I was never polluted. It just felt that way because of the evil intentions of the people near me. What I had held inside me was the pain, terror, shame and helplessness I felt. We had labored together and that was all out of me now. She burned some grass over the little flame and smoke went right up to God who is both the judge and the forgiver. I understood by the "incense" that it wasn't my job to carry the sins of the people against me either. It was God's, and what an ever-unfolding richness this taste of salvation is.

At the end of this healing time we went outside together. It was not dark in the visioning prayer. There were so many stars stretching to infinity. The sky was all a shimmer with a moving veil of light. (I had seen photos of the Northern Lights, but didn't know they moved.) Either Matushka Olga said, or we both heard in our hearts—I can't remember which—that the moving curtain of light was to be for us a promise that God can create great beauty from complete desolation and nothingness. For me it was proof of the healing—great beauty where there had been nothing before but despair hidden by shame and great effort.

This account is full of details rooted in Alaskan life, like the little "hill house," the grass burning, and the tea, but also with emblems of another world, of heaven. The Mother of God is present, looking, of course, just as she does in the icons in church and at home. Mother Olga speaks with reassurance and warmth, as she did in her village, but she is now "St. Olga." The narrator has quite naturally relocated and reidentified her. No approved liturgical hymns are required, nor icons, because the dead are still part of the tribe. In some tribes the "spirit houses" on top of the graves signify the enduring presence of the dead. They are not really departed but are members of the community.

John Shimchick concludes that it is hard to assess the significance of these and other accounts of Olga and her life. While so ordinary as to be inconspicuous, her holiness was nonetheless real and immediately after her death was if anything recognized as both everyday yet wonderful. However, Shimchick recognizes that in the increasingly "saintly" stories of appearances, visions, and healings, one must read the start of an authentic local veneration of Olga by her community.[3]

Here is a more intimate account from a native Alaskan Orthodox Christian who presents a "local" or "natural" interpretation. I find it striking that from the start the simplicity of her sanctity, a "hidden holiness," is recognized.

It is a joy to write to you about Blessed Mother Olga. She is a wonderful blessing to us and a model of the simplicity and spirituality possible today, even in the midst of modern life. I think her piety is best revealed in the Judgment Sunday gospel about Jesus separating the sheep and the goats. She led a very quiet life full of this kind of Christian love. Her life of deep and continuous prayer is evident through her actions while she was alive. Whatever the need and whatever the opportunity, she always put love of the other first.

She had deep empathy and discretion for all the people who came to her in need, especially the women she served as midwife. Often situations of sexual abuse would be made known only to a midwife. She would be the only person they could turn to and then only if they really trusted her. There were no resident Doctors and for a long time only a very small dispensary. I'm not at all sure how much of her healing, especially of women from abuse and rape, will ever be known to anyone other than the ones she healed. People in a small villages keep silent about this kind of pain even these days.

There is something specifically Yup'ik in her faithfully fulfilling roles of caregiving and healing in her community, as the narrator emphasizes below. Being a midwife gave Olga unique access to women in the most intimate experiences of their lives. One could almost say that beyond her physical midwifery she was also a spiritual midwife, helping others to self-understanding, even in coming to terms with some aspects of tribal life that were cruel and destructive. Her own experiences growing up as well as in her own marriage—experiences of abuse by some accounts—did not destroy her but rather furnished her with the compassion and insight with which she assisted others, functioning both as their advocate and therapist. The exquisite sense of the financial and physical needs of others was an important aspect of Yup'ik culture. However, it also had to be incarnated, enacted, and Olga's seemed to be a particularly radical version, one which imprinted itself on the memory of fellow villagers as well as her own granddaughter, as we will hear. The account continues, and I have decided to cite most of it because, despite its length, it is a relatively unembellished and free of pious interpolation, a direct first-person description of what holiness looks like.

> Theirs was a poor family too, but somehow that did not count with her. She lived in a three room house with no running water, no sewer connection and no furnace. This life style is still quite common in rural Alaska. She had to carry water every day for her eleven children. Her children remember her giving away their clothes, before they had outgrown them, to children in their village who were in greater need. She used to say to them, "If you see your dress on someone else, please don't mention it or say anything about it."

As Mother Olga becomes known to more and more people, her radical sense of our common life and sharing will become an important part of her gifts to us. God reveals his saints to us fully themselves and fully glorified. Mother Olga's Yup'ikness is part of her gift to us.

> The Yup'ik Eskimos have a sense of community that I find quite amazing and is definitely part of the goodness of God that she brings to us. Very much like the early church, Yup'iks believe in sharing what they have. The worst thing I heard someone say to a two and half year old is that she was stingy about sharing her cookie . . .

Mother Olga's Yup'ik life also models for us the eternal value of understanding our relatedness one to another. God will use the example of her whole life to draw us closer to His goodness, His bounty and His loving will for us. Our ways of honoring that relationship will be different, but I think her example asks us to examine the depth of our love for each other and our faithfulness to the call to love God in our neighbor.

It is her deep spiritual life that guided her through the transition from a completely traditional life style to one comfortable in the modern world. Here, too, her example of inner calm and spiritual steadfastness is a strong part of her gifts to us. She hid her life in Christ, was very humble and unassuming, very quiet. Visitors to her house, while her husband was the priest in Kwethluk, say that she was almost invisible, so gentle and complete was her sense of hospitality and service.

She lived a life of deliberate generosity. Once she told one of her daughters to invite a specific girl home to play. This child was being neglected and badly treated at home. Alcohol and child abuse happen in small villages too. Mother Olga knew that the girl had been told not to eat at anyone's house so she cooked potato pancakes and, keeping her back to the table, kept piling them on a plate from the stove. Her daughter whispered to her that the little girl was stealing the food. This is a big no-no in a culture which sees greed as a major failing. Mother Olga put her finger to her lips and shushed her daughter asking if the little girl was still eating. With each yes, she cooked more pancakes and put them on the table until the little girl was full. For her love came first even above cultural norms and supposed righteousness. This little story is very healing for anyone who has suffered from deprivation and neglect as a child. Blessed Mother Olga is a saint they can turn to for healing from the pain and loneliness, and especially the lost self-esteem that is the result of neglect and abandonment.

She never criticized her children and gave them great freedom and respect. One of her daughter's friends told me that they used to go over to play at her house and leave all their toys out, but Mother Olga never said anything. After a few years, the girls realized that they had been making a lot of work for her and began to put the toys away themselves. Blessed Mother Olga's way was to understand what children were capable of doing and let them become responsible for themselves. She believed in not forcing them to conform to her set of rules whenever possible and never using shame to discipline. This, too, is a very Yup'ik way of child care when the cultural expression of that is intact.

As they grew so did the expectations. When her girls were big enough, she would ask them to accompany her to do housework for the ill and old people in the village. When they were old enough, they went wherever she saw the need. Sharing didn't just mean clothes and food but also time and effort. She taught what it means to be a fully alive human being, connected to people through love and service by example. She was good at many kinds of hand work, sewing and knitting mostly.

People remember her stopping whatever she was doing in order to help anyone with just about anything. I think she was aware of Jesus in all the people she saw but I think she was very simple about it. She didn't talk a lot. She just would go ahead and do what was needed. She would stop whatever she was doing to finish a snow boot sole that was too difficult for her friend, knowing a leaky boot meant death for the wearer.

For many years several times a week, she hauled wood and water to make a steam bath to share with a friend who was blind. She used to make traditional fur boots and parkas as donations to be raffled by other communities around Alaska which were trying to raise money.

Mother Olga was in the first generation of people in her village to be baptized Orthodox as a child. She was probably one of the few people who lived both in the traditional ancient world of the Yup'iks and in our modern one. So it isn't surprising that when the Theotokos (the Mother of God) revealed her to us the context of the healing was so traditionally Eskimo . . .

Mother Olga was a midwife and a healer. She was known for her foreknowledge of who was pregnant even before they had missed a period. The current priest's wife, Matushka Helena Nicholai, told me that Mother Olga had told her not to carry any more water buckets for a while because she was pregnant. Matushka Helena didn't have any idea she was pregnant. Mother Olga also knew who would need to plan for a difficult pregnancy.[4]

Over and over Olga typifies Yup'ik ways and values. She seems not to do anything unusual, with the exception of a kind of sixth sense for pregnancy as a midwife. She seems to be so ordinary as to be invisible when company came to her house. Her hospitality, her sensitivity to others' needs, whether of food or clothing or listening, were remarkable yet also very much characteristic of her people and their ways. Her faith did not stick out but was nevertheless always present. There was a beautifully transparent quality to her personality. Nothing was concealed and nothing was trumpeted.

Olga's case is in many ways illustrative of some of the issues about holiness discussed here. While there is already ample evidence of faithful discipleship in her life, it is nevertheless ordinary, woven into the life of her Christian community and culture. She was a woman of prayer, of loving service to her neighbor. She was a faithful worshipper and communicant, and she exercised the ministry of a "matushka," alongside her already sizable roles and activities as spouse, parent, and grandparent. One could say she was a saint, but no one would really notice or call her that. All of the accounts, it is important to say, come from after her death.

Yet after her death more classic signs of sanctity begin to emerge— unusual climatic conditions around the time of her burial, then the visions of her as a companion of the Mother of God and her continued activity as a healer. I have no intention of criticizing or in any way belittling the developing cult of Mother Olga. In part it appears to be a natural continuation to the great affection and regard in which she was held while still living. It is also noteworthy that one can see a development of natural communal veneration for her during her life into an abiding memory of her after her death. However, the addition after her death of unusual appearances, of almost miraculous actions and events, indicates that ordinary holiness is not quite enough. Extraordinary events and characteristics seem to be required.[5]

Her granddaughter's brief memoir is I believe a strong testimony to Olga's "hidden holiness," perhaps even more poignant than the ones above, which are longer, more reflective of traditional ecclesial piety toward saints. In Elizabeth Michael Ruppert's account we have the memory of a much loved grandmother, yet in it is there not the image of someone "very much like" God?

Often I think of my Grandmother Olga Michael and I do feel her presence. Even though I cannot see her physical form, I know she is there spiritually. I feel so blessed to have known her in the way that I did.

I learned unconditional love from her because she loved me without any conditions. Just loving me because I was me.

My mother Minnie told me that I moved in with my grandparents when I was three years old and lived with them until I was in high school. I remember one time that she got angry at us for being so noisy and it was the only time that I heard her yell. She treated me and the rest of her grandchildren in gentle and loving ways.

Grandmother Olga (Ma) fed us and made sure we went to school on time. She helped me with my homework even though she did not know much English. I would get upset with her at times because she was constantly trying to help me, but that was the way she was, always helping other people.

The best thing about my grandmother was how she held me as we were laying in bed, with her arm over my stomach. I knew that she loved me. Because I loved her, I would hold her in the same manner. She was the main reason why my childhood was happy and carefree.

My Grandmother Olga made sure that I was safe. The best thing anyone can do for a child is to make sure that they feel loved, and that is precisely what she did for me. I know how to love unconditionally through the example of my Grandmother Olga. That is something so valuable, nobody can take that away. Not even death can fade that kind of love.[6]

ARTIST, NUN, AND PILGRIM: SISTER JOANNA REITLINGER

Another case is also instructive here, that of artist and nun Joanna Reitlinger.[7] Although she was close to the center of church life in the Russian emigration community of Paris and to Fr. Sergius Bulgakov, and a well-known name in the beginning of the renewal of iconography, she has virtually been forgotten. Julia Nikolayevna Reitlinger, as her autobiographical sketch indicates, came from an upper middle class, professional family. Born in St. Petersburg in 1898, she had the most extensive education girls could receive: private instruction from a tutor, Western languages, girls' gymnasium curriculum. Family affluence enabled her artistic gifts to be recognized and nurtured in art school and the Society for the Advancement of Artists.

The revolution brought flight to the Crimea and then the road of emigration communities in Prague, Belgrade, Warsaw, and finally Paris. In the Crimea she met and began a lifelong spiritual relationship with Fr. Sergius Bulgakov. Her studies in art, according to Elizabeth Roberts, produced nothing remarkable in the 1920s in Belgrade and Prague. But her attraction to iconography set her apart from other icon painters of the emigration. Having studied closely Igor Grabar's monumental *History of Russian Art,* she took whatever courses in art and art history were offered. She studied iconographic technique with Cyril Matkov as well as Sofronov and Stelletski, but it was not until actually viewing copies of the Vladimir Mother of God, the Rubliev Trinity, and other medieval icons in Munich in 1927 that she experienced a kind of breakthrough. Her time in the atelier of Maurice Denis was extremely important. While she was not interested in the direction of his Catholic sacred art, she acquired both compositional skill as well as the freedom to again be creative in iconography. Unhappy with mere copying of ancient icons in the Old Believer mode, Julia displayed both traditional form as well as ingenuity in icons made for the Russian church at Meudon and the Church of the Presentation of the Mother of God in Paris, which included icons of the head of John the Baptist; the Russian pietá, "Do Not Lament Me, Mother"; frescoes of creation, with numerous, playful animals; end-of-time scenes from the Book of Revelation; and the feasts of the church year. A new catalog of her work captures these large-scale works and many of the small, personal icons Sister Joanna made over the years for friends, such as St. Seraphim with his bear and St. Gearsimus with his lion. The playfulness of her depiction of animals, especially in the Meudon creation fresco and in small icons, eventually led to her work in crafting illustrations for children's books.

She was received into monastic life by Metropolitan Evlogy in 1934, much like he had received Mother Maria Skobtsova a year earlier. Because she was living with the Bulgakovs and assisting the often ill Matushka Helena Ivanova Bulgakov, she was made a simple *riassa* nun—"Sister," since it would not be appropriate for Matushka to call her "Mother," given their difference in age and status.[8] Julia, now Joanna, referred to herself the rest of her life as Sister, even long after she stopped wearing the monastic habit.

Sister Joanna explicitly mentions the precedent of Mother Maria's "monasticism in the world/city" as a great encouragement. Like Mother Maria, Sister Joanna's life was not to be a typical monastic existence. Mother Maria reflected extensively in her writing on the need for a new form of monasticism. In a world torn by revolution, forced apart by immigration, economic depression, and unemployment, she reconnected monastic life with the suffering of people, a link understood and a ministry practiced by the desert fathers and mothers of the third and fourth centuries. Her founding of hostels to shelter and feed the marginalized in Paris was not unlike the early work of a Sergius of Radonezh or a Francis of Assisi, the compassion of a Seraphim of Sarov to the afflicted who lined up to see him in the monastery. One could add here Peter Maurin and Dorothy Day at the Catholic Worker houses in the Bowery.

Yet Sister Joanna's journey in faith would be even more unusual and more of a challenge. Given the task of helping to care for Fr. Sergius Bulgakov and his ailing wife and family, she was also called on to continue her work in making icons. And she would do this while progressively losing her hearing. She would pursue this for years, completing icons for Mother Maria's chapels at Rue de Lourmel and Noisy-le-Grand, also for Fr. Euthymius Wendt's chapel at Moisenay. On commission from the Fellowship of Sts. Alban and Sergius, she did a triptych of Christ and Saints Alban and Sergius in memory of Bishop Walter Frere, a founder of the aforementioned fellowship, for the the Mirfield (UK) monastery church of the Community of the Resurrection, of which Bishop Frere was a monastic member. There is a photo of Sister Joanna working on the Meudon frescoes along with another important renewer of iconography, Fr. Gregory Krug, and her own sister Katia.

Joanna did several large icons still in the Orthodox cathedral in Prague as well as many icons for individuals' homes and for both Orthodox and Greek Catholic churches in eastern Slovakia, where she moved after Fr. Bulgakov's death. Perhaps her greatest work was a series of panel icons for the Fellowship chapel at St. Basil's House, painted in 1947. These depicted the saints of Russia, France, and Britain, as well as important Latin and Greek saints, the last judgment, and scenes from the Book of the Apocalypse. Some of the icons, such as those of the Mother of God and Christ, are inscribed on the back in memory of Fr. Bulgakov's pioneering work towards restoring unity in the churches.

Sister Joanna was one of those who cared for Fr. Bulgakov in the weeks he lay in a stroke-induced semi-coma before his death. She wrote an account of these forty days, including the description of light surrounding the dying theologian-priest.[9] But afterwards, she lost her connection to the church, at least to the services and the sacraments. She returned first to Czechoslovakia and then the Soviet Union. She supported herself for years by painting scarves and by teaching graphic and commercial art at an industrial school in Tashkent. In the summer she would live in Moscow with friends, the Vednerikovs, who were active in church life and in the circle of Fr. Alexander Men. The death of her spiritual father, Fr. Bulgakov, appears to have thrown Sister Joanna into a crisis of faith. Only in her later years did she return to the church's sacramental life and to the painting of icons, this first through the priest she had known in Paris, Fr. Andrei Sergienko, but later mostly through meeting a contemporary giant of a priest, like her old spiritual father. It was through her relationship to Fr. Alexander Men that her spiritual journey came full circle back home.[10]

In several reminiscences of Sister Joanna, Ella Layevskaya and Dimitri Baranov, among others, find little that is extraordinary about her as an older woman, already deaf since her twenties, in the last years before her death on May 31, 1988, when she was also going blind.[11] Her life back in the Soviet Union was hard. Living on a pension in Tashkent, she began again, after meeting Fr. Men, to paint icons for many people. She would send these hidden in boxes of candies or in books, since most were very small, easily fitting into the palm of one's hand.[12]

But iconography was not all she did in her later years. A circle of young people gravitated around her there. Several of the authors of reminiscences assembled quotations from letters. What is fascinating about these is the utter freedom from the often stylized piety of Russian Orthodox faithful. She writes of Christ as if he were living in her apartment, about prayer as though it were the same as breathing or eating. All of the details of Orthodox liturgy and church life, often obsessively observed, are absent from Sister Joanna's letters and talks. The Christian faith is quite simple. Absolutely accessible. In the end, I myself wonder whether or not she had a crisis of faith at all. Perhaps hers was a kind of "desert" or exile experience.

Dmitri Baronov gathered some quotes in his memoirs of Sister Joanna:

There was another conversation—I can't remember what it was about. Suddenly she said: "You think God's somewhere up there, in the heavens, a long way from us? No, He's here, with us, He's right here" she pointed to her heart. "I've only just begun to feel that and understand it; but do you understand?"

"It seems to me that we can even pray for people using the Jesus prayer—and perhaps it becomes more concrete for us? Or, conversely, in between all our concerns, we can sometimes simply 'appeal' not just to Jesus but to some saint close to our souls—there are more of these times than we think. It is important to apply our will to helping in some way. But to make up our minds that prayer will 'beat' in our hearts all the time we are working—perhaps that is beyond our powers."

"[W]e do not know what is good for us and what evil, but there must always be prayer and—not mine, but Thy will be done."

"Only one thing is needful—to strive for unity with Christ, again and again and for ever and continually and everywhere and in everything to seek to be one with God, everything else will come by itself . . ."

"As far as Lent is concerned, I think we each need to set ourselves some kind of small personal objective, specially suited to us individually—that's important, but we always take on everything and then achieve nothing."

"You know, penitence isn't always the same thing as confession, nor is a tortured conscience the same as prayer, even if perhaps one either precedes the other or comes after it."

"Of course, the most important thing is faith and 'receiving the Kingdom of God like a child.'"

Contrary to what one might expect from Fr. Bulgakov having been her confessor, and from having spent so much time in the company of the Paris émigré intellectuals, this upper-class, well-educated artist had a very practical, simple approach to prayer, to fasting, church services, in fact to all of life. The criterion for all aspects of life, not just the spiritual, is human

honesty. If the Gospel does not become woven into everything human, it
is not real, not made incarnate. This make sense, coming from an artist
who all of her life sought to use color, line, and form as expressions both
of the divine and the human. Her iconography is at once most creative and
dynamic—the playfulness of the animals in her icons, the psychologically
distinctive features of the faces of the saints, whether John the Baptist,
Francis, Seraphim, or her portrait of Fr. Bulgakov. There is a great deal of
resemblance between the brooding, fiery countenance of John the Baptist
and Fr. Bulgakov, almost certainly the latter becoming a real-life model for
the former. She was able to express equally the real human affection between the Christ child and his mother, and the naiveté of young women
martyrs Blandine or Joan of Arc. In the scenes of the Apocalypse she created for the Fellowship chapel at St. Basil's House, much of the sheer terror of the civil war and Russian revolution as well as the Nazi occupation
of Paris comes through. One also sees in this cycle of icons the vision of
the triumph of God in the New Jerusalem. The saints of the now-divided
church seem not to know any schism or separation, united as they are in
friendship and in God. Joanna somehow remained a child herself as witnessed by the docile lions, bears, giraffes, and camels in her icons of creation and of desert saints like Gerasimos and Seraphim.

Challenged all her adult life by loss of hearing, she was fully engaged
in a number of circles, as we see from photos of the fraternity of the Holy
Trinity or that of Holy Wisdom, of gatherings in the apartment of the Bulgakovs, and of meetings of various other intellectual or student groups in
Paris. In some, the sensitive, pensive artist's face is what we see; in others, an
open, radiant one. And the accounts of her later years always suggest warm
hospitality toward guests, a genuine desire for company, the solicitude of
a grandmother for those to whom she sent her miniature icons.

Ella Layevskaya gathered these sayings, very much in resonance with
the others.

"Christ, whom we can meet in the Church, in the Gospel, reveals himself as Love, Kindness, Mercy, Helper, with an ardent concern for our
well-being. He is the only One Who understands us to the end, pities
us, loves and helps us when we turn to Him."

"Only one thing is needful—to strive for unity with Christ, again and again and for ever and continually and everywhere and in everything to seek to be one with God, everything else is embraced in that."

"Of course, the most important thing is faith and 'receiving the Kingdom of God like a child.' "

"But 'there are different gifts and services.' And your particular work, if you do it as of the Lord and place it in His hand, is also service, not just a job. After all, you are serving people in it."

"Besides, to put it practically, it is clear to me that our efforts are necessary for grace, surely our whole spiritual life consists in praying all the time, and by prayer we call forth this grace."

"We must avoid a magical flavor in prayer, when we put our own will in first place. This is 'religious violence', wishing to take by force that for which we ask . . . 'Nevertheless, not my will but Thine be done.' "

"Without faith and the help of Christ we are weak. We wish well, but we cannot overcome the evil in ourselves. But with him we can. He is the way to overcoming ourselves, our weaknesses and our failings. The way is *real*, I know."

In Sister Joanna's life, her gifts of artistic ability were paired with disabilities. In the "Russian Paris," wonderful visions were combined with great poverty, material as well as spiritual. For all the clarity on the icon, on prayer, on being the church, there was also intense conflict and division among Christians, even if they were both Russian and Orthodox. In addition to losing her hearing as a young adult, later in life came crippling arthritis, failing eyesight, and finally blindness. Some of the quotations above come from her last years when she could neither paint nor read. Situated in the midst of the Russian émigré community in Paris, she learned from great minds like Berdiaev, Bulgakov, Mother Maria, and the others who lectured for the religious Philosophical Society and for the Russian Christian Students' Association and published in journals such as *Put'* (*The Way*). She was held in high regard by fellow artists and iconographers Leonid Ouspensky and Fr. Gregory Krug.

Despite all this, her path led her far way from Paris, and she went through some kind of crisis of faith, an exile from what had been dear to her, including iconography. Yet even more astonishing was her return to the sacraments and icons through friendship with Fr. Alexander Men. But maybe we should be more cautious in assessing her "crisis," for even at the end of her life, when age and illness made many things impossible, she clearly was devoted to prayer, living in God. Perhaps the deeper truth is that she had remained in communion with God even though distant from the church. Those who were face to face with the poverty and personal tragedies suffered in migration, the Great Depression, and the war—like her colleague Mother Maria—became forgiving and generous toward less than observant Christians. This "economy" of love hearkens back to the tax collectors, prostitutes, Gentiles, and Samaritans seen as thundering their way into the kingdom in the Gospels.

GRANDMOTHER, SCHOLAR, TEACHER, AND ACTIVIST: ELISABETH BEHR-SIGEL

It is essential . . . to respond to evil's argument, an argument fundamental to the atheism of today and tomorrow, by pondering the *kenosis,* the kenotic love of God, the vision of "God suffering" evoked by Fr. Lev Gillet, "the vision of a God whose omnipotence, his almighty love, is inseparable from his all-weakness." It is by death, as the Orthodox sing at Easter, that Christ has conquered death.

An awareness of global human solidarity is one of the marks of modernism, though this can still meet with resistance. Could not the task of Christian theology be "to deepen solidarity in communion," the certainty that there exists "one single man, one unique Adam who is constantly broken by our sins yet constantly restored in Christ, in whom we are all consubstantial," a certainty that must be incarnated in love and the humble service of our neighbor?

The task in which all this of which I have spoken is contained is the ongoing understanding and diffusion of the mystery of God, one in three persons, the mystery of the living God who is so utterly one that he bears in himself the reality, the heartbeat of the other. The task is to reveal, in this vision of the one-in-three, the basis and paradigm of all true human relationships. For God became man so that man, created in his image, might become god, a personal being in communion, in the image of God who is himself communion. These are some of the points that are today of extreme urgency in our thinking about the faith.[13]

It surely was someone in tune with the times who wrote these lines, a person who constantly saw the relationship between God and the world, faith and life. Elisabeth Behr-Sigel was the author, in a paper at the 1998 inauguration of the Institute of Orthodox Christian Studies at Cambridge University. Anyone who knew her recognized that she was a free spirit, despite her fidelity to Christian tradition. She was an indefatigable writer and lecturer, and an incurable optimist, even in her late nineties, after a life that saw numerous wars, social upheavals, and personal suffering. In her last years she appeared several times to speak — at conferences on the anniversaries of St. Sergius Institute and the passing of her friend, Fr. Lev, and at diocesan assemblies of the archdiocese of Russian parishes in Western Europe. She published an open letter to Seraphim Rehbinder on the crisis provoked by the Moscow Patriarchate among the Orthodox parishes in Western Europe and was a signer of an open letter on the status of men and women in the church in 1979. She also was active in the effort to glorify as a saint her friend and collaborator, Mother Maria Skobtsova. She was one of the last living links with the renaissance of Orthodox theology and church life in the early decades of the twentieth century. The walls of her apartment in Épiney-sur-Seine, I can attest, were covered with photos of those who were the giants of the church and theology for decades in Europe.

She had a life both colorful and untypical for a theologian. She was resistant to the idea of writing and publishing memoirs, and even indifferent to the idea of someone else doing her biography. Elisabeth did write autobiographical sketches and eventually allowed her future biographer, Olga Lossky, to regularly have lunch — and interview her. Having studied hagiography and done her first dissertation on it, Elisabeth continued in this specialization all her professional life. Her most comprehensive book was the biography of her friend Lev Gillet.[14] She did her doctoral dissertation on the nineteenth-century Russian theologian Alexander Bukharev and wrote a number of other biographical essays.[15] Elisabeth wrote an autobiographical overview, although it is more taken up with her theological work later in life than with her life as a whole.[16] Later, she also did a short sketch for *St. Nina Quarterly*.[17]

Olga Lossky eloquently sums up her personality and her vision of the church and Christian life.

> "Let yourself be astonished," Elisabeth would say philosophically. "Thank God for the beauty of the world," she would add theologically. To examine one's life in order to discern the presence of God there—this was her dynamic depth. This was the spirit she showed throughout all her reflections in response to my questions whenever we met [trans. note: every Saturday for lunch, among other times]. Elisabeth grappled with the question of how it was possible to integrate the Gospel in one's life if one did not hear it in the Church's preaching. How could you live out Christ's words: "All will know that you are my disciples, if you love one another," if our divisions reached down even to our own bishops? How can there still be discrimination toward women, she wondered, women made in the image of God just like men? Surely one can review all the different dimensions which evolved in Elisabeth's work, in particular the dialogue among religions and the place of women in the church. But beyond all the specific themes, it seems to me that her principal, her unique contribution was anchored above all in what she saw as the one thing necessary, namely to go into the depths of oneself, to make one's being, with all one's singularity and personal history, permeable to Christ in order to witness to his existence to as many as possible. For me, this is really Elisabeth's legacy.[18]

Michel Evdokimov, whom Elisabeth Behr-Sigel held at his baptism, says that all in France call her their "mother" in the church.[19] Whether "mother" or even "grandmother," she has given a striking witness to the vocation of a layperson who is a member of the royal priesthood of all the baptized.

Elisabeth was born in Schiltigheim in Alsace-Lorraine on July 21, 1907. The perfunctory religiosity of her family—a nonobservant Jewish mother, Emma Altschul, and equally nonobservant Lutheran father, Charles Sigel—made her hunger for deeper faith. This she began to discover in her adolescence, in the wake of the suicide of her closest friend's father during the post–World War I turmoil. Baptized in the Lutheran church, the regular

Christmas gifts from the pastor who baptized her, a friend of her father's, were the rare connections with the church. Yet her mother did teach her to say her prayers every night. As a teenager she began to attend Sunday services by herself and thereafter demanded that her parents register her for catechism classes in order to be confirmed. She also joined a French branch of the World Christian Student Federation.

After completing a degree in philosophy, she was among the first women allowed to study at the Protestant theology faculty at Strasbourg. It was there that immigrant Russian students first introduced her to the Orthodox Church. Later, she attended her first Orthodox Paschal Vigil in 1928, with Fr. Bulgakov as celebrant, at St. Sergius Institute in Paris. Drawn irresistibly to enter the Eastern Church, she transferred to the Protestant theology faculty at Paris for one year. Elisabeth attended both Lutheran and Orthodox churches on alternating Sundays and studied with Louis Bouyer, a Lutheran pastor and theologian who later entered the Roman Catholic Church. Father Lev Gillet, himself a Benedictine monk and later a Greek Catholic monk, had recently been received by Metropolitan Evlogy into the Orthodox Church. Father Lev received her as well during a liturgy he celebrated at Strasbourg for Orthodox students there. Elisabeth was chrismated in the apartment of the engineering student who would become her husband, André Behr.

After finishing her theological degree (*maîtrise*) in Paris, with the blessing of Fathers Lev and Sergius and Metropolitan Evlogy, she accepted the request of the Reformed Church ecclesiastical supervisor in Alsace-Lorraine, and from 1931 to 1932 she was "delegated" though not ordained to serve as an "auxiliary pastor" in rural Ville-Climont, given the shortage of clergy resulting from the war. This she did, already having been received into the Orthodox Church.

This remarkable act of ecclesial openness and love was only one of the singular breakthroughs among divided Christians who had previously had little to do with each other.[20] Brandon Gallaher has documented the equally remarkable discussions about sharing of prayer and even of the Eucharist in the early days of the Anglican-Orthodox Fellowship of St. Alban and St. Sergius in the UK, deliberations involving, among others, Bishop Walter Frere, Anton Kartashev, Nicolas Zernov, and, in particular, Fr. Bulgakov.[21] Although the proposal of common sharing of the Eucharist at each others' liturgies after confession and the blessings of each others' bishops did not occur, the very impetus to it in the early 1930s, the recognition that there might be simultaneously a maximum and minimal profession of faith, remains an encouragement to us today. Active in the Russian Christian Students Movement (ACER), Elisabeth also participated in Fellowship meetings through her friends Vladimir Lossky and Fr. Bulgakov and was among the founders of the Orthodox Fraternity in France.

Elisabeth and André, along with Paul and Natasha Evdokimov, Vladimir and Madeleine Lossky, the Kovalesky brothers Evgraph and Pierre, were members of the first Francophone Orthodox parish in Paris, led by Fr. Lev Gillet. Relocating to Nancy, André worked as an engineer while Elisabeth taught in the public school system. The couple started a family as well as an ecumenical study group. Daughters Nadine and Marianne were born respectively in 1934 and 1936 and their son, Nicolas, in 1944. During World War II this group became a resistance group, sheltering those fleeing Nazi persecution in the time of occupation, Jewish people in particular. After the war's end, she continued to teach but also attended St. Sergius Institute adult education courses in theology taught by Lev Zander, Olivier Clément, and Evdokimov.

While some believe that her scholarly career, in particular her writing and publishing, only began much later in life, it is important to remember that in the 1930s, in 1939 to be exact, she wrote on Bulgakov's focus on Divine Wisdom in his theological project.[22] Her first and perhaps most important book is still in print after more than a half century.[23] Her other studies in hagiography date from the early thirties and were influenced by Fedotov and his pioneering work in this field.[24] Anyone who would regard her as a "late bloomer," interested mostly in feminist themes in theology, needs to inspect carefully the bibliography of her publications assembled for the *festschrift* presented on her ninety-sixth birthday in 2003.[25] Her overview of Orthodox spirituality, based on her course at St. Sergius Institute, was paired with Bishop Kallistos Ware's essays on the "prayer of the heart."[26] Perhaps her best known book—on women in the church— gathered papers and essays spread out over almost two decades.[27] This was followed again by a joint work with Bishop Kallistos on the question of the ordination of women in the Orthodox Church.[28]

André Behr died in 1968 after a long struggle with depression and alcoholism. Olga Lossky, using Elisabeth's letters and journals, traces the destructive atmosphere and the enormous struggles of Elisabeth to survive financially, emotionally, and spiritually in the 1950s and '60s. She had to maintain her family by teaching in the national education system, often living apart from both André and the children. After her children were raised and grown and out of the house in 1968, she embarked upon yet another stage of her life. Long since emotionally and otherwise abandoned by her husband, Elisabeth leaned on her old pastor and counselor, "the monk of the Eastern Church," Fr. Lev Gillet. But she also had to struggle to stabilize her close friendship with the emotionally turbulent Fr. Lev in these years, finally achieving a strong, mutually enriching relationship.[29]

She had served on the editorial board of the French Orthodox journal *Contacts* since 1959. With her children grown and producing grandchildren and then great grandchildren, Elisabeth continued to write and lecture. She completed her doctoral dissertation at the University of Nancy under Pierre Pascal in 1975. Throughout the 1970s and 1980s she offered courses at l'Institut supérieur d'études oecuméniques of l'Institut Catholique in Paris as well as at St. Serge, the Ecumenical Institute at Tantur, and the Dominican College in Ottawa. Alongside teaching and writing she became an important voice for the Orthodox Church in the World Council of Churches (WCC). She presented papers at the consultation on women in the church at Agapia, Romania, in 1976 and the 1981 Sheffield consultation on the community of men and women in the church.

Elisabeth continued her scholarly activities well into her nineties. She was a signer of a petition asking the Ecumenical Patriarchate to consider the restoration of the diaconate to women. She was the Orthodox vice-president of the Christian movement for the abolition of torture (ACAT). She was a consultant to the French Orthodox Bishops Conference. In 2003 she was chosen to give the Florovsky lecture at the annual meeting of the Orthodox Theological Society of America and subsequently spoke at gatherings of the *St. Nina Quarterly* at St. Vladimir's Seminary in Crestwood, New York, and at Hellenic College in Boston.[30] She was present in the cathedral of St. Alexander Nevsky in Paris on May 1 and 2, 2004, for the canonization services of her friend Mother Maria Skobtsova and her companions.

In a photograph of her after the canonization, she is holding several prints of the icon of the newly canonized saints, made by Marie Struve—a few of which she sent to me, since I had asked her to get me one.[31] In March 2005 she participated in a conference at St. Sergius commemorating her friend Fr. Lev. She was also present and spoke at a conference there celebrating the Institute's eightieth anniversary. Just a couple weeks before her death she was scheduled to lecture on Fr. Lev at a commemoration sponsored by the Fellowship of St. Alban and St. Sergius in Oxford. A fall and injury to her leg made it impossible for her to give the lecture.[32]

She died in her sleep in her apartment, with books, journals, letters, and other work spread out around her. Still actively lecturing and writing to the end, she surely did not think like a woman of many years. She held on to her driver's license well into her nineties, though it was hard for her to see the road any longer due to her shrinking height. I recall that on a visit to her apartment outside Paris my wife and I arrived much later than she expected us. We were lost, due in part to the absence of street signs in her neigborhood, and her reply was, "Well we don't need them. We know where all the streets are!" No sooner had we seated ourselves but Elisabeth broke out the port and asked if we minded her smoking. It was an inspired visit to be sure, one in which I was complimented on my publications but criticized for my lousy accent—in English, my native language. Elisabeth said she preferred the only really acceptable accent, the "public school" British one. This was some little lady! Around the room were icons by Sister Joanna Reitlinger and the wedding icons by Evgraph Kovalesky, paintings of Strasbourg, including one of her as a very young woman now on the cover of her biography, plus photos of all the friends she treasured. She considered herself a nobody but, she said, "I have had some very notable friends."

Elisabeth may not have been a household name, but she was hardly a nobody. She was a living icon of the great vision all her friends and colleagues had of the church in our time. She was, in her own writing and lecturing, a bridge to their work and a continuing witness to their hopes, not only for Christians of the Orthodox Church but to Christians of the Western churches. Elisabeth rejoiced in her Lutheran roots, citing Fr. Lev's insistence that we all are brought to Christ by many paths in the churches. She was like her friend Paul Evdokimov, in Olivier Clément's description, a *passeur*, one who ferries people back and forth—between the churches.

As Olga Lossky observed, the relationship of the world and every person to Christ could be the leitmotif of her writing, whether in tracking the Russian forms of holiness and spirituality, as evidenced in the lives and saying of holy people, or in the insistence on the mission of the church in and for "the life of the world." The conversation that Bukharev sought to establish, between the church's tradition and the consciousness of modern people—she affirms this forcefully.

> Bukharev's free-flowing theological reflection rooted in the tradition of the Church along with his personal spiritual experience allowed his early intuition to deepen. "God is love," . . . [he] proclaimed with the Apostle John. His love is a love of generosity or mercy that never ceases to flow out on creation to sustain it, restore it to its original beauty since its fall. This love is also a crucified love offered from the beginning and victorious in its self-giving. This is a love which is entirely concentrated on and revealed in Christ Jesus whose name, wrote Bukharev's first biographer, "never left his lips." The Lord upon whose face Bukharev gazed looked like the Christ in the Rubliev icons. It was the object of contemplation for the young monk, a divine and human face filled with both gentleness and an infinite majesty, radiating a love stronger than death. It is in the radiance of this face that Bukharev invited an encounter with each man and woman across time, from ancient history to our contemporary world. He characterized modern man as enclosed in his own hell, in a universe of things which have become opaque to the divine light shining in the darkness that the darkness cannot overcome. Modern man is walled off in his own autistic ways, incapable of a sincere dialogue with the other.
>
> Today, to become one with Christ means descending into this hell armed only with the weapons of faith, hope, and compassionate love, Bukharev affirmed. Neither crusades against the modern world nor flight nor prostration before it will change its course, but simply interior illumination enlightened by the light that enlightens all coming into the world.[33]

As steeped in history as she was, Elisabeth fought an ongoing battle with many Orthodox theologians about the authentic meaning of tradition.

Love for the past, wanting to return to the past, despising the modern world, its culture and people, believing that in the Eastern Church nothing can or ever does change—she rejected all of these as true appeals to tradition.

> I want to say a few more words about that faithfulness that must not be confused with an ossified traditionalism . . . Fr. Sergius Bulgakov . . . writes . . . "The Church of Christ is new life with Christ and in Christ, guided by the Spirit." And a little further on . . . "Tradition is not an archeological wall or a dead deposit!"
>
> Tradition is the memory of the past, but this past must be living Tradition . . . True Tradition is always living Tradition. It changes while remaining ever the same. It changes because it is confronted with different situations, while its essential content remains unchanged. This content is not an abstract proposition. It is the living Christ who says, "I am the truth." . . . I could quote others, such as my friend Vladimir Lossky, who saw in Tradition the critical spirit of the Church. It allows the Church to discern, in the Holy Spirit, the authentic from the non-authentic, to distinguish the essence of the message of the Gospel from non-essential and therefore ephemeral historical additions . . . Will the Orthodox church be capable of responding to one of the greatest challenges of our time, the desire of women, in accordance with the revolution in the understanding of the Gospel, to be recognized as free and responsible persons, capable of participating in various ways in the responsibilities and consequently the authority exercised in the Church? I hope so. And hope, together with faith and love, is a theological virtue, a grace that we must not cease to implore.[34]

It was most courageous to maintain such a position on tradition and on the question of women in the Orthodox Church, even with Metropolitans Anthony Bloom and Emilianos Timiadis, and Bishop Kallistos Ware supporting her. It is significant that the questions Behr-Sigel raises with respect to the place and ministry of women in the church are not only about the theology and practices of the past but about how we think and act in the church today.

The greatest of souls in the ancient Church recognized that the hierarchy of spiritual gifts had nothing at all to do with sex. The apostle Paul, for instance, counted among his closest collaborators in apostolic work women such as Phoebe, Priscilla, Junias, and the others named in his epistles. Basil the Great of Caesarea and Gregory of Nyssa called their sister Macrina their *didaskalos,* their master or teacher. For these brothers in their youth, she played the role, as they said, of "mother and father" at the same time. The cultural context of the age did not permit any institutional expression of such a recognized spiritual equality. Today the cultural context is much more favorable, at least in the West. Orthodoxy ought not to remain a stranger to this, as Metropolitan John Zizioulas notes. The mission of a "Western Orthodoxy," he affirms, is to "reconnect Tradition to the problems of modern Western humanity which are, for that matter, more and more the problems of humanity in the global dimension." Among the problems of modern Western man, one of the most important concerns the restoration of an authentic partnership, a true reciprocity, without loss of their identity, between men and women.[35]

Elisabeth Behr-Sigel does not at all exaggerate her place as a continuing spokesman for a group of theologians who sought to understand tradition as both alive and renewing. For her, the question of the ministry and place of women in the church was never the only or even the principal issue for theology in our time. It was but one of a number of issues that raised the question of what really was the "tradition" of the church—an unchanging perspective in everything or a dynamic, living vision guided by the Spirit, the "mind of Christ" that always "tested the spirits to discern whether they were of God."

But does this theological view not succumb to the critique of many Christian initiatives of the past several decades, namely that it is an outright concession to culture, that the world itself is dictating what the church should believe, teach, and do? How could this be the stance of one who saw not only the horrors of two world wars, of the Nazi occupation and the Holocaust, of the innumerable local conflicts that employed both torture and genocide as in Africa, but also watched the witness of a

Maria Skobtsova and an Alexander Men, a person of faith in the Resurrection, "whose joy and triumph the Eastern Church sings of on Pascha like no other," in Lev Gillet's words.[36]

> Does the Church's teaching change, is it called upon to change with the centuries? The task of Orthodox theological teaching in the twenty-first century, as in the preceding centuries, is the faithful transmission of the faith of the apostles, as expounded by those with the title Fathers of the Church and given its dogmatic form by the ecumenical councils. Could we have the sacrilegious presumption to change anything, as though it were ephemeral? Divine truth transcends time. The letter to the Hebrews proclaims "Jesus Christ, the same yesterday, today and forever" (13:8). And the apostle Paul exhorts the Christians "not to be like children tossed to and fro by every wind of doctrine" (Ephes. 4:14) . . . The task of Orthodox theological formation, it seems to me, is both ever the same and yet always new, always being renewed. It consists in the faithful transmission (an action not "rational" but "intelligent," in the sense of being the "Eucharist of the mind"), of the evangelical *kerygma* [proclamation], of the original apostolic message. To be living, this transmission, this Tradition (giving the term its active meaning) must, in fidelity to the original and fundamental message, attempt to find answers to the new questions asked of the Church in its new circumstances.[37]

It may seem, after listening to her theological vision, that Elisabeth Behr-Sigel is possibly out of place here in this look at hidden holiness. True, she is a published author here and in France, beloved and now the subject of a major biographical study. Some years ago, I introduced Elisabeth to Sarah Hinlicky Wilson, the daughter of a Lutheran pastor, now a wife, mother, and ordained Lutheran pastor herself. Elisabeth became very fond of Sarah, telling her she saw herself as a young woman in her. Providentially, as it turned out Sarah also went on, in October 2008, to defend her doctoral dissertation at Princeton Theological Seminary on Elisabeth's theology, the first we know of anywhere.[38] Elisabeth Behr-Sigel is, to be sure, not a household name for most Orthodox Christians, much less the wider public. Because of her unflinching theological commitment to the place of women in the church, her name is anathema to many traditionalists. But I consider myself privileged, indeed blessed, to have met and known her, to have corresponded with her in the last years of her life, and to have known a great mind and truly singular personality, all less than five feet of her! I have a thick folder of her hard to decipher handwritten letters. And I have a priest's wooden pectoral cross that she had hanging in her apartment, a gift to her from a monk. When I asked if it was really a priest's cross, her face lit up and she said that of course it was, why shouldn't she have accepted it as a gift! I was again fortunate to receive it as a souvenir of her after her death, from her daughter Nadine. It is a great gift to have known a holy person—but I can hear Elisabeth saying, "But no, no, although I too have known many, many holy people,"—as she gestured to the photos all over her apartment walls.

As we look for some discernment in the encounter of the church with the complex, troubled world of the beginning of the twenty-first century, we would do well to pay attention to her. But I would also argue that despite her important contribution in her theological work, her effort against torture, her advocacy of the place of women in the church, her life itself was one of the ordinary struggles to follow Christ.

YMCA Staffer in Revolutionary Russia and Beyond: Paul Anderson

Most people who have been eyewitnesses to history-making events are eager to trumpet having been there. Not so for a modest Iowan such as Paul B. Anderson (1895–1985), a YMCA staffer, deployed in China, Russia, Paris, and elsewhere from 1913 until his retirement in 1961. He continued to work for church unity and human rights long after.

His memoirs, published only a couple years before his death, begin with a fascinating narrative of his presence at the legendary event, the actual declaration of the Soviet era. Those who remember the film *Reds*, based on Jack Reed's life and adventures, will particularly appreciate the following account.

Early in 1956, when I was in Moscow, I was taken to the tsars' palace in the Kremlin. At the reception suite, there was a huge painting by Gerasimov called "Lenin at Smolny 25 October 1917." In the center is Lenin gesturing vigorously and saying: "We shall now proceed to construct the socialist order!" I remarked to nearby journalists, "It was not quite like that." Daniel Schorr of CBS asked, "How do you know?" I replied, "I was there!" I saw Lenin on the platform only a few feet from the journalists' table where I sat with my friends Jack Reed, Rhys Williams and Louise Bryant.[39]

Matter-of-factly, Anderson goes on to describe, with remarkable recall, almost seventy years later, how his famous journalist colleagues informed him that the Soviets had taken the Winter Palace in Petrograd, arrested the Kerensky government's cabinet, and that the Soviet would be meeting that night of November 8, 1917 (not October 25!), at the Smolny Institute. Anderson's fluent Russian made him their interpreter, and after hours of waiting, amid banners with slogans and all sorts of workers, peasants, professionals from the Petrograd, and the All Union Soviets, not to mention Red Guards and other functionaries, and after a rather ascetic borscht supper, Anderson indeed did see Lenin and translate for his comrades. Only after 10:00 p.m. did the assembly come to order, but still there was bickering about the amount of time for each speaker. At last,

> Kamenev then called Lenin, who had been sitting unnoticed among the praesidium members. He came to the podium amidst tremendous applause. Some may not have recognized him, as he had shaved and appeared with only a stubble in place of the familiar moustache and trimmed beard . . . Gradually the chairman restored quiet. Lenin began. He read slowly and clearly, without Gerasimov's "gesturing." Initially came the draft resolution on peace. Then came the resolution on nationalization.[40]

Only later did a peasant mount the podium to cry: "Comrades! We have won the revolution!" Anderson not only corrects the date but more accurately records what became an iconic event.

For the next five decades of his life, Anderson dealt with the consequences of the Revolution—from the starvation and poverty brought on by World War I to the many intellectuals and religious leaders who were either expelled or decided to flee the Soviet regime. His account of living through the next several months is both riveting and terrifying. Nevertheless Anderson and his colleagues from the YMCA did whatever they could to provide food for prisoners of war, refugees, and others displaced by revolutionary violence. But the growing threat not only to their work of feeding others but to their own safety led to their escape across the Finland border. The torture chamber of Lubyanka, headquarters and prison of the KGB's predecessor, the Cheka, are vividly described, the result of Anderson's own detention there with dozens of others, foreign and Russian, and his interrogations, one at 2:30 a.m., not knowing the charges against him. Nightly disappearances of people became permanent, after forced confessions. Thousands would end up in the gulag, thousands more exterminated; later, millions starved to death in Ukraine and Belarus.[41]

Never shrill in reporting the atrocities of war and political upheaval, there is a serenity and determination throughout Anderson's memoirs. He has very little to say about himself. There is never self-promotion, self-serving judgments, or sentimentality. Having already moved from YMCA relief and educational work in China to Russia, the 1920s and '30s found him in Paris and across the continent. From evening and correspondence schools for Russian emigrants to the printing of books for their vocational education and cultural lift, he encounters all the great minds in the Paris émigré community: Feodor Pianov, the philosophers Boris P. Vycheslavtsev, Symeon L. Frank, and Nikolai A. Berdiaev. He assists them in renting space for the lectures and classes of their "Free Philosophical Academy" in Berlin, based on the one set up in Moscow after they had been expelled from the universities.[42] Anderson meets and begins long working relationships and friendships with the head of the Russian Church in Western Europe, Metropolitan Evlogy (Georgievsky); as well as Berdiaev; theologian and future dean of St. Sergius Institute, Fr. Sergius Bulgakov; and chaplain of the Russian Christian Student Movement, Fr. Sergius Chetverikov. In time, such relationships would lead to the establishment of and financial support for the Russian Christian Students Movement, to the financing of St. Sergius Theological Institute, and to support for the faculty who taught there: Frs. Cyprian Kern, Nicolas Afanasiev, Sergius Bulgakov, Basil Zenkovsky, and George Florovsky, as well as professors Boris Sové, Lev Zander, Anton Kartashev, and George Fedotov. These scholars would seek to renew theological work and bring it into contact with Western Christians through many different institutions. Early students who would become scholars themselves were also assisted with scholarships: the later Bishop Cassian Bezobrazov, Paul Evdokimov, Constantin Andronikov, and the later Frs. Alexis Kniazeff, Alexander Schmemann, John Meyendorff, and Boris Bobrinsky, among others.[43]

Paul Anderson's accomplishments went on to include the establishment of a publishing house for the St. Sergius faculty and other émigré writers—the YMCA Press—and finally the most influential journal of the emigration, *Put'* (*The Way*), edited by Berdiaev and published from 1925 to 1940, with virtually all the theological minds of the emigration contributing at one time or another. The YMCA Press also sponsored the liberal journal *Novy Grad* (*The New City*), edited by Berdiaev, Fedotov, and Ilya Fundaminsky.[44] The latter, also Mother Maria's treasurer and fundraiser, was arrested by the Gestapo with Mother Maria, Fr. Dmitri Klepinine, and Yuri, Mother Maria's son. Eventually all were sent to concentration camps where they died. The four were canonized in 2004 by the archdiocese still based in Paris and under the Ecumenical Patriarchate of Constantinople.[45]

Throughout his career, Anderson, an American Anglican, displayed the most profound ecumenical sensitivities, striving to enable the poor, disorganized, and often divided Russian community to find its own way in shaping the Russian Christian Students Movement. It was in this group that Mother Maria Skobtsova, then Elizaveta, along with Fr. Lev Gillet, Sophie Kolumzine, Elisabeth Behr-Sigel, and Paul Evdokimov all found the rooting for their theological and diaconal work in the liturgy. To this circle was added in time a Religious and Philosophical Academy that met in Mother Maria's hostel each Sunday for presentations and discussion. Further conversation went on in the Fraternity of the Holy Trinity, which included Boris Vycheslavtsev, Lev and Valentina Zander, George Fedotov, Frs. Basil Zenkovsky and Nicolas Afanasiev, the iconographer Sister Joanna

Reitlinger, Mothers Blandine and Eudoxia who after Mother Maria's hostel went on to found the still active monastery in Bussey-en-Othe, and Nicolas and Sophie Zernov. Eventually among the various groupings of the academy, the fraternity, the St. Sergius community, and the Russian Christian Students Movement, as well as the Orthodox Action board of Mother Maria's hostels and the Fellowship of St. Alban and St. Sergius, connections were made. Individuals saw each other on numerous occasions, as the many photographs of these various groups meeting attest. Ideas were exchanged, challenged, rejected, modified. Above all, Anderson points out, using the very term these émigrés themselves used, the effort of the Russian Christian Students Movement, the Religious and Philosophical Academy, and St. Sergius Theological Institute was to "church" daily life, that is, to allow the Gospel to permeate all of existence, to integrate Christian faith into all aspects of existence. As a fellow Christian, though of the West, he clearly shared this fundamental goal.

By pursing the Gospel works of love in feeding the hungry, sheltering the homeless, visiting the sick and abandoned, Paul Anderson also sustained the most creative and progressive collection of scholars, clergy, artists, and activists ever assembled in the modern history of the Eastern Orthodox Church. The "Paris school," if one extends this label of identity generously enough, surpasses even the Silver Age or "renaissance" of religious thought and philosophy in Russia in the first decade of the twentieth century in opening conversation with modern culture and in promoting prayer, study, and conversation among the Eastern and Western churches for the first time in centuries. It is not surprising that Anderson also supported the establishment of the first ecumenical group, the Orthodox-Anglican Fellowship of St. Alban and St. Sergius in the UK in the 1920s. Had he been a midwife to this confraternity alone—the locus of the most serious theological research and discussion about reunion of the churches in the modern era—he would have done the church a very great service.

The discernment with which Anderson profiles his friends—Nicolas Berdiaev and Fr. Bulgakov in particular—is remarkable. After summarizing Bulgakov's tumultuous life, his ordination, and the controversy that his theological writing evoked, Anderson reveals his own insight about this great theologian.

But he [Fr. Bulgakov] was not the type of professor who separated himself from his students. On the contrary, he had great personal influence on each of them. He was not a dreamer in an ivory tower, although he was certainly what one might call a creative theologian and philosopher. He was basically a priest and a prophet in God's temple. While some priests or ministers go through the prescribed readings, prayers and sermons by rote, Father Sergei's every liturgy was an authentic renewal of the Last Supper of Our Lord. When he, with arms uplifted, faced the elements on the altar to pray that they might be truly transformed and received as the Body and Blood of Christ, it was as if this was the first liturgy since that fateful Thursday when Jesus fed his disciples the bread and wine of communion.[46]

Anderson goes on at length in striking detail to dissect the charges of heresy brought against Bulgakov, the attack on his earlier work in social and economic theory when he was a Marxist. But just as a faculty panel cleared Fr. Bulgakov, so too does Anderson, noting in detail his adherence to the church's tradition. Anderson also notes Bulgakov's growth in understanding that authentic Christian faith was to be found beyond the Orthodox church among Anglicans and other Protestants. Bulgakov became an influential participant in the Fellowship and the proto-ecumenical gatherings: the 1925 Stockholm Life and Work conference, the Faith and Order meeting at Lausanne in 1927, as well as those in Oxford and Edinburgh in 1937—all of these the predecessors to the World Council of Churches.

Anderson likewise witnessed to the genius and faith of Berdiaev.[47] He recognized the passion of Berdiaev for freedom in all things as God's greatest gift, combined with that for creativity. For Anderson, Berdiaev's explusion by force from the so-called "Philosophers' ship" in 1922 was not just the guarantee of life and further work for Berdiaev but indeed a great gift for Western culture, just as Bulgakov's exile meant the same for the churches. Berdiaev was able to recognize what was in fact useful and reforming and positive in socialism, shorn of the Soviets' brutality. He likewise wrote boldly against the rise of the fascists in the 1930s.

After World War II, Anderson was deeply involved in European reconstruction, working with the Eastern European Fund of the United Nations Relief and Rehabilitation Administration (UNRRA), keeping the YMCA

Press running in Paris, and even finding support for the Tolstoy Foundation here in the US from his own Episcopal Church. As if his close friendships with so many of the Russian émigrés were not enough, Anderson became a close friend and for the rest of his life an advisor to Greek Archbishop in America, then Ecumenical Patriarch Athenagoras I.[48] But Anderson's intimate friendships do not end with this monumental promoter of ecumenical healing—the one who embraced Pope Paul VI in 1966, prayed with him, and then mutually laid aside the condemnations of the eleventh century. Anderson also describes without fanfare his close friendship with Archbishop Iakovos, who for almost fifty years would head the Greek Orthodox Church in America, as well as Patriarch of Moscow Aleksei I.[49]

Anderson was revered and sought out by the hierarchy of his own Episcopal Church, presiding Bishops Lichtenburger, Sherill, Hines, and Allin, as well as by the great theologian and archbishop of Canterbury, Michael Ramsay. He was involved in the negotiations which led to the granting of autocephaly to the Orthodox Church in America (OCA) by the Moscow Patriarchate, having brought together Russian Patriarchal and Metropolia leaders. He was involved as well in the formation of the Standing Conference of Orthodox Bishops in America (SCOBA). Dr. Eugene Carson Blake of the Presbyterian Church in the USA, Dr. Franklin Clark Fry, president of the then Lutheran Church in America—there was no denominational leader Anderson did not know or assist. The names of church leaders in Anderson's memoirs really are the who's who of American church life and beyond in the twentieth century.

He was an observer at the 1956 Anglican-Orthodox meeting in Moscow and continued to be intensely active after retiring from the YMCA in 1961, serving as a volunteer consultant for the National Council of Churches (NCC) and also for his own Episcopal Church in the US. The 1976 Anglican-Orthodox Agreed Statement owed a great debt to his work over at least four decades in supporting ecumenical dialogue. There is an entire other chapter in his retirement years—a major commitment to the improvement of Soviet-US relationships.[50]

But in the end, Anderson returns to the basics. As he prepared his memoirs in the years of attempted détente, before the fall of the Soviet regime, he deplored the suffering caused by war and totalitarian government, the suppression of religion and brutal treatment of believers in the

Soviet Union. But recalling that in the nearly fifty years of his work as a YMCA official he tried to maintain human rights and the culture and church of the East, he also underscored how important were essential humanitarian services such as food, shelter, medical care, and then education. In addition to these, Anderson saw reconciliation, not only of East and West politically but also of the divided churches, as among his principal aims. He continued this work of reconciliation, bringing together American Episcopal and Russian Orthodox clergy and theologians, despite all the diplomatic and political obstacles of the cold war period, and despite all the hesitation of church groups unsure of themselves in ecumenical encounters.

> The world has changed greatly since I heard Lenin proclaim the Soviet State, when I first met that string of brilliant émigré intellectuals and could only hope that some way might be found for their nurture, when I sat at the Life and Work Conference in Stockholm in 1925 and wished that it might achieve a World Council of Churches. And yet my witnessing and response only reveals that the goals remain to continue to work for greater unity, to protect human rights, and to strive for further East-West reconciliation. Now I often think of my mentor and great friend, Nicolas Alexandrovich Berdiaev, and I ask myself—as so often he did—what has been the meaning of it all? I take deep comfort in that though the tasks be great, we must seek for "a power to move men *in extremis*" while being sensitive to the great issues of our day. For however much the world may betray our efforts, we must not betray the world. We must actively love one another, and make this love known through the power of good works, as Berdiaev often said, and love God so strongly that in doing so we are able to put aside our petty differences and live together, in peace and unity, on this tiny planet.[51]

Paul Anderson wrote those concluding lines to his memoirs when he was more than eighty years old, after almost three-quarters of a century of intense Christian engagement and witness. It turns out that he rubbed elbows and was friends with quite a few holy people, some already declared saints, more likely to come. But as unpretentious as the accounts of all these individuals, programs, and groups are in Anderson's memoirs, one begins to see what "hidden holiness" looks like in precisely the simple, matter-of-fact attitude toward his life. There are no healings from terminal disease, no resurrections from death, no sitting atop a pillar or feats of bilocation or geographic or temporal boundaries being surpassed. There was however an extraordinary life, lived in a most ordinary way.

ORDINARY LIVES?

To the extent that their lives have been observed and to some extent written, that their writings have been published or other work such as paintings and icons have been catalogued and exhibited, how can we claim that these four holy people are examples of the kind of everyday, ordinary, even hidden holiness we are reflecting upon here? For one thing, during their lives, Olga, Joanna, and Elisabeth were at the very least relatively invisible outside of their families and immediate circles of friends. To some extent, they were pioneers in a church that is patriarchal, in which women as either icon painters or theologians were unheard of until their time. As for Olga Michael, to the outside observer she might appear to be the most ordinary, even insignificant, of the three, yet within the dense relationships of the Yup'ik, she was a revered matriarch, a healer and counselor. Paul Anderson was known to many luminaries of the intellectual and ecclesiastical worlds, but he moved among them gracefully, without fanfare. How much recognition would his name have today, in a seminary or church body headquarters, even in the NCC or WCC?

And yet—there are no spiritual acrobatics evident here, no exemplary piety of an unusual sort. Quite the opposite. These four seem to have deeply assimilated their faith and then gone about their lives. And, as one looks more closely, these were hardly lives chronicled in children's books about the saints. For years both Olga and Elisabeth lived with husbands afflicted with alcoholism and sickness. Despite this, or maybe because of it, their strength of character made them strong parental figures both within their large families and outside, in the parish and beyond. All of Joanna Reitlinger's life was marked by loss: loss of hearing early on and sight toward the end, loss of first her father and then her mother, loss of her comfortable home, artistic training, and security in the wake of the revolution, loss of her homeland, loss perhaps of her faith. Paul Anderson worked in China, Russia, Paris, and many other locations. He very clearly knew deprivation, separation from his spouse and children, hunger, fear of his fate at the hands of the Cheka, criticism or indifference from church colleagues.

Did their life stories have "happy endings"? Yes and no. Old age and illness came to them all. Some suffered more severe loss of faculties and energy, all eventually suffered the loss of family and friends. Only after her death do the stories of unusual happenings and appearance commence for Olga Michael. There may have been the forty days of Fr. Bulgakov's dying and the unusual light that radiated from his face during those weeks for Sister Joanna, but all the years of his teaching and preaching and even this light did not save her from her own exile and years of spiritual emptiness. She did return to Russia and eventually to her faith, but her last years were ones of isolation and loneliness due to her loss of both hearing and sight. Elisabeth Behr Sigel's indefatigable lecturing and writing—about the place of women in the church, and the need for the church to follow the signs of the times, to listen to and serve the world—these made her friends but also enemies. Perhaps by the year before his death Paul Anderson saw the ecumenical hopes declining, the positions of the churches hardening—a winter, rather than the spring he experienced in Paris, setting in. We have been living in that long, cold winter for decades now, not only in ecumenical work but within the very life of the church, now divided by traditionalism and the "culture wars" division.

Yet these four lives show that the call to holiness can indeed be followed in very different, very ordinary, yet surprising ways in our time. We have to accept that the lives of holy people as well as their personalities—if they are to be taken honestly—do not conform to the patterns for sanctity of the past. Neither are these lives of complete perfection, nor lives full of interesting events or unusual deeds. They may even be forgotten, discarded— as the writings and lives of many of the Paris thinkers are these days, both in Russia and in Orthodox communities elsewhere. Yet those lives continue to offer encouragement and illumination.

CHAPTER FIVE

Equipment for Holiness

Liturgy in Life, as Life

Metropolitan Anthony Bloom, widely recognized as a master in the spiritual life, and himself a most complicated personality, regularly urged his listeners to use the treasury of prayers of the holy people of the past, whether the texts of the liturgical services themselves or the many prayers gathered in various prayerbook collections.[1] For him, these were a living connection with our sisters and brothers in the faith. We may be separated from them in many ways—by time, by culture and language, now by ecclesial divisions. Yet we can still make their prayers our own, as we continue to create prayers ourselves. It is important to realize that prayer is not separate from the rest of life, something sacred distanced from the dirty, messy, ordinary, and profane. In all the religious traditions, ritual or liturgical celebrations link the divine and the human, the material and spiritual, and these rites knit together not only the believers of today but all those who have gone before.

Aside from the common liturgical texts for the Eucharist, baptism, the daily cycle of prayers, and the Divine Office, Eastern Orthodox Christians have used for years standard collections of prayers for the morning and evening as well as for preparation before holy communion and thanksgiving afterwards. Virtually every Christian church does likewise, the Lutheran, Methodist, Anglican, Presbyterian, Roman Catholic, the Oriental churches. The Anglican Communion uses now a growing number of worship books created by churches alongside the historical *Book of Common Prayer* in its various editions. Increasingly it is possible to find ecumenical collections. The ecumenical monastic community of Bose has produced a beautiful book of daily commemorations of holy men and women from a variety of Christian traditions complete with brief biographical sketches, excerpts from writings and the prayers used by their communities to commemorate them.[2] In the US the Lutheran and Episcopal churches have published similar volumes to enrich the celebration of the holy men and women on their liturgical calendars. One also finds that such liturgical commemorative lists are themselves becoming more ecumenical. Anglicans remember the medieval Russian monastic saint Sergius of Radonezh as well as the twentieth-century German Lutheran pastor and martyr Dietrich Bonhoeffer. Lutherans commemorate Anglican theologian and martyr Thomas Cranmer as well as late-nineteenth-century Anglican and Catholic Ugandan martyrs. Along with the remembrance of universally recognized figures—apostles, church teachers, and martyrs—the calendars of many churches today also commemorate contemporary holy ones as well, like John XXIII, Oscar Romero, and the Reverend Dr. Martin Luther King Jr.[3]

While there is debate, even sharp disagreement, over the many aspects of Christian life—how much their traditional forms should be preserved, how much freedom we have to modify them to our own time and needs—one anthropological certainty remains. The basics I am thinking of, the tools of the holy life, remain present and in use. Emergent church communities gather on Sunday evenings, with all sorts of music and practices from the past as well as the present. Yet their assembly is unmistakably shaped by the eucharistic liturgy of the word and the table. The "tools" of the spiritual life remain, not surprisingly, the same both over time and throughout the Christian churches. Following the insight of Sergius Bulgakov's essay from more than seventy years ago, "By Jacob's Well," these tools—themselves the basics of the Christian life: prayer, the Word of God, the spiritual life, and the sacraments—rather than being ecumenical obstacles or points of division, are God's gift of continuing unity among believers.[4]

Liturgy, Prayer, and Life (and an Excursus on Icons)

In our time there has been a profound renewal of the liturgy. No longer understood solely as a means of individual piety, in liturgy there has been a rediscovery of the church as the people of God, the community of the Kingdom. Nicolas Afanasiev urged that we recognize once again that the church is eucharistic and that the Eucharist is ecclesial. In the liturgy we have also rediscovered not just the study of the scriptures, their use in preaching and personal prayer, but also how they shape our lives. How is it that liturgy is both a resource for as well as an expression of holiness? It is the case that we today are able to access liturgical texts, music, iconography from many different historical periods and traditions. Could this not enhance both our prayer and our lives? Is it possible that quantity of prayer, adhesion to precise forms, and frequency of attendance at services are less crucial for us today, compared with the liturgical lives of saints in the past? Might we also want to enlarge the scope and meaning of liturgy and prayer to extend beyond church services into other forms of artistic expression, engagement with the culture and with the sufferings of others?[5]

In her essay "Types of Religious Lives," in addition to a penetrating critique of various forms of spirituality and piety, Mother Maria Skobtsova makes a case for life as liturgy, that is, for how one lives out liturgy beyond and after the liturgy itself. Here she draws upon an ancient perspective, one that goes back to the first texts we have about the liturgy in the community and life of Christians, the *Didache* and the witness of Justin Martyr in the *Apology,* and of course the New Testament letters themselves. All of this literature culminates, as it were, in John Chrysostom's powerful sermons, especially those on the Gospel of Matthew, in which he argues that the liturgy offered upon the altar of precious silver or marble with altar vessels of gold or silver must then be celebrated upon the even more precious altar—the hearts of our brothers and sisters in need. Contemporary liturgical theologians such as J.-M.-R. Tillard, Ion Bria, and Alexander Schmemann echo this "liturgy after the liturgy," the "sacrament of the brother/sister."

In order to fully appreciate what Mother Maria Skobtsova writes, it seems good to look briefly at the place and meaning of icons in Eastern Church piety and worship. In Orthodox churches, icons abound.[6] There are the icons that form a screen (*iconostas*) before the altar: of the Mother of God, Christ the Ruler of All, and deacon saints like Stephen or Lawrence, and sometimes the archangels Gabriel and Michael appear on the side door, while on the center or "royal" doors will be the Annuciation, the four evangelists Matthew, Mark, Luke, and John, and the Last Supper. There also may be higher levels of icons on the screen, with the major feasts of the church year: the birth of the Mother of God and her entrance into the temple, the exaltation of the Cross, the birth of Christ, his baptism in the Jordan, the events of holy week, Easter, Ascension, and Pentecost. In some churches there may also be levels still higher with the apostles and the prophets. In the dome, if there is one, will be again Christ the Ruler of All, and perhaps the evangelists, apostles, and prophets along the diameter. On the walls of the church building there can be other feasts or scenes from the Old and New Testaments, as well as from events in church history or the lives of saints, especially the patrons of the particular church. And there will be icons placed out for veneration, usually once more Christ and the Mother of God, the feast being celebrated, or the patron saint of the church. Most Western Christians will take such elaborate placing of icons as ornamentation and education, and these surely are accurate functions.

Eastern Orthodox Christians, however, understand another, personal dimension and meaning of the icons. Those depicted in them are understood to be spiritually present in the church, especially during the liturgy, since in the services the kingdom of heaven is open—the royal doors are open—and those in heaven praise and thank God along with those on earth. It is an assembly of the entire communion of saints. Orthodox Christians kiss the icons as a way of offering love and prayer to God through the holy persons there depicted. People who are ill also light candles or oil lamps in front of the icons as a way of expressing veneration and as signs of prayer to God through these holy ones in the icons. Moreover, during many of the services the same affection and respect are demonstrated by the censing of the icons by one of the liturgical ministers.

In an essay, "The Mystery of Human Communion," Mother Maria notes that when the deacon or priest incenses the church it is not only the icons inscribed on panels or in fresco, on the walls or icon screen, that are offered the prayer and praise of the smoke but also the assembly of "living stones," the "living icons," as she calls them, the holy ones who form the community, the saints already and in the making.[7]

> During a service, the priest does not only cense the icons of the Savior, the Mother of God, and the saints. He also censes the icon-people, the image of God in the people who are present. And as they leave the church precincts, these people remain as much the images of God, worthy of being censed and venerated. Our relations with people should be an authentic and profound veneration . . . We like it when the "churching" of life is discussed, but few people understand what it means. Indeed, must we attend all the church services in order to "church" our life? Or hang an icon in every room and burn an icon-lamp in front of it? No, the churching of life is the sense of the whole world as one church, adorned with icons that should be venerated, that should be honored and loved, because these icons are true images of God that have the holiness of the Living God upon them . . . [T]he liturgy outside the church is our sacrificial ministry in the church of the world, adorned with living icons of God.[8]

Mother Maria's vision, one shared by so many others in our time, is not just of the cosmic expanse of the liturgy, that the prayer of the church encompasses the entire world. She also recognizes the implications of this. It is not so much that "secular" or profane life and activity are somehow sanctified, "baptized," or blessed by the church and the individual Christian. Rather a more ancient and biblical realization is recovered, namely, that all of creation is holy, that all of the sacrament using material and human elements such as bread, wine, water, oil, touch, sound, light, and movement reveal the holiness of bread, wine, eating, communication, song, and community. Teilhard de Chardin also achieved this cosmic vision of faith and worship, and Alexander Schmemann carried this theme through his liturgical theology.[9] Sister Joanna Reitlinger, an exact contemporary and fellow Russian émigré with Mother Maria had a special gift for including animals in her icons, whether the array God produced at creation or those entering Noah's ark, or the lions and bears befriended by saints like

Gerasimos, Jerome, or Seraphim of Sarov. Her simple and playful icons affirm the cosmic nature of faith, that we are united not only in the communion of saints but also with all creatures of the Lord, as the psalms and canticles of the Hebrew Bible sing.

Mother Maria further forces us to see that it is most definitely a communal holiness that we are given by God. We cannot see God alone, but, as the desert fathers and mothers put it, when we see our neighbor, we see the Lord. Mother Maria has become known as a martyr for her protection of those hunted down in the Nazi occupation of Paris. Her courageous efforts to assist the captured Jewish Parisians at the Vel d'Hiver in June 1941 and her rescue of several children from deportation have now become a children's book.[10] She is also known for her administrative skill in renting space and obtaining funding, provisions, and even governmental aid for her hostels and nursing homes. Her commitment to the service of those in need was not theoretical but most particular. One can almost see the figures, hear the names: Vanya, Dima, Katya, Olga.

> We get from the world and from man what we count on getting from them. We may get a disturbing neighbor in the same apartment, or an all-too-merry drinking companion or a capricious and slow-witted student, or obnoxious ladies, or seedy old codgers, and so on, and relations with them will only weary us physically, annoy us inwardly, deaden us spiritually. But, through Christ's image in man, we may partake of the Body of Christ. If our approach to the world is correct and spiritual, we will not have only to give to it from our spiritual poverty, but we will receive infinitely more from the face of Christ that lives in it, from our communion with Christ, from the consciousness of being a part of Christ's body . . . Social endeavor should be just as much of a liturgy outside the church as any communion with man in the name of Christ . . . Everything in the world can be Christian, but only if it is pervaded by the authentic awe of communion with God, which is also possible on the path of authentic communion with man. But outside this chief thing, there is no authentic Christianity . . . He who rejects the sorrowful face of Christ in the name of the joys of life believes in those joys, but tragedy is born at the moment when he discovers

that those joys are not joyful. Forced, mechanized labor gives us no joy; entertainment, more or less monotonous . . . gives us no joy; the whole of this bitter life gives us no joy. Without Christ the world attains the maximum of bitterness, because it attains the maximum of meaninglessness. Christianity is Paschal joy. Christianity is collaboration with God, an obligation newly undertaken by mankind to cultivate the Lord's paradise, once rejected in the Fall; and in the thicket of this paradise, overgrown with the weeds of many centuries of sin and the thorns of our dry and loveless life, Christianity commands us to root up, weed, plow, sow, and harvest.[11]

Mother Maria sketches this out further in a most concrete and personal way. She looks to the Mother of God and sees in her the willingness to suffer for and with the other. She speaks of the ways in which the life of the Mother of God serves as a model for each person not only to bring Christ forth but to sustain Him, to love Him in the person before us in need. In a way both radical and years before its time, as Natalia Ermolaev points out in her groundbreaking study, Mother Maria argues for the "motherhood of God" (*Bogomaterinstvo*) as a way of understanding the infinite compassion.[12] This is close to what Evdokimov called along with Nicolas Cabasilas God's "absurd" or "foolish" love for his children.[13] However, the Mother of God is not just a model of heroic virtue or love for Mother Maria. Rather, the Mother of God is an image of how each Christian should act, should sacrifice self, should do for the one before us. Every person is therefore a "bearer of God" or *Theotokos*.

If a man is not only the image of God but also the image of the Mother of God, then he should also be able to see the image of God and the image of the Mother of God in every other man. In man's Godmotherly soul not only is the birth of the Son of God announced and Christ born, but there also develops the keen perception of Christ's image in other souls. And in this sense, the God-motherly part of the human soul begins to see other people as its children; it adopts them for itself . . . The human heart should also be pierced by the two-edged swords, the soul-cutting weapons, of other people's crosses.

Our neighbor's cross should be a sword that pierces our soul . . . To my mind, it is here that the authentic mystical bases of human communion lie.[14]

Thus, the liturgy is not exhausted in its gathering of the community, in the community's prayer of praise and thanksgiving, in the shaping of each person by the word of God and sustaining each with the heavenly bread and the cup of life. The liturgy propels the believer out and dismisses her or him, Aidan Kavanagh emphasized, to mission, to the loving service of the world, the people around, not just those in the liturgical community.[15] There is a centrifugal direction of the liturgy, drawing all to Christ in the Spirit as the center and beyond into the abyss of the Father. But the community is also centripetally launched out into every kind or work, every state in life and profession and place to be what they have received: the bread for the life of the world.

So often defined, even obsessed by the details of liturgical worship, as Mother Maria also described in her "Types" essay, Christians should rather be like Mary Magdalene and the other women who brought myrrh to the tomb. It is not a coincidence that they carry with them the oil and spices not only of burial but of healing and life, for it was precisely these women who fed and cared for Christ and the disciples in the first missions to proclaim the Kingdom in Palestine. These holy women fed not only the soul or spirit but also the body. Having cooked and fed people, they are equal-to-the-apostles, in fact the first witnesses and preachers of the Resurrection. What does this tell us about our faith? And what would Christ do, Mother Maria asked, if he walked into one of our church buildings today?

Christ himself departs, quietly and invisibly, from the sanctuary protected by a splendid icon-screen. The singing will continue to resound, clouds of incense will still rise . . . But Christ will go out onto the church steps and mingle with the crowd: the poor, the lepers, the desperate, the embittered, the holy fools. Christ will go out into the streets, the prisons, the hospitals, the low haunts and dives . . . The most terrible thing is that it may well be that the guardians of beauty . . . will not comprehend Christ's beauty, and will not let him into the church because be-

Father Nicholas Afansiev.
Photo courtesy of Dr. Anatole Afansieff.

Paul Anderson.
Photo from the
YMCA archives,
University of Minnesota.

Father Sergius Bulgakov.
Icon by John Reves,
from the author's
collection.

Elisabeth Behr-Sigel
in 1999. Photo by
Jeanne Berggreen Plekon,
from the author's
collection.

Dorothy Day in February 1968. Photo from the *Milwaukee Journal*, courtesy of Marquette University.

(below)
Charles de Foucauld at the Beni-Abbès, Algeria, taken between 1901 and 1905.
Photo courtesy of the Little Sisters of Jesus.

Thomas Merton.
Photo by
John Howard Griffin,
used with permission of
the Merton Legacy Trust
and the Thomas Merton
Center at Bellarmine
University.

Etty Hillesum.
Photo courtesy of the
Jewish Historical
Museum, Amsterdam.

Paul Evdokimov.
Photo courtesy of
Mrs. Tomoko Faerber-
Evdokimov.

Sara Miles.
Photo courtesy
of Sara Miles.

СВ҃ ПРМЦА   МАРІА

МАТЬ НЕ БОЛЬШЕ ДЕТЕЙ, А ЧАСТО И МЕНЬШЕ

Mother Teresa. Photo courtesy of the Mother Teresa Center.

(left)
Mother Maria Skobtsova. Icon by John Reves, courtesy of the artist.

MATUSHKA OLGA ARSAMQUQ

Photo of Olga Arsamquq Michael. From the collection of Heather MacKean.

(left)
Olga Arsamquq Michael. Icon by Heather MacKean, private collection.

Icon of dancing saints from the frescoes at St. Gregory of Nyssa Episcopal Church, San Francisco, California. Courtesy of Daniel J. Simons, All Saints Company.

Figures include (from left): Bartolomeo de las Casas (1474–1566); Miriam, the sister of Moses; theologian and preacher Origen (185–254); Malcolm X (1925–65); Elisabeth I of England (1533–1603); and Iqbal Masih (1982–95), Pakistani martyr.

Icons by Sister Joanna Reitlinger, of the creation of Eve *(left)* and the Logos creating. Courtesy of Christ the Saviour Monastic Trust of the Holy Trinity Monastery, West Sussex.

Sister Joanna Reitlinger in 1980. Photo courtesy of Sergei Bessmertney.

Kathleen Norris. Photo by Garry Yamamoto, courtesy of Kathleen Norris.

Darcey Steinke.
Photo by
Maude Schuyler Clay,
courtesy of
Darcey Steinke.

Simone Weil.
Photo courtesy
of Sylvie Weil.

Rowan Williams,
Archbishop of Canterbury.
Photo by Eleanor Bental,
courtesy of Lambeth Palace
and the Archbishop of
Canterbury.

Father Alexander
Schmemann during
the 1970s.
Photo by Dr. Connie
Tarasar, from the
author's collection.

hind him there will follow a crowd of people deformed by sin, by ugliness, drunkenness, depravity and hate. Then their chant will fade away in the air, the smell of incense will disperse, and Someone will say to them: "I was hungry and you gave me no food, thirsty and you gave me no drink, a stranger and you did not welcome me."[16]

The liturgy brings us into communion with the Lord, with each other, and with all the rest of the church and the world. St. Basil the Great and St. John Chrysostom preached the impossibility of coming only to the altar in church for communion. That communion continued on the altars of the hearts of our neighbors.

[W]e must offer the bloodless sacrifice, the sacrifice of self-surrendering love not only in a specific place, upon the altar of a particular temple; the whole world becomes the single altar of a single temple, and for this universal liturgy we must offer our hearts, like bread and wine, in order that they may be transformed into Christ's love, that he may be born in them, that they may become "divine-human" hearts and that he may give these hearts of ours as food for the world, that he may bring the whole world into communion with these hearts of ours that have been offered up . . . Then truly in all ways Christ will be all in all.[17]

Mother Maria's words are echoed in those of other church teachers, emphasizing how essential this sacramental outreach is to the church, what others have called in Chrysostom's phrase, the "sacrament of the brother/sister."

Would you see His altar also? . . . This altar is composed of the very members of Christ, and the body of the Lord becomes an altar. This altar is more venerable even than the one which we now use. For it is . . . but a stone by nature; but become holy because it receives Christ's Body: but that altar is holy because it is itself Christ's Body . . . [which] you may see lying everywhere, in the alleys and in the market places, and you may sacrifice upon it anytime . . . When then you see a poor believer, believe that you are beholding an altar.[18]

"Take This Bread": Eucharistic Conversion and Mission

If the Eucharist, as Afanasiev, Zizioulas, and others have argued, is what constitutes the church, how might the Eucharist shape daily holy living?[19] Of all of the "means of grace," the Eucharist is the "sacrament of the church." The eucharistic bread and cup form the pattern for "God's humanity," his continuing presence among us. In St. Augustine's words, though, "we must become what we receive." The work of preparing a meal, the action of feeding, as Robert Farrar Capon has emphasized, is godly, Christ-like labor.[20] Is our everyday eating and drinking connected with the Eucharist and the Lord who is both host and food? Here is where saints of our time make it clear that the table of the Lord extends into the everyday, into soup kitchens and dining rooms and restaurants, fine and simple.

Too much religion has evaporated into spirituality, leaving behind the material bases of human life. The liturgy, with the tangible realities of bread and wine, water and salt, oil and wax, is the "primary theology." This was Schmemann's assertion. When we recall how the Eucharist transformed people like Maria Skobtsova and Dorothy Day, turning them into fiery prophetic writers and activists, we should not think this was the result only of the era of the Great Depression and the two great wars. Sara Miles has recently documented her own eucharistic conversion experience in her spiritual memoir.

One early, cloudy morning when I was forty-six, I walked into a church, ate a piece of bread, took a sip of wine. A routine Sunday activity for tens of millions of Americans—except that up until that moment I'd led a thoroughly secular life, at best indifferent to religion, more often appalled by its fundamentalist crusades. This was my first communion. It changed everything.

Eating Jesus, as I did that day to my great astonishment, led me against all my expectations to a faith I'd scorned and work I'd never imagined. The mysterious sacrament turned out to be not a symbolic wafer at all, but actual food—indeed, the bread of life. In that shocking moment of communion, filled with a deep desire to reach for and become part of a body, I realized what I'd been doing with my life all along was what I was meant to do: feed people. And so I did. I took communion, I passed the bread to others, and then I kept going, compelled to find new ways to share what I'd experienced. I started a food pantry and gave away literally tons of fruit and vegetables and cereal around the same altar where I'd first received the body of Christ. I organized new pantries all over my city to provide hundreds and hundreds of hungry families with free groceries each week. Without committees or meetings or even an official telephone number, I recruited scores of volunteers and raised hundreds of thousands of dollars.

Sara would soon discover that the life of the Gospel, Christian life, was more than the ecstatic experience of liturgy, of the sacrament of the bread and cup. Her own very material sensitivity probably alerted her to this as she was first receiving the sacrament, but coming to the Eucharist immediately locates one within a group—communion leads to community. And community, in turn, further draws one into a tradition, its history, a straification system, a jargon, and most of all, the holy mess of humanity that is church.

My new vocation didn't turn out to be as simple as going to church on Sundays, folding my hands in the pews and declaring myself "saved." Nor did my volunteer church work mean talking kindly to poor folks and handing them the occasional sandwich from a sanctified distance. I had to trudge in the rain through housing projects, sit on the curb wiping the runny nose of a psychotic man, take the firing pin out of a battered woman's .357 Magnum, then stick the gun in a cookie tin in the trunk of my car. I had to struggle with my atheist family, my doubting friends, and the prejudices and traditions of my newfound church. I learned about the great American scandal of the politics of food, the economy of hunger, and the rules of money. I met thieves, child abusers, millionaires, day laborers, politicians, schizophrenics, gangsters and bishops, all blown into my life through the restless power of a call to feed people, widening what I thought of as my "community" in ways that were exhilarating, confusing, often scary.[21]

Sara Miles's description of her unlikely eucharistic conversion is not far from that of the twice married-and-divorced Maria Skobtsova. Perhaps reactions from some churchgoers would also be skeptical or negative. Sara's experience took place at St Gregory of Nyssa Episcopal Church in San Francisco. There she discovered what others we have mentioned preached — the indissoluble linkage among liturgy and life. She found another community in addition to those she had known previously, that of *koinonia:* the rediscovery of life shared in prayer and community with others. No one had to tell her; rather, she immediately was led from the eucharistic bread and cup to *diakonia,* to life lived in the service of others. She discovered that *martyria* is not restricted to the shedding of one's blood but extends to a much larger witness to the Gospel and to Christ in one's life. Evdokimov insisted that we are not so much people who say prayers but "ecclesial beings" who become what we pray. We should not be surprised that Sara's eucharistic conversion reached back into her life.

Mine is a personal story of an unexpected and terribly inconvenient Christian conversion, told by a very unlikely convert: a blue-state, secular intellectual; a lesbian, a left-wing journalist with a habit of skepticism. I'm not the person my reporter colleagues ever expected to see exchanging blessings with street-corner evangelists. I'm hardly the person George Bush had in mind to be running a "faith-based charity." My own family never imagined that I'd wind up preaching the Word of God and serving communion to a hymn-singing flock.

But as well as an intimate memoir of personal conversion, mine is a political story. At a moment when right-wing American Christianity is ascendant, when religion worldwide is rife with fundamentalism and exclusionary ideological crusades, I stumbled into a radically inclusive faith centered on sacraments and action. What I found wasn't about angels, or going to church, or trying to be "good" in a pious, idealized way. It wasn't about arguing a doctrine — the Virgin birth, predestination, the sinfulness of homosexuality and divorce — or pledging blind allegiance to a denomination. I was, as the prophet said, hungering and thirsting for righteousness. I found it at the eternal and material core of Christianity: body, blood, bread, wine poured out freely, shared by all. I discovered a religion rooted in the most ordinary yet subversive practice: a dinner table where everyone is welcome, where the poor, the despised and the outcasts are honored.

And so I became a Christian, claiming a faith that many of my fellow believers want to exclude me from; following a God my unbelieving friends see as archaic superstition. At a time when Christianity in America is popularly represented by ecstatic teen crusaders in suburban megachurches, slick preachers proclaiming the "gospel" of prosperity, and shrewd political organizers who rail against evolution, gay marriage and stem-cell research, it's crucial to understand what faith actually means in the lives of people very different from one another. Why would any thinking person become a Christian? How can anyone reconcile the hateful politics of much contemporary Christianity with Jesus' imperative to love? What are the deepest ideas of this contested religion, and what do they mean in real life?[22]

Sara was propelled into extending the communion she received, not just as a deacon helping to lead the services and distribute holy communion but in the extended communion of setting up a food pantry for those in need. This would not be a purely paradisiacal experience, as we saw earlier. Just as a chef she worked under had colorfully put it, she found the public who lined up on the pantry day to be aggressive and grating. Her culinary mentor's favorite label for the public is the epithet one hears on the streets that insults one's mother. Yet, every night this cook chopped and sauteed to feed them. No less difficult to deal with were the fellow Christians of her own parish, some of whom recoiled at the idea of the hungry filling their sanctuary right after Sunday liturgy. Sara's eucharistic enthusiasm was real, but so were the anxieties it stirred up at her church.

James Martin reminds us, as do other writers on the saints, that some holy people we hold dear, whose statues, icons, or stained glass window we venerate, were hardly revered in their own time. But no matter how notoriously bad or boring and ordinary, the encounter with God in their lives made for their sanctity. It is, as a monastic friend has emphasized to me, not so much what they said or who they were but what they did, their actions, that makes men and women saints.

A Simple Pattern and Second Thoughts about "Religion": Alexander Schmemann's Vision

Alexander Schmemann continues to intrigue those who read him, although we do not know all of what he said and did in his very full life. Well known as a spokesman for Eastern Orthodoxy until his death in 1983, he remains an important voice in the more specialized field of liturgical theology. But it was the publication of a journal he kept in the last decade of his life that most recently provoked interest in his keen, discerning observations on life and religion. Both in his journals and in several essays, he had a great deal to say about excessive piety. Few escape his scrutiny—bishops and other members of the clergy, and the laity and fellow theologians as well.

Schmemann's name continues to be connected to liturgical theology, to the renewal not only of liturgical celebration but more widely of Christian life and of the church with the Eucharist at the core. There is always a thrust from the liturgy to life in his thinking. It is no surprise that some of his most important writings were titled *For the Life of the World, Liturgy and Life, Church-World-Mission,* and *The Eucharist: Sacrament of the Kingdom.* Far from being sectarian, the very reason for the church's being was to be the sign, the doorway, to the Kingdom. All of the words and actions of the eucharistic liturgy, as Mother Maria Skobtsova observed in the Paris community in which Fr. Schmemann grew up, were directed toward a "liturgy outside the church building," the "sacrament of the brother/sister," as John Chrysostom called it.

> The Church, the sacrament of Christ, is not a "religious" society of converts, an organization to satisfy the "religious" needs of man. It is *new life* and redeems therefore the whole life, the total being of man. And this whole life of man is precisely the world in which and by which he lives. Through man the Church saves and redeems the world. One can say that "this world" is saved and redeemed every time a man responds to the divine gift, accepts it and lives by it. This does not transform the world into the Kingdom or the society into the Church. The ontological abyss between the *old* and the *new* remains unchanged and cannot

be filled in this "aeon." The Kingdom is yet *to come*, and the church is not *in* this world. And yet this Kingdom to come is already present, and the Church is fulfilled *in* this world. They are present not only as "proclamation" but in their very reality, and through the divine *agape*, which is their fruit, they *perform* all the time the same sacramental transformation of the *old* into the *new*, they make possible real action, real "doing" in this world.[23]

During the years in which Schmemann was most active and in which he kept the journal, there was a spurt in interest in Eastern Church spirituality, the monastic life in particular. Having grown up with monastics in Paris, authentic men of prayer, and having visited monastic communities in Europe, Schmemann could not agree that America was hopeless as a location for real monastic life. On the contrary, he had some sharp critiques of the "museum" monastic phenomenon, that is, attempting to replicate in absurd detail the liturgical, ascetical, and monastic life of past centuries and other countries. He rejected such efforts as eccentric, inauthentic, and deeply damaging to those involved and others who would be misled. Instead, he supported American communities such as the nuns and monks at New Skete and the women's communities in Ellwood City, Pennsylvania; Otego, New York; and Rives Junction, Michigan.

Of particular interest is that Schmemann in several places, both in his journals and in talks and a booklet, outlined how monastic life might be shaped and lived honestly in our time. In a journal entry from Tuesday, January 20, 1981, he begins by leveling what can only be called a ruthless attack on religious fanaticism passing as traditionalist piety. His journals are filled with similarly cutting observations.

Yesterday, a whole day of suspense about the epilogue of the hostages in Iran. Will they or will they not release them before Reagan's inauguration?

Two nuns left convent A (which had 8 nuns), went to convent B, then went further to create convent C. And so, all the time, everywhere, "sketes of Transfiguration," and pretty soon each of them will have one monastic. There will be as many sketes as there are monastics!

More and more often it seems to me that reviving the monasticism that everybody so ecstatically talks about—at least trying to revive it—can be done only by liquidating first of all the monastic institution itself, i.e., the whole vaudeville of *klobuks* [monastic hoods], cowls, stylization, etc. If I were a *starets*—an elder—I would tell a candidate for monasticism roughly the following:

—get a job, if possible the simplest one, without creativity (for example as a cashier in a bank);

—while working, pray and seek inner peace; do not get angry; do not think of yourself (rights, fairness, etc.). Accept everyone (coworkers, clients) as someone sent to you; pray for them;

—after paying for a modest apartment and groceries, give your money to the poor; to individuals rather than foundations;

—always go to the same church and there try to be a real helper, not by lecturing about spiritual life or icons, not by teaching them but with a "dust rag" (cf. St. Seraphim of Sarov). Keep at that kind of service and be—in church matters—totally obedient to the parish priest;

—do not thrust yourself and your service on anyone; do not be sad that your talents are not being used; be helpful; serve where needed and not where you think you are needed;

—read and learn as much as you can; do not read only monastic literature, but broadly (this point needs more precise definition);

—if friends and acquaintances invite you because they are close to you—go; but not too often, and within reason. Never stay for more than one and a half or two hours. After that the friendliest atmosphere becomes harmful.

—dress like everyone else, but modestly, and without visible signs of a special spiritual life;

—be always simple, light, joyous. *Do not teach.* Avoid like the plague any "spiritual" conversations and any religious or churchly idle talk. If you act that way, everything will be to your benefit.

—do not seek a spiritual elder or guide. If he is needed, God will send him, and will send him when needed;

—having worked and served this way for ten years—no less—ask God whether you should continue to live this way, or whether change is needed. And wait for an answer: it will come; the signs will be "joy and peace in the Holy Spirit."[24]

It is noteworthy that as with many of his journal entries, even fairly intricate observations of church life—points about our relationship with each other and God—that these are framed by observations and reflection about everyday life, matters political, cultural, social, economic. Schmemann started off the day with the *New York Times,* voraciously read literature of all sorts, Russian, French, American, often in preference to professional theological publications. In these journals covering the last decade of his life, when he was at the summit of his careers as seminary dean, advisor to the bishops, international spokesman for Orthodox Christianity, husband, parent, and priest, he consistently attacked the artificial and unhealthy separation of church life from the rest of existence. He is repulsed by obsession with clerical hats, cassocks, beards, the ostentatious bows and signs of the cross in church, the deliberate trumpeting of difference and distance by the wearing of prayer ropes, crosses, as well as a jargon of theological and spiritual terms. He not only perceived all of this, and the accompanying nostalgia for the Orthodoxy of the past and of "authentic" Orthodox mother countries, not just as psychologically pathological but as outright rejection of Christ and the Gospel. He repeatedly observes the absence of caring or joy among such devotees. He is not afraid to voice his own inner distance from what many, including seminarians, find attractive about piety.

> Back to what I wrote on Thursday, the falsity and fear that makes my work at the seminary so difficult . . . Where does this falseness come from? From the psychological style of Orthodoxy—a style quite foreign to me, not only to my nature but to my perception of Orthodoxy. I am not a so-called "pious" man. Not only do I feel alien, feel repelled by the unctuous, grief-stricken mixture which constitutes the style of Orthodoxy and which our students take to so easily. But one must live in that style, thus—falsity, mannerisms, a necessity to pretend. Hence, fear, a faint-hearted fear that I will be caught, that people will see through me, what I really am. I feel "at home," I am

myself only while lecturing. It seems to be my only talent. The rest—
confessions, guidance, spiritual help—it all follows someone else's example, and therefore it's quite burdensome . . . While lecturing, I don't
ever compromise with my conscience because somebody else is in me
lecturing. Quite often I am surprised: Well, so that's how it is! That's
the faith or the teaching of the Church! Sometimes I feel like getting
up and saying, "Brothers and sisters, whatever I have to say, whatever
I can witness to—it's all in my lectures. I don't have anything else, so
please don't look for anything else from me." In everything else, it's
not that I lie, no, but I don't have the "anointing" which is needed to
be genuine. Maybe that's what the Apostle Paul meant when he said
that God sent him not to baptize, but to "spread the good news." All
of this is to explain why everything is so troublesome for me the
whole year long. My soul hides from people and all that I can do, except "spread the good news," is so difficult. I play a role and I cannot
not play it. "Father, teach me to lead a spiritual life." This is where my
difficulties start with this spirituality that everyone talks about. Here
I am blind and deaf. I don't have any "spiritual talent." Spirituality has
become an academic discipline and nobody seems to chuckle at the
title, "Spirituality 101."[25]

After taking a few shots at citations of the *Philokalia,* a collection of
ancient spiritual texts, in the bulletin of the French language parish at the
Paris cathedral and at people regularly flying to London for confession
with Metropolitan Anthony Bloom "because he is their 'guide,'" and at a
three-hundred-page dissertation on "Solitude in the Ascetic Tradition,"
Schmemann laments:

Here I stumble against some kind of wall—not only because my
intuition tells me this student is possessed by fear of solitude and a
passionate longing for friendship and love; not because I never saw
tangible results from this spiritual guidance; on the contrary, I saw
quite a few spiritual catastrophes—but because I consider erroneous
the singling out of this spirituality as a thing in itself (*Ding an sich*),
into a sort of (or does it only *seem* to me?) refined narcissism in all

of this . . . [T]he more they come to confession, the more intensely they study (!) spirituality, the stronger the religious madness which I loathe.[26]

The honesty in some passages, such as Schmemann's feelings both about the excesses of Orthodoxy and of the ecclesiastical culture more generally, is so stinging one wonders how it passed through the editorial process. The real Schmemann is visible in the selection of entries, perhaps despite efforts to avoid his most venomous entries. He is cranky—who wouldn't be with his job as dean of a seminary, sought-after confessor and counselor, fund-raiser, scholar, and advisor to the bishops. He also had his failures of vision. A reviewer of these collected journal entries notes both the absence of comments on racism and poverty, frequent irritation at programs to make social and political changes, and an impatience and lack of compassion for the problems of society strangely out of synch with Schmemann's other sensitivities. Clearly, Schmemann had a circle of family and friends he treasured, and beyond it there is hardly an individual he doesn't criticize in one way or another, from presidents to patriarchs, celebrities to seminarians. He has opinions—and strong ones—about feminism and the civil rights movement, about Solzhenitsyn's obsessive Russianism and the superficiality of Ronald Reagan. But despite the edge, the negativity, the sometimes quick, impulsive, and judgemental reactions to social engagement and political involvement, there is also a discerning, rich expression of what we have been looking at throughout this book, namely, the neither pious nor churchy seeking for God and the very ordinary living in his joy, which is Schmemann's definition of holiness. To start with, not everything in a tradition, even that of the Eastern Church, is valuable or important.

In my case, I feel every year more and more strongly my own Westernism—not metaphysically, not dogmatically, but in the West I feel at home, while I have the impression that the East is hopelessly entangled in itself. Yesterday I had this feeling while listening to the Canon of St. Andrew of Crete. This flow of words, this deluge of allegories, metaphors, various ornaments is rather tiresome. But once in

HIDDEN HOLINESS

116

awhile a simple, deep, bright thought comes as a breath of air on a hot exhausting day. An Orthodox person will not say, will not acknowledge that Orthodoxy can be decadent, that a great part of the heavy volumes of the liturgical *Menaion* [texts of the services] consists of imitative and often meaningless rhetoric. An Orthodox person will condemn the very thought as heretical and sinful. Thus a man who comes close to the church, who has become churchly, constantly struggles to fit into a very narrow garment not of his size, while assuring himself that he is right and despising anyone who does yet question anything but might do so. Such a man easily burns what he adored; leaves and throws everything away.[27]

Then there is the deeper question of where to draw lines and what these means. For Schmemann, the church exists "for the life of the world." He recoils from the sectarian, cultic piety that wants to separate itself from all culture and life outside church boundaries. The tendency to this exclusivism is strong in the Eastern Orthodox "world," with historically different languages and practices of immigrants seen as "colorful" and "mysterious," yet also foreign and esoteric. To become infatuated with the rubrics and the other details would be to miss the point of Christianity as such. Schmemann's reflection is direct and disarming.

If one could apply the Gospel's basic principle, "for the tree is known by its fruit" (Matt. 12:33), to the history of the Church, one would see that what happened was the reduction of the Church to a mysterious piety, the dying of its eschatological essence and mission, and, finally, the de-Christianization of this world and its secularization. But, it seems that there is an impulse precisely to return to this very legacy. It's time to acknowledge to myself: I feel part of this secularized world and I feel strange and hostile in the world that calls itself Christian. The secular world is the only one that is real. Christ came into this world and spoke to this world; in it and for it He left us the Church. If one would speak in paradoxes, one could easily say that any religious world, as well as the Christian world, easily manages without God, but cannot spend a minute without gods, i.e., idols. Little by little, the

Church and piety and the way of life and faith itself become such idols. The secularized world, by its denial, clamors for God. But, captivated by our holiness, we do not hear that clamor. Captivated by our piety, we despise this world, escape it with priestly jokes and hypocritically pity those who don't know "our" churchliness. And we fail to notice that we, ourselves, failed and are failing all our exams—of spirituality, of piety and of churchliness.[28]

What are taken as signs of the spread and the success of Orthodox Christianity in America, the running toward "any *credo quia absurdum*" (I believe because it is absurd) toward any *typikon* (book of rubrics) or "spirituality" is for him not the faith of the Gospel. "In America, suspicious sketes and rather meaningless charismatics are sprouting like mushrooms, in which everybody is condemning everybody else and trying to outdo the other."[29]

While the critique of the "vaudeville" of monastic hats, hoods, habits, and other paraphernalia is the point of departure in the entry cited earlier, it is crucial to note what follows. This is one of the extremely rare instances of Schmemann making very specific recommendations. It is a simple statement of the basics of monastic life not only as found in ancient rules but in contemporary efforts at monastic renewal, such as the rules of Bose, New Skete, Taizé, and the Community of Jerusalem.[30]

These specific recommendations, as well as various published writings, reveal Schmemann's "return to the sources" in recognizing Christian life as the Gospel put into practice, lived out in the concrete circumstances of this place and this time. Thus his scorn for imitations of nineteenth-century Russian practices or the glorification of the pre-revolutionary "Holy Russia" mystique. He knew all too well the history of that time, its decadence and the church's own urgency for reform, reform asked for as early as the bishops' responses to the synodal questionnaire in 1905 but most especially the reforming work of the Moscow Council of 1917–18. Schmemann is best known for the planning and receiving of autocephaly of the Orthodox Church in America in 1970 and for his work in the developing of an authentic liturgical theology. Yet in order to accomplish these he also had to craft a renewed understanding of the qualities of the "local church," as well as Orthodox liturgical practice and spirituality. In these the influence of his teachers at St. Sergius Institute are much in evidence as are the efforts of a wide array of Western scholars.

While intentionally too general to be seized upon as a "recipe," and not without some questionable details, Schmemann's perspectives do point precisely to the universal and ordinary qualities of a "hidden" holiness in our time. Along with prayer and liturgy, these qualities are ways of giving witness and serving. They are the outlines of the holy life that each of us creates with God. The contents, however, will be particular to each one. Schmemann sketches out very roughly the qualities of an authentic Christian life as opposed to contrived efforts of spiritual seekers. These include above all simplicity in one's dress, home, and lifestyle. To be avoided are peculiarities of dress or behavior that would single one out as "spiritual." Also to be avoided are special study or discussion groups on the spiritual life or on texts like the *Philokalia*, the lives of elders. Schmemann very much wanted to discourage the "cult" of stereotypically holy people and the obsession with spiritual literature and practices.

Schmemann encouraged reading beyond specialized theological and ascetical material, a practice he followed in his own life. An authentic Christian life would embrace the best of both classic and contemporary literature, drama, music, film. The theme of openness runs throughout all of his writing. Again, in a very practical sense he counseled resisting the urge to find the ideal spiritual elder or guide. It would be better to mix with all kinds of people, at work, in the community, at church, not just those interested in ecclesiastical matters or in the techniques of spiritual things. Stay in your parish, he also advised. Fight the temptation to shop around for the perfect priest or liturgy. Live with joy, Schmemann preached— and lived. Live in an ordinary way, rather than with much pious posturing and sentimentality. Do not look down on any job or work as less than spiritual, rather, do it to the best of your ability, remaining open to all those around you as the face of God himself. And if after a significant time living in such a simple manner one still felt called to more, then one could ask God to show how and if one's life should be changed, if another path were to be taken. It was crucial to discern that true life in and with God is marked by peace and joy, in the Spirit. If what you find is anger, impatience with the weakness or mistakes of others, restlessness, then something is very wrong.

If one lives waiting, with openness, one will inevitably find how God intends that life to be lived.

Schmemann also suggested three "vows" or commitments that might constitute the core of Christian life today. First, he called for a practical discipline or regular form for *prayer*. Next, he advised *obedience* or a commitment to stay in the ordinary community of the church rather than retreating to more interesting, unusual, or demanding forms of monastic life or liturgical groups. And finally, he underscored *acceptance* of one's place in life.[31] Any spirituality of authentic substance could only be found in the locations of one's work, family, parish, in short, in one's world and time, rather than in a relentless search for better locations or more "interesting" books, services, clergy, or church activities.

One can read traditionalists' criticism or even attacks on virtually every aspect of Schmemann's person and writing, from the length of his beard to how much he did or did not wear the cassock to his alleged negative attitudes toward monasticism, liturgy and its celebration, and the relationship of the church to the world. While himself a discerning but not uncritical product of the "Paris School"—the thinking of a number of his teachers at St. Sergius Institute in Paris—Schmemann exemplified one of the principal features of its outlook: openness to and a desire for dialogue with the modern world. Paul Valliere better than anyone else has captured this stance in his masterful study of several of its proponents.[32] The very title of an anthology of essays by Berdiaev, Bulgakov, Afanasiev, Kern, Kartashev, and Zenkovsky, among others, of the "Paris school," published in 1937 reveals their vision: *Living Tradition: Orthodoxy in the Modern World*.[33] Bulgakov, in his contribution to this collection, claimed that the fathers themselves sought dialogue with the intellectual life, the political and economic institutions of their time and world. He went even further, holding open the door to both doctrinal and dogmatic development. Schmemann, despite disagreements with the ideas of his teacher, Sergius Bulgakov, nevertheless shared a discerning critical sensibility with him on society. There is much insightful assessment of American consumerism and conformity in Schmemann's essays, more than one would expect from a liturgical theologian. But perhaps precisely because he saw Christianity as a liturgical reality, that is, a public and communitarian enterprise,

Schmemann saw the profound social implications of Christian life. His thoughts about how a person might live—simply, honestly—while discerning a vocation in life only confirm the ordinary as well as diverse forms that holiness takes.

THE EXPERIENCE OF CONTEMPORARY MONASTICS: BOSE AND NEW SKETE

In their attempt to describe the spiritual life from their own experience, the monastic communities of New Skete in Cambridge, New York, and Bose, near Magnano in the Piemonte, have emphasized that the traditional elements—the liturgical calendar, the feasts and daily services, the Sunday and festal liturgies, the *lectio divina* and meditative reading of scripture and other sources, personal prayer, and meditation—are all indeed handed down from the earliest days of Christian communities whether local or monastic.[34] These basic elements are woven into the fabric of monastic life and, more broadly, all of Christian existence. They are inseparable from our daily work, our jobs, our families, as well as from the service and care for the neighbor and the witness of all this as our life in Christ.

The founder and prior of the Bose community, Enzo Bianchi, is a prolific lecturer and writer.[35] With weekly columns in Milan's *La Stampa* plus regular conferences at the Bose monastery, which have turned into numerous volumes over the years, he has constantly held up daily life in our time to the Gospel. Often, he finds much to criticize about our materialism, our indifference to faith, the deep loneliness that is found in so many relationships. Yet Brother Enzo has also been acutely aware of the weakness, the many failures of institutional Christianity. He has taken aim at the retreat into spirituality as a way of avoiding the hard realities of life in our time. In a recent book he has heralded the "difference" that Christian faith makes not only in our perception of the world around us, but more importantly in how we choose to live, in how we act (or don't) in this world of ours. In the forty years of its existence, the community of Bose that Brother Enzo founded has been an experiment in returning to the sources of monastic life but also in finding the ways in which these can be lived today.

[M]onastic life, it is *to be there* and *not for the accomplishment of a particular task* in the Church and the world and because of this it ought to be an evangelical life, one modeled on the Gospel. And this is never easy or obvious, especially because the evangelical character of a life must be continually recreated and established, *as all Christian life.* What monastic life needs to absolutely establish or rediscover is where it has been lost or distorted in the following of Christ in everyday communal existence, in the concreteness of a life which is a human life in a form that is the most ordinary and shared in by most people in the context where monastics find themselves. It is necessary, really most urgent that monasticism become rigorously Christian, opposed to any gnostic tendencies, faithful both to the world and the Church. The monastic ideal ought to become once more the radical form of Christian life but a life which is not some other "state" or "way of life," but a life that seeks to be very basic, humane, the most human and which abandons the alibi that says it is impossible to lead a holy life in the normal, the ordinary life in the world or in the Church. There is only one calling to holiness, as there is but one hope in the Church; the time has truly come for monasticism to body and soul wage a war against gnosticism (as an insightful theologian Pierangelo Sequeri demands).[36]

Just as at Bose, the monastic communities of New Skete have, since 1966, sought to live this particular form of the Christian life in authenticity and simplicity.[37] Their rule or typicon is a statement of this aim, rooted first in the Gospel and then in many of the ancient monastic rules of the church. It is the pattern for the particular communal life we call monastic, but, especially by drawing upon the most ancient monastic documents and witnesses, the communities of New Skete powerfully affirm the unity of the life of holiness in the church and in the world.

The monastic life has but one rule, the Gospel of our Lord Jesus Christ, and one goal, our salvation. Accordingly, the monks, nuns and companions of New Skete are endeavoring to live the Christian life as fully as possible by becoming true disciples of the Gospel. In the community life of our respective monasteries, we not only profess the Gospel, but manifest our intention of seeking sanctification with God's help through growth in wisdom and spiritual enlightenment. In so doing, we witness to the Kingdom of God which is to come and the fulness of the promises made at baptism to every Christian. Thus, we hope to be responsive to the prophetic character of our vocation, which from the very inception of monasticism in the desert of Skete, has made monks and nuns responsible not only for their own salvation, but for that of all God's people.[38]

Anyone who has visited, prayed, eaten, and talked with the New Skete communities is struck by the basic humanity of the brothers and sisters, the sense that one is not dealing with radically other or different people, but fellow Christians. At New Skete, members wear the monastic habit for services in church but otherwise ordinary clothes suited to work, the season, and a frugal budget. In this they are only following the lead of the first mothers and fathers of the desert, who wore the ordinary clothes of Egyptian farmers, shepherds, and peasants. (The same is true at Bose.) A visitor is always welcomed as Christ himself would be. While food and time and conversation, as well as prayer, are shared, a guest is neither interrogated nor lectured in the spiritual life. One immediately thinks of the reluctance of early monastics even "to give a word," preferring, rather, to show through one's actions what one believed and lived for. There is great diversity among those who visit—some are married, others single, some young and just starting their lives, others caught in the midst of family and work pressures, still others heading toward retirement. Likewise at both New Skete and Bose, the members of the communities come from different educational, professional, and family backgrounds. What emerges as common and most important is not some set of ascetic practices or detailed rules for prayer but the integrating of liturgy and life, prayer and work, faith and care for others—precisely the signs of the Kingdom.

> Living, praying, and working together, therefore, in harmony with the teachings of our elder, we strive to make the Kingdom present among men and women today. By our mutual love and understanding as sons and daughters of the same father, we hope to demonstrate the possibilities open to all people everywhere of living in peace and concord for the benefit and welfare of all . . .

By seeking God in solidarity with our confreres and with all people
of good will, by training in the monastic way of life of the Orthodox
Catholic Church, and by personal repentance, i.e., changing our minds
and hearts, our manner of life, in favor of progressive interior responsiveness to the words of Christ: we illustrate and fulfill our desire to
foster true peace and compassion as the genuine roots of justice in the
world.[39]

Just as the New Skete communities look for the authentic practice of
the Christian life in monastic existence, so too with Bose monastery (and
some others in the Benedictine and Cistercian traditions). Both of these
experiments in the renewal of monastic life (as I know from friendship
and time with both communities) place great value on their connections
to the rest of the church and the world, not only through families, friends,
and retreat and conference guests, but also through their own efforts to
be part of the wider community where they live. It is also characteristic of
both that they see a distinction of form but not of substance between their
monastic existence and that of the universal Christian vocation, a point
emphasized by John Chrysostom in the fourth century and echoed more
recently by Paul Evdokimov.

It is beyond the scope of this book to examine the ongoing questions
and efforts at adapting monastic/religious life to our time. That would
entail many volumes in fact. Suffice to say that the growing number of as-
sociations of oblates or lay associates of Cistercian, Benedictine, and other
communities attests to a usually unexamined corollary to the continuing shrinkage of numbers and vocations to religious life, namely, the increasing number of ordinary Christians who want to follow the patterns of
prayer, study, spiritual reading, and work that monastic rules have historically used to frame everyday life. Rather than this being a drift toward monastic holiness by lay people, it seems to be what many writers have recognized, Evdokimov but André Louf as well, that is, the rediscovery of the
common elements of Christian life for all.[40]

CHAPTER SIX

Holiness, Hidden, Ordinary, Yet New

Simone Weil wrote on May 26, 1942, a letter to her friend Fr. Perrin titled "Last Thoughts." It offers typically insightful yet provocative observations about holiness in our time.

> We are living in times that have no precedent and in our present situation universality, which could formerly be implicit, has to be fully explicit. It has to permeate our language and the whole of our way of life.
>
> Today it is not nearly enough merely to be a saint, but we must have the saintliness demanded by the present moment, a new saintliness, itself also without precedent.
>
> Maritain said this, but he only enumerated the aspects of saintliness of former days, which, for the time being at least, have become out of date. He did not feel all the miraculous newness the saintliness of today must contain in compensation.
>
> A new type of sanctity is indeed a fresh spring, an invention. If all is kept in proportion and if the order of each thing is preserved, it is almost equivalent to a new revelation of the universe and of human destiny. It is the exposure of a large portion of truth and beauty hitherto

concealed under a thick layer of dust. More genius is needed than was needed by Archimedes to invent mechanics and physics. A new saintliness is a still more marvelous invention.

Only a kind of perversity can oblige God's friends to deprive themselves of having genius, since to receive it in superabundance they only need to ask their Father for it in Christ's name.

Such a petition is legitimate, today at any rate, because it is necessary. I think that under this or any equivalent form it is the first thing we have to ask for now; we have to ask for it daily, hourly, as a famished child constantly asks for bread. The world needs saints who have genius, just as a plague-stricken town needs doctors. Where there is a need there is also an obligation.[1]

This quotation perhaps can serve as a book end, as it were, along with the short, playful poem that started the first chapter, "Saints," by Matthew Brown. The passage is vintage. Weil, full of her brilliance and urgency, has absolute clarity but also is reluctant to spell out this new saintliness in detail. Of course, as was the case most of the time, I believe she was thinking about her own life, about herself. It would never have been too proud or presumptuous for her to think about becoming a saint. Not to do so, in Léon Bloy's words, is the only real tragedy in a person's life.

Simone Weil, as singular and personally difficult as she was, would resonate with many of the others we have met and heard here. After all, she inhabited the same historical period as most of them, even the same countries. Though a classicist, she read many of the same authors who challenged traditional faith both in the past and in the twentieth century. She experienced firsthand, like many of them, the Great Depression and the horrors of World War II. For her, as for them, despite all sorts of foundations and certainties and civilities being shaken, even shattered, she nevertheless embraced the swirl of modernity, the rush of changes, terrors, and hopes that characterized the twentieth century many of us would come to know.

Weil recognized the value of the tradition of faith in the past. But she was also herself in profound struggle with religious tradition, whether the Judaism which her family never practiced, the Christianity that surrounded her in France, and the thought of the ancient Greeks which she revered, not to mention the many more recent social and philosophical movements, including Marxism. For all her complex relationships and estrangements, ideologically and personally, she was able to glimpse what would be new and different in living the life of holiness in our time. Something of an outsider, a marginal person given to a solitary life, she kept herself outside the borders of ordinary family life and romantic connections. She rejected the ordinary career path for a top graduate of the leading school for humanities, École Normale Supériere.[2] She had mystical experiences at Assisi and Solesmes, felt the presence of Christ in her heart as she recited a George Herbert poem, corresponded for years with Dominican Fr. Jean-Marie Perrin, but could not enter the church. She never felt the worthiness nor the calling to be baptized, though her faith united her to Christ and to many others.

She was a person of great intellect, as her writings still witness, and also of immense passion.[3] Her refusal to accept more than wartime rations may have contributed to the illness that cut off her life quite prematurely. She was a difficult person, not only with respect to friends and family, but in regard to her own life and behavior and thinking.[4] It is painful to read of what appeared to be an estrangement from both family and friends that increased during her short life, leaving her very much alone. It might not seem like her stints of teaching or her profound efforts at connecting classical philosophical thinking to our time are the works of a saint.[5] Even the best known of her writings seem to have no central theme but, like letters or journal entries, dart around to the issues or impasses into which her reading (and her writing) seemed to lead her.

For these reasons, I think her words about the need for a new saintliness, one of genius, are particularly eloquent. Moreover, it is remarkable that she refuses to state in explicit terms the shape or content of this holiness, allowing for the diversity of its genius and, perhaps, its less than obvious presence. A stickler for precision when she taught in the lycée, almost eccentric in her adhesion to the ancient Greek thinkers, what could she have had in mind in attaching such importance to the need for new and creative forms of holiness, without specifying any characteristic of sanctity? She does fault Maritain, albeit gently, for only being able to envision holiness in the categories of the saints of the past.

Perhaps careful scholar that she was, Weil, much like Evdokimov, sensed something different about the terrain of the twentieth century—the unexpected trauma of World War I, the pathetic aftermath that in many ways set the stage for further violence and hatred. Some have seen Weil almost as a secular nun, dressed in nondescript, virtually uniform or habit-like clothes, uncomfortable with romance, fashion, the diversions, and rich life her family's wealth and both Paris and New York could surely have afforded her. Several career paths seemed open to her. Her writing and teaching and degrees from the best schools could have taken her either into academic life or into the flourishing scene of public intellectuals, the world of another Simone, de Beauvoir, as well as Sartre, Gide, and other French intelligentsia. She could have moved equally into politics, or even into the kind of humanitarian service that attracted Mother Maria Skobtsova or the recently deceased Abbé Pierre. Instead, she remained marginal, chosing much less than her status and achievement could have brought her, choosing paths her family could not understand. And then there was the mystical dimension, only mentioned briefly, without elaboration, in her letters, and finally the asceticism of her last months, refusing any more than the rations those in occupied France had to survive on, also rejecting medical treatment until it was too late.

Simone Weil's personality and life hardly stand out as models to be held up as exemplary. She could not bring herself to enter the Christian community of faith, even though she prayed regularly, meditated, and often desired to receive communion. If one closely reads her letters as well as her more formal essays, this reluctance had nothing whatsoever to do with doubts about the existence of God nor about the reality of God's presence in the Eucharist nor the testimony of the gospels nor even the lives of the saints. She copied out the text of the Lord's Prayer, the "Our Father," from the Greek New Testament text and used it in her daily prayer, which included the rest of the scriptures.[6] What Weil leaves us, however, is both a troubling yet very important realization about piety. I think we heard this quite powerfully, and for some possibly also in a disturbing way, from Schmemann's journals. Simone Weil could not allow prayer nor any other religious action to become an escape for her, a legitimation for looking away from the troubles of the world around her, from the terrible ma-

terial suffering caused by the Great Depression and then the war, particularly the Nazi occupation of her own country, France. Her parents were
among those of Jewish background able to flee Europe for New York. But
Simone Weil found herself unable to remain in the safety of America, much
like Dietrich Bonhoeffer, who agonized over the same safety in his room
at Union Theological Seminary in the summer of 1939. Bonhoeffer could
have stayed in New York, several offers were made to him, precisely to protect him, but he concluded that if he did not suffer with his people in the
inevitable way he could not be part of the reconstruction when the Nazi
regime was destroyed.[7] Whether her time on the assembly line in a Renault
factory or with the Republican Army during the Spanish Civil War or her
final work for the French provisional government in England from November 1942 to her death in a sanitorium at Ashford, Kent, on August 29,
1943, Weil claimed she was never actively or consciously seeking God, but
rather "waiting in patience" for him while working for the oppressed, the
forgotten. She gathered an entire spiritual autobiography in her letters to
Fr. Perrin. She wrote essays on the forms of the implicit or hidden love of
God, as well the relationship of suffering to God's love. It is impossible to
perceive anything but an intense spiritual life and relationship with God
in her writings, both the more analytical essays and the personal letters.
But she distanced herself both from the institutional church's excesses and
the equally delusional retreat into pious activities because of the division
it would mean for her from others. She wrote to Fr. Perrin:

> It seems to me that the will of God is that I should not enter the
> Church at present. The reason for this I have told you already and it is
> still true . . . I cannot help still wondering whether in these days when
> so large a proportion of humanity is submerged in materialism, God
> does not want there to be some men and women who have given them-
> selves to him and to Christ and who yet remain outside the Church.
> In any case, when I think of the act by which I should enter the Church
> as something concrete, which might happen quite soon, nothing gives
> me more pain than the idea of separating myself from the immense
> and unfortunate multitude of unbelievers. I have the essential need,
> and I think I can say the vocation, to move among men of every class

and complexion, mixing with them and sharing their life and outlook, so far that is to say as conscience allows, merging into the crowd and disappearing among them, so that they show themselves as they are, putting off all disguises with me. It is because I long to know them so as to love them just as they are. For if I do not love them as they are, it will not be they whom I love, and my love will be unreal . . . It is the sign of a vocation, the vocation to remain in a sense anonymous, ever ready to be mixed into the paste of common humanity. Now at the present time, the state of men's minds is such that there is a more clearly maked barrier, a wider gulf between a practicing Catholic and an unbeliever than between a religious and a layman.[8]

Despite the affection and the trust in which she held Fr. Perrin, Simone did not blunt the force of her convictions and negations. She loved Christ, the faith, the liturgy, hymns, and the saints, but not the church. She could not accept the violence it had perpetrated on people over the centuries. Further, for Weil to belong to the church would cut her off from so many others, from the world. Do we not hear in this a description of ordinary and thus hidden holiness? Is there not also present in the following lines a sense of belonging to God and his family more resonant with the Gospel's freedom, with the expansiveness of the Kingdom Christ preached and demonstrated?

The children of God should not have any other country here below but the universe itself, with the totality of all the reasoning creatures it has ever contained, contains, or ever will contain. That is the native city to which we owe our love. Less vast things than the universe, among them, the Church, impose obligations which can be extremely far-reaching. They do not, however, include the obligation to love. At least that is what I believe. I am moreover convinced that no obligation relating to the intelligence is to be found among them either. Our love should stretch as widely across all space, and should be as equally distributed in every portion of it, as is the very light of the sun. Christ has bidden us to attain to the perfection of our heavenly Father by imitating his indiscriminate bestowal of light. Our intelligence too should

have the same complete impartiality. Every existing thing is equally upheld in its existence by God's creative love. The friends of God should
love him to the point of merging their love into his with regard to
things here below.[9]

In that last line is a beautiful description of holiness. Perhaps the erratic,
perfectionist, sometimes antisocial character of her life, when coupled with
the idealism that burned in her writings, leaves us with an image of modern holiness that we could easily overlook. Only years after her death did
her writings and life become remarkable.

Everything I have learned about Paul Evdokimov as a person — of
course the originator of the idea of "hidden holiness" — connects here with
Simone Weil. Evdokimov was in the first graduating class of St. Sergius In-
stitue. He had a Sorbonne degree and would later earn two doctorates. And
yet until his fifties he held no faculty position, had none of the access that
the academic profession or status of intellectual offered. He helped raise
his children and worked with the Resistance during World War II and then
with the ecumenical group CIMADE afterwards, administering hostels for
the homeless and later for students from the Third World. He never sought
ordination, yet those who lived in the hostels experienced him as both a father and a pastor. Later in life he became known, mostly outside his own
Orthodox Church, among both Catholics and Protestants, as an insightful
interpreter of liturgy, sacred art, the history of the spiritual life, and the
connections between monasticism and marriage, among other areas. He
worked to open theological education to all who were interested, mostly
behind the scenes through correspondence and summer courses, and bringing scholars out into the parishes, religious houses, and the wider community. With colleagues like Elisabeth Behr-Sigel and Olivier Clément, Evdokimov sought to create an indigenous Orthodox Christianity in France, while
at the same time deepening the ecumenical relationships, study, and dialogue begun in the 1920s. Clément brought together in his book all that
Evdokimov did, quietly, often imperceptibly, to bring the Christian tradition into dialogue with the modern world, a lifelong effort crowned by
Evdokimov's appointment as an official ecumenical observer at Vatican II.[10]
Clément rightly notes the impact of Evdokimov's thinking on the council's

pastoral constitution on the church in the modern world, *Gaudium et spes.* As mentioned earlier, Evdokimov's collaboration with his St. Sergius colleague, Fr. Nicolas Afanasiev, provided a crucial tool for emphasizing the universal vocation to holiness, namely, the priesthood of all the baptized. As Metropolitan Evlogy urged Mother Maria to make all of Paris, indeed the whole world, her monastery, so did Evdokimov see that there was no place in which the life of the Gospel could not thrive. The last chapter of Evdokimov's *Ages of the Spiritual Life* is devoted to the priestly calling of all to be witnesses, to be saints—women and men, laity not just clergy or religious, young and old, in every profession and state of life. This is not just a lyrical, religious dream but a worldly vision, one of holy realism.

> During the liturgy, the bishop collects the prayers and the gifts of the faithful and bears this offering to the Father, and pronounces the *epiklesis,* the calling down of the Holy Spirit on behalf of all. But the presence of the lay person in the world is also a perpetuation of this *epiklesis,* which sanctifies every inch of the world, contributes to the peace of which the Gospel speaks, and gives to all the liturgical "kiss of peace." According to the litanies prayed in the liturgy, our prayer is directed to the day ahead, to the earth and its fruits, to the efforts of all. In the immense cathedral that is the universe, we, the priests of this life, whether workers or scholars, make of everything a human offering, a hymn, a doxology . . . According to the spiritual writers, such a person is described in the final words of St. Mark's gospel: the one who will tread on serpents, cure all sickness, move mountains and raise the dead, if such is the will of God. If we live our faith simply, to the end, we will arrive at our goal unshaken . . . We are invited to live our faith, to see what is not seen, to contemplate the wisdom of God in the apparent absurdity of history, and to become light, revelation and prophecy.[11]

MERTON AND REALISM

Thomas Merton could well be called a religious genius of our time, but he also occupied a liminal or border place both in monastic life and in the church. Very much a scholar and teacher of ecclesial and monastic tradition, he gradually came to recognize the dynamic nature of Christian life, its capacity to take new shape and direction in the latter half of the twentieth century. In the conference he gave in Bangkok on the day of his death, he quoted the words of a Tibetan abbot to a monk asking what to do, now that the Communists had come and his monastery and way of life were gone. "From now on, Brother," said the abbot, "everybody stands on his own feet." Merton repeated it, adding that if everything else he had said would be forgotten, this "extremely important monastic statement" should be remembered.[12]

Rather than bemoan the declining numbers of those taking up a vocation to priestly and religious life, Merton recognized something providential and very promising. He had seen the numbers of candidates even in his own monastery soar during the 1950s and early 1960s. But as he rediscovered the world, and, as well, the great problems of racism, nuclear arms proliferation, cultural unrest, and the Vietnam war, he did not become despondent as he saw many leave monastic life. God remained, and so too did the church and monastic life, though both needed renewal and reform. Merton saw that the Spirit would not cease to be given to all and abide in them. However, the forms and ways of living the Christian as well as the monastic life could no longer repeat the patterns of the past, and this Merton had much to say about, especially regarding change and renewal in Christian life generally and in monastic life more specifically. As Simone Weil, Merton saw the need for creativity, genius, and courage—all of which he displayed himself.

In the freedom of his hermitage on the grounds of Gethsemani monastery, Merton also celebrated in detail the quotidian liturgy, the liturgy of everyday life tasks such as making breakfast and doing the dishes, gathering the laundry to be done, folding the clean clothes, sweeping the room, and chopping firewood. In his "Day of a Stranger," an extended account of "a day in the life" of a hermit—himself—written on request of a poet friend, he exclaims:

> This is not a hermitage—it is a house. ("Who was that hermitage I seen you with last night? . . .") What I wear is pants. What I do is live. How I pray is breathe.[13]

Of course he also wore the Trappist habit and in church the monastic cowl and in celebrating the liturgy, vestments. At the monastery he still taught novices, but more and more in his life, he welcomed back the world from which he had fled, which he criticized in his autobiography. An "epiphany" or conversion experience in downtown Louisville opened his eyes again to the essential connection of faith and prayer to life and to others. What was rejected by others as profane, he was able to integrate and recognize as holy.

> In Louisville, at the corner of Fourth and Walnut, in the center of the shopping district, I was suddenly overwhelmed with the realization that I loved all those people, that they were mine and I theirs, that we could not be alien to one another even though we were total strangers. It was like waking from a dream of separateness, of spurious self-isolation in a special world, the world of renunciation and supposed holiness. The whole illusion of a separate holy existence is a dream . . . This sense of liberation from an illusory difference was such a relief and such a joy to me that I almost laughed out loud . . . It is a glorious destiny to be a member of the human race, though it is a race dedicated to many absurdities and one which makes many terrible mistakes: yet with all that, God Himself gloried in becoming a member of the human race. A member of the human race! To think that such a commonplace realization should suddenly seem like news that one holds the winning ticket in a cosmic sweepstakes . . . There is no way of telling people that they are all walking around shining like the sun. There are no strangers! . . . If only we could see each other [as we really are] all the time. There would be no more war, no more hatred, no more cruelty, no more greed . . . The gate of heaven is everywhere.[14]

This is a later, more embellished version of the journal entry for March 19, 1958, the day after Merton was in Louisville and had his experience on the street corner.[15] Yet in the original journal entry, the basic experience is still all there—the realization that monasticism was not a retreat from the world, that holiness was not an effort isolated from real life and other people. To be sure, in his journals before this, Merton was sensitive to the grounding of the spiritual life in the everyday round of life, but for him this was mostly monastic observance. Now, the walls came down, the distance disappeared, his vision expanded and the world outside, with all its turmoil, was not to be fled from but embraced.

The Louisville experience of March 18, 1958, most likely was not the first moment of a change in perspective for Merton, and it surely would not be the last. There is an echo here of Simeone Weil's similar vision of holiness open to the entire world and all people, not just those in the church. And there is resonance of Merton's experience here with so many others to whom we have listened.

Merton connects singing the psalms in the middle of the night in his hermitage to the SAC bombers flying overhead, to the booms of weapons testing he can hear from Ft. Knox, to the coverage of the violence in the civil rights movement he reads about in such places as Selma and Birmingham. He can write of translating the poetry of Nicanor Parra while having his morning coffee but also reading the thirteenth-century Cistercian Isaac of Stella and the early church theologian Tertullian. But along with such intellectual and liturgical endeavors there is carrying water to the hermitage, worrying about the presence of snakes in the outhouse, feeling the cold in his arthritic joints in the minimally insulated and heated rooms. In hundreds of pages of journal entries the hermitage would replace the expansive monastery buildings as his daily home, his world. And they would contain not only Joan Baez's singing and Daniel Berrigan's antiwar strategizing but Merton's own agony as he fell in love (and out of it) with a Louisville hospital nurse, and came to terms with his monastic vocation.

After so many years, so much theory, so many essays and books, so much reading, discussion, and analysis, Merton seemed to have achieved the wholeness, the integrity of self, that he restlessly sought. At least I find this in the journals as well as in the articles and the conferences he gave in the last year of his life, not just those on his trip to the East, but also in the Asian journal and that last talk at the monastic conference. The presence of a Dutch television crew filming his talk made Merton visibly nervous. The film footage affirms this: a somewhat hestiant presentation, very different from his many other conferences where he is confidently in command. Perhaps also the material, a radical thinking about the connections between

Marxism and monasticism, made for some uneasiness in the demanor of the largely monastic audience, and thus also in Merton. When he finished, Merton quipped "So, I will disappear from view and we can all have a Coke or something. Thank you very much." Questions and discussion were to be at the evening session. The remark would turn out to be eerily accurate. He did disappear, dying of an electric shock after lunch that afternoon, December 10, 1968. But his many questions and ideas certainly remain.

A year before his death, Merton gave a retreat to a group of contemplative nuns, actually superiors, at his Gethsemani monastery. The task of transcribing and then editing this very spontaneous collection of talks and question-and-answer sessions yielded nothing like the usual lyrical, powerful Merton prose. And now, some forty years later, details of the conversation seem antiquated. But what is striking is the honesty of what Merton had to offer as well as the honesty of the responses, the questions posed back to him by the sisters. The monk who wore pants, loved his beer, who best described prayer to a correspondent as simply breathing with God, also took on the basic, almost daily question we all have about our faith, and thus about holiness. The question itself is in italics.

> *It is amazing to me that Christianity is the most wonderful thing that has ever come to us and yet it seems to have touched the lives of most people very little.*
>
> Isn't that the way it is all through the Bible? It seems to me that that is part of the message. Maybe that's the meaning of "Many are called, but few are chosen." It isn't that people are consciously bad. Maybe they respond on one level but just do not follow through. Scripture teaches us basic things, God's thoughts about human beings. We have to remember that no one does everything right. We are all sinners. God speaks and we do not listen. On the other hand, the mercy of God is constant. It cannot be overcome. God's promises are absolute. Being Christian doesn't mean "being on the right side." A Christian does not always know where justice lies, does not always see clearly. But the Christian is aware that, while in the human being there is falsity and infidelity, in the mercy of God there is always ab-

solute fidelity. So we reject no one, but still try to dissociate ourselves from anything that is going to hurt other people. Every Christian has to stand up for the truth that God's mercy is without repentance. God never takes back mercy.[16]

Here is Merton's vision of holiness in our era. It is not so much what we do as the constant presence and the power of God's mercy. The more we are aware of this, the more urgent it will be not to run off into "religious" practices such as prayer, reading, services, and fasting, believing that these exhaust the meaning of holiness. As a young monk, Merton was entranced by all the details of religious life, particularly those of monastic observance. Not only in his autobiography, *The Seven Storey Mountain,* but in his journal selections, *The Sign of Jonas,* certain activities and objects form the framework of his thinking and writing: the daily services, feasts, intricacies of fasting, monastic clothing. Later, he would be his own harshest critic in seeing the romanticizing obsessiveness of his early years. Yet he did not reject these practices entirely but came around to see that they originated in the realities of everyday life and had to be redirected there.

To reassess and reform liturgical and ascetic practices is a way to honor them as living traditions, not a brutal rejection of them. For example, as important a place as fasting has had in the Christian tradition, Evdokimov suggests that it might take new forms in our time: fasting from substances that can be addictive, fasting or reining in of our many everyday addictions—to work, to consumption of all kinds, to sound and information and gratification. There certainly would be an everyday, hidden holiness in how we manage time with our friends and families—to assure them some! Evdokimov's friend, Fr. Lev Gillet, further noted that fasting might better take the form of eating simple, cheap food rather than that allowed by ancient Eastern Church fasting rules such as lobster, shrimp, scallops, caviar, which are now quite expensive. (A Greek friend tells me that such seafood was considered to be fit only for the poor or fasting, even in the mid-twentieth century. There are other, less convincing theological explanations too.) Both Evdokimov and Fr. Lev noted the great difficulty in listening to anyone today, especially those coming to us with problems, sadness, or rage but without belief in our God. Perhaps this can be a more useful form of fasting, namely, slowing down, making a gift of our time and attention to others. As his biographer Elisabeth Behr-Sigel observed, Lev Gillet, both in Paris and in London, exercised a street ministry that was then quite unconventional. He most likely learned it from Mother Maria, accompanying her to taverns and bistros. Father Lev's habit of mixing in city parks and cafes with so many different people and with those who could not use his language of belief enabled him to find a different language for the content of faith, for even God. His writings on "Limitless Love" stem from these encounters and from his intense desire to listen and then respond without falling back on stale, conventional language.[17] We can only imagine how many people felt welcomed and respected by this inconspicuous little man, only a notch above a street person in his clothing despite his possessing the highest rank a monastic priest could be granted. His park bench companions would have been startled to know they were talking with a well-known author, also a confidant to many bishops and theologians. They would however have called him a friend.

HOLY REALISM

Kathleen Norris has beautifully described in her writings her time with Benedictine nuns and monks, her own pilgrimage as a writer, the meanderings of her spiritual life, her marriage, and the recent illness and death of her husband.[18] She has also spoken very beautifully of the very mundane yet "holy realism" of the spiritual life in our time.

> The popular wisdom is that the words "[holiness]" and "realism" don't go together. Holy people, like poets, are dreamy and sentimental. Never get places on time . . . Holy people are not of this world. [They are not real about life]. Their mind is always on higher things, including perhaps the old pie in the sky . . .
>
> My goal today is to overturn [these] false notions of holiness, for I believe that it surfaces in human beings precisely when we are being most realistic, most grounded, most down to earth. Holiness is never fussy or sentimental. Neither is a good poem; it's ultimate realism.

My evidence for this belief is that holiness endures, persistent as a weed through the depredations of all the ages, throughout all the terrors that we human beings can inflict on each other and have inflicted over our history on this earth. Holiness prevails, and poetry. Religion and poetry are among the most ancient of human activities, predating even agriculture. And battered as they are today by secular indifference or co-optation ... by legalism, fundamentalism, or terrorism, by right-thinking ideologies, [or] tyrants; religion and poetry are with us still, still witnessing to hope at the dawn of the 21st century. Both holiness and poetry [may seem] anachronistic, ... [but they are] peculiar forces with a life of their own in the face of the dog-eat-dog world we know too well, and as necessary as breath, giving us the hope that evil does not have the last word.[19]

As down-to-earth, practical, and realistic as holiness (and poetry) are for Norris, she is the first to tell us that her experiences of these are also powerful, life giving as well as life changing. They may at one moment serve as a strong alternative to a weak, self-indulgent attitude that tells us to do what we want, when we want. But at another moment, holiness and poetry console us, lift us from where suffering and grief have left us flattened. We have to be reminded of what we hold dear, of what we really live for, what we believe and love.

[Another] point about holy realism is that it is grounded in the present, in the real world, and especially not in our heads. We have in our society so many temptations to live in our heads. We're constantly invited to live our lives through the carefully packaged lives of celebrities, even people who are famous only for performing some infamously stupid or vulgar act ... Holy realism rejects these false images of the world and human life, and it reminds us of who we really are ... Holy realism asserts that life does matter, how we live it matters. It's not willing to accept ... that the endless daily drudgery is all there is to life. Holy realism takes a stand for awe and wonder and beauty even in the midst of ordinary daily activities. That is asceticism to me, I think.

Although she knows the history of monastic life very well, Kathleen Norris does not draw upon it for an illustration of mundane holiness. She takes us, rather, into Kate Daniels's kitchen.

> [Poet] Kate Daniels . . . writes of a burgeoning poem that she was forced to set aside, in a typical day of teaching, and couldn't get back to [that] night because her children and her husband were coming home and had to be fed. "Like me," she wrote, "they are tired and over stimulated. The events of the day are clamoring inside them. The good events want to be shouted out, the bad see the inside or are precipitously acted out in ferocious sibling wars. We have all come home to each other to be healed and hailed, to be soothed as a victim, chastised if a perpetrator, and morally realigned. But we are so tired and we lash out in irritation, frustration, anger." That sounds very familiar to me. In the midst of chaos in her kitchen, the children doing homework are littering the floor with paper scraps, the dog overturning the garbage pail, Kate Daniels takes a stand. "Try as I may, and I do, I have a hard time browning the ground turkey I'm planning to mix with canned spaghetti sauce for the glory of God. I try to find the poetry that exists even here. I know that God is here but in the chaos and the noise, I can't seem to find Him."
>
> Now this is a woman who can find God in the midst of changing a diaper, so we know she's morally realigned and very strong. But now in that kitchen she feels bereft of any consolation. And I connect with that very much. I don't have children, but I have been a caregiver for my husband for about three or four years. And so I really do understand that you sense that God is there but you really can't find God . . . But even the fact that Kate Daniels or I am aware of the absence of God is a form of holy realism. We can have faith and hope that there is something better than the ordinary pains and frustrations of life. Holy realism is grounded defiantly in the daily chores of life . . .

Browning ground turkey to combine with a can of spaghetti sauce, restless kids, a messy house—what do these mundane items have to do with holiness? Kathleen Norris startles us with the force of the very ordinary images pulled out of everyday life. Even if you have not labored over a stove, preparing a meal for family members who may be ungrateful, it is clear that in the midst of tasks like that—taking another phone call, answering a student's question, responding to numerous emails, or forcing yourself to keep putting words on a page—there arises the feeling: "I could be doing something else, something better, something more enjoyable than this!"

It is true, and in many ways sad, that religion becomes a distraction or a diversion for many of us. The scripture lessons or other readings we do in our daily prayer, the music, smells, and movement of the liturgy in church, the limitless resources now available online for further reading, sacred art for viewing, music for listening—all of this very often tastes better than the meal set before us. Not just the meal someone else (or we ourselves) have prepared. And not just the food items but all the other ingredients of a typical work day. The idea of days at a retreat house or monastery, even just visits to huge urban churches or museums—just about any of these stand up better than the drill of our everyday chores and obligations. Here is where the extraordinary lives and actions of some saints, the unusual pull of the numinous, become attractive.

Holiness for All of Us: Evdokimov's Vision Again

> It was revealed to Abba Anthony in his desert that there was one who was his equal in the city. He was a doctor by profession and whatever he had beyond his needs he gave to the poor, and every day he sang the *Trisagion* with the angels.[20]

Evdokimov provides a discerning point of view in *Ages of the Spiritual Life*, evoking in detail the rich heritage of holiness we have in the traditions of both the Western and Eastern churches. Any listing of examples would be long, from perennially attractive figures like Francis and Clare of Assisi to Sergius of Radonezh and Thérèse of Lisieux. Perhaps today others would more readily think of Padre Pio or Mother Teresa. There are also the more difficult figures like pillar-dwelling Simeon and Daniel, holy fools Isaac of Moscow, Pelagia of Diveyevo, Xenia of St Petersburg, and Peter Maurin of the Bowery, or mystics like Marthe Robin.

Evdokimov's point is that while the saints of the past have shaped us and our thinking about the Gospel life, even influenced how we live, there are nonetheless some significant disjunctures. It is difficult for us to return to the patterns of the past in our lives today. It is also the case that we need to recall the historical context of earlier saints and the ways in which hagiography depicts their sanctity. Thus what would easily be understood as renunciation or single-mindedness or utter dependency upon God for them, in the sixth or the twelfth or the nineteenth centuries, may sound simply bizarre or even pathological for us today. Clairvoyancy and the stigmata may characterize the ministry and life of Padre Pio, but so too does his compassion for those suffering people who came to him. His keen insight into the many causes of pain both spiritual and physical and his tireless attention to the suffering—these may speak more clearly to us today, though the other marks of holiness remain.

Likewise for Seraphim of Sarov, some accounts of his activities and remarks in the *Diveyevo Chronicles* might strike us today as strange if not antic.[21] But at the same time, we see many of the features of modern existence in his own shifting forms of life. Changes in his lifestyle need not be read as inconstancy or distraction but rather as responsiveness to the Spirit. That he would plot out the dimensions of the convent and church to be built at Diveyevo with no architectural training and upon apparent direct revelation from the Mother of God—this might not be listened to with such sympathy if a monk-priest were to present the same demands today from the Blessed Virgin. Yet might one not consider that Seraphim's father was a contractor, that he may very well have worked with him and learned the building trade as a young man and then demonstrated at least some of this expertise in his early monastic days in woodworking and furniture craft? Rather than react to extraordinary even questionable spiritual traits or happenings, Evdokimov tells us that the vernacular of the past can find its counterpart in the present.[22]

Yet Evdokimov's principal arguments go further.

It appears that a new spirituality is dawning. It aspires not to leave the world to evil, but to let the spiritual element in the creature come forth. A person who loves and is totally detached, naked to the touch of the eternal, escapes the contrived conflict between the spiritual and the material. His love of God is humanized and becomes love for all creatures in God. "Everything is grace," [Georges] Bernanos wrote, because God has descended into the human and carried it away to the abyss of the Trinity. The types of traditional holiness are characterized by the heroic style of the desert, the monastery. By taking a certain distance from the world, this holiness is stretched toward heaven, vertically, like the spire of a cathedral. Nowadays, the axis of holiness has moved, drawing nearer to the world. In all its appearances, its type is less striking, its achievement is hidden from the eyes of the world, but it is the result of a struggle that is no less real. Being faithful to the call of the Lord, in the conditions of this world, makes grace penetrate to its very root, where human life is lived.[23]

Without in any way rejecting the models of holiness in the past, Evdokimov nevertheless calls for holy lives for our time, lives firmly set in the homes, offices, schools, streets, and towns of our era. Not unlike Evdokimov, Bonhoeffer sees the circumstances of the late twentieth and early twenty-first centuries calling forth a holiness faithful to the Holy One, but like Him, willing to be part of society and culture, one with our bodies and time. In a "world come of age," Bonhoeffer saw the need for a recovery of the concrete, bold faith we see in the scriptures.[24] He was thinking, I am sure, of the warriors and kings, the prostitutes and tax collectors, the radical revivalists and ecstatic prophets and apostles we too often tame or whose worldliness we ignore.

Holiness in the Ordinary: Rowan Williams on Bonhoeffer

Likewise, Rowan Williams both in his writing and preaching has sought to probe the difficult situation of the life of faith today. We have already heard from him. He refuses to retreat into spiritualities of evasion and escape. He seeks to connect us, as a good teacher would, with the figures of the past, as well as the frictions, thereby showing that today we too must encounter God in all the mess of twenty-first-century living, all its horrors and all its joys. When preaching on the centennial celebration of Dietrich

Bonhoeffer's birth, Williams saw in this theologian and pastor an image of the struggle to be holy in our time.

> [I]n a letter to Eberhard Bethge written in July 1944, Dietrich Bonhoeffer recalls a conversation many years earlier with the French pastor, Jean Lasserre. "He said he would like to become a saint (and I think it's quite likely that he did become one). At the time I was very impressed, but I disagreed with him, and said, in effect, that I should like to learn to have faith." And he continued, "I discovered later, and I'm still discovering right up to this moment, that it is only by living completely in this world that one learns to have faith."[25] [This text speaks] of involvement, the involvement of believers with each other and their involvement with the world. [It] is the kind of remark that has made Bonhoeffer the hero of a certain kind of "modernising" Christianity (specially, I must confess, in the English-speaking world): involvement in the world takes precedence over the search for holiness. But this is to misunderstand Bonhoeffer fundamentally. He is not replacing one model of good or heroic behaviour with another. As that letter to Bethge makes clear, he is asking us to forget models and images, the attempt to "make something of oneself." We are not to aim at effective, modern involvement in the place of prayer and praise or sacrifice. For Bonhoeffer, involvement in the world is not undertaking a bold programme of service or reform; it is simply doing what has to be done, in awareness of God—more specially in awareness of God's presence with us in the form of Jesus in his agony in Gethsemane. We are to live out the obligations of our daily life conscious of how all around us is the presence of the suffering Christ. God has promised and chosen to be with us in our most serious need. And, as Bonhoeffer spells out in a well-known poem written in prison, we go to him in his suffering and need. We stay awake with him. That is faith: neither hectic, self-justifying action nor private piety, but abiding in Gethsemane.[26]

No matter how often we admit that it does not have to be "churchy" work or explicitly religious activity, it does seem the case that the mundane, profane realm makes many suspicious. How many times we hear in sermons and lectures that the world of the early twenty-first century is amoral or immoral, that outside the communities of faith the world is not only secular but full of violence and destruction.

Noah Feldman has made the point from the perspective of modern Orthodox Judaism.[27] Despite the effort to be well educated according to both yeshiva and university standards, in bridging the gap between the world of faith and the other worlds beyond it, differences cannot always be reconciled. Contradictions abound. There remains an almost impenetrable wall constructed by the Talmud and rabbinical opinion. The opinion and its logic cannot be made acceptable outside, redeemed in some oblique manner. Sharing a meal with one who is "other" is very difficult if not impossible, the rejection of a most basic human action. Feldman points out that even the acceptable reason for violating the Sabbath work restrictions to help or save a non-Jew must be concealed. It is only to maintain good relations with the non-Jewish community, not because of any inherent value in the life of the non-Jewish person. (Feldman notes that rabbinical opinion remains divided on this.)

The more we live and work with those not of our faith and community, the more we ourselves internalize and understand different points of view not reconcilable with our own, the more we sense the walls, the borders, the distances. Yet, it is a mark of the sanctity of our time being examined here, of "hidden holiness" that it is lived out precisely in the diverse world of our culture. Rowan Williams continues:

> So, to become a human being and a Christian, to use Bonhoeffer's words in the same letter, is not to separate ourselves and work to become holy in a space that is defined and protected by religious convention; nor is it to seek for perfection by ordinary social or political activism. It is to be present with Christ in the world. It is to be there in God's name and God's presence in both confusion and order alike, standing with Christ, standing in that place in the world where God has chosen to be. And this is not a place of power or influence; it changes the world not by force but by patient endurance, by making room for the truth of God's alarming compassion to be there in the midst of everything.

So if we ask about the nature of the true Church, where we shall see the authentic life of Christ's Body—or if we ask about the unity of the Church, how we come together to recognise each other as disciples— Bonhoeffer's answer would have to be in the form of a further question. Does this or that person, this or that Christian community, stand where Christ is? Are they struggling to be in the place where God has chosen to be? And he would further tell us that to be in this place is to be in a place where there are no defensive walls; it must be a place where all who have faith in Jesus can stand together, and stand with all those in whose presence and in whose company Christ suffers, making room together for God's mercy to be seen.[28]

I quote Williams at length here because he is so discerning in seeing past the "versions" of Bonhoeffer to which we have become accustomed. In these few lines we are reminded not of "religionless Christianity" or of "religion-come-of-age" as we may have learned in courses or texts but of a pastor-theologian who returned to Germany from a safe haven at Union Theological Seminary in New York City and who engaged in teaching at the Confessing Seminary at Finkenwalde and in the effort to remove Hitler. For this he accepted both his prison time and execution, rather than the marriage he had longed for and to a life as a tenured academic and pastor.

Williams, like Evdokimov, underscores the significance of Bonhoeffer's refusal to replace prayer and praise with social service or reform. Some get frustrated with Rowan Williams himself for regularly using this kind of nuance, for they see in it his unwillingness to take one side or the other. However, this is not borne out in Rowan Williams's words or actions. One must not flee one's daily place, whether in a kitchen, classroom, library, or office, thinking that a monastery or cathedral would be "more spiritual."

What I have tried to show throughout is that the "cult of celebrity" will not soon go away. Our culture thrives on the "lifestyles of the rich and famous" and those of the spectacularly saintly. I confess that for me it was very moving to stand before the tomb where the relics of St. Ambrose lie, along with those of the earlier martyrs Gervasius and Protasius, on whose grave he built the basilica that now bears his name: San' Ambrogi. It was deeply moving to stand before the side altar at St. Sergius Institute chapel in

Paris where Fathers Bulgakov and Afanasiev celebrated weekday liturgies, to stand on rue de Lourmel where Mother Maria's hostel once was, to worship in places like Canterbury and San Vitale where saints have prayed for centuries.

Some of those saints now look down from the walls, like Ambrose himself in the mosaic of the "golden chapel" of his basilica in Milan, or the Mother of God, the fathers, and other saints in the twelfth-century mosaics in St. Sophia cathedral in Kiev. Others continue to speak to us, their voices now for the most part coming through their words in print. It is a gift to have known a saint, talked to him or her, been given a word of insight. Elisabeth Behr-Sigel recalled Fr. Lev Gillet this way, as well as Mother Maria Skobtsova. Nikita Kolumzine most often remained in the shadow of his wife, Sophie, whose books made her a figure of some renown among Orthodox Christians in the US.[29] I think of Nikita as a saint of "hidden holiness" whom I had the privilege of knowing. I remember when I showed him my book *Living Icons:* he kissed all the portrait photos in it as though they were icons of saints, having known all the persons of faith profiled. Of Fr. Bulgakov he said in particular, "Now THAT was a priest!"

In my observation, these are saints revering saints. I vividly remember Elisabeth Behr-Sigel, looking around the walls of her apartment at so many photos, pointing out all the really remarakble people, all the holy people she had known: Mother Maria Skobtsova, Frs. Sergius Bulgakov and Lev Gillet, Paul Evdokimov, and Vladimir Lossky, among others.

Simone Weil insisted that holiness today has to be a reality of *our genius and invention.* In other words, holiness is by definition the life we create, out of our own gifts, personality, work and experiences.[30] But the definition of holiness does not end here. While it most surely is the product of our own genius and invention, it is also the gift and work of God. Holiness is the result of our interaction with God and with the others in our lives. This is not new in religious history, but what this looks like and how it is accomplished may be different today. Lacking the glitz, the unusual features of patterns of sanctity from the past and perhaps the romance as well as the cultural and social supports, I think that the believer today has a greater challenge but also greater possibilities.

HOLINESS AND FAILURE: CHARLES DE FOUCAULD, THE LITTLE BROTHERS, AND THE HIDDEN LIFE OF JESUS

If the human factor—what is imperfect, fallible, weak—is truly a part of the gift of holiness and the journey both in and toward it, the figure of Charles de Foucauld (1858–1916) must be mentioned.[31] If anything, one would have to judge his efforts as inspired but impractical. A soldier, explorer, linguist, Trappist monk, priest, then hermit near Tamanrasset in Algeria, his life is both an adventure worthy of dramatization but also without any recognizable rationale or achievement. Having tried several different professions or vocations, he turned toward "going native," an indigenization among the Tuareg, aiming either heroically or irrationally at a life somewhere between theirs and what he imagined to be the life of Jesus and his family in Nazareth in the early years of the first century. For a solitary Christian monk-priest to attempt this in North Africa in the first years of the twentieth century strikes one immediately as implausible, impossible. The further plan of gathering a monastic community to follow him in this path was equally futile. One brother came . . . and went. And at the end of his life, what was there to show for his efforts to live a poor, simple life among the poor, after the model of Jesus's "hidden life" in Nazareth? It was only after the death of Brother Charles that the community of little brothers and sisters emerged and grew, remaining over the decades, small in numbers and very simple and poor, radically so, in their way of life.

A colleague gave me a contemporary assessment of the life and legacy of Brother Charles, who was made a "Blessed" by Pope Benedict XVI in February 2005.[32] It came from a member of the community that Brother Charles wrote and dreamed about but never saw in his lifetime. This little brother is so unknown that he would be a striking example of "hidden holiness" himself. I only know that he is in his eighties and presently in Japan. This essay presents both de Foucauld's vision of the "hidden holiness" of the "hidden life" of Jesus of Nazareth before his public ministry and de Foucauld's decision to follow for himself the example he saw in Jesus. De Foucauld's path, as difficult as it was to follow, eventually became the path of others in the communities he inspired: the little brothers and sisters of Jesus.

Our brother notes that there has always been a difficulty in communicating clearly what Charles de Foucauld experienced in his solitary life in the Sahara, in his mostly ineffective effort to reach out to his Muslim neighbors with love that bridged the divisions between Christianity and Islam. Though he dressed as they did, spoke their language, and rejected the conversion-oriented approach of late-nineteeth- and early-twentieth-century Christianity, his effort to return to the utter simplicity of Jesus' own life seemed to make no difference. Our brother further links de Foucauld's vision to that of the community of little brothers and sisters founded only after his death. And he then examines the ways in which Brother Charles's singular idea of a hidden life, doing Jesus's work, remains elusive today but is capable of being put into practice.

For more than 70 years we have not progressed very much in the understanding and unified expression of the charism of Brother Charles. We love it, we live it, we are still clumsy in expressing it . . .

What has helped me is a question that we are shy of asking: why did the good God fill the head and the heart of Charles with Nazareth?[33] What is the goal that God desires? For us little brothers of Jesus, the constitutions say that the contemplative life is mysteriously fertile for the journey to and in the Kingdom. I imagine without difficulty that the Good God could have obtained the same fecundity by keeping Charles [a Trappist monk] at La Trappe. Charles would have dynamited out what was needed and dynamized the rest . . .

We have a concrete experience that neither Brother Charles, Rene nor Madeleine [the founders of the little brothers and sisters] had. We have discovered in real life the treasures of the fraternal life with the "little people" and the poor . . .

I believe that **now** we can divine how Brother Charles was transformed, despite himself, through his immense faith in **the hidden life** of Jesus. He always tried to imitate better the humble carpenter of Nazareth . . . Suddenly, the hidden life of Charles, in the far reaches of the Sahara, becomes the window onto the hidden life of Jesus of Nazareth.

With Brother Charles, the "mystery of the hidden life" has come out of the shadows. In the 30 silent years of God-made-man in order to save us, there is a great mystery to contemplate, to love! The beloved

Brother and Lord Jesus is only one of the inhabitants of Nazareth. Mary and Joseph are the only ones to divine a little of the secret of his face. It is the human face of God.

We stammer in order to say it, but we all know that the charism given to Charles is to help the Church as a whole to understand better what it knows in faith, to explore more fully the height, the breadth and the depth of the silent and humble life of the beloved Brother and Lord Jesus at Nazareth.

The slow development of the legacy and vision of Charles de Foucauld, in part supported by his friend the great Islamic scholar Louis Massignon, was not unlike the journey of the communities gathered by Francis of Assisi or Sergius of Radonezh or, closer to our time, by the tradition-bridging efforts of Dominican, priest, bishop, and martyr Pierre Claverie.[34] Sheer existence, the struggle for an identity as well as a status in the larger church, the inevitable disagreements over strategy and practice—our brother implies all of these burdens and more. In the particular case of Charles de Foucauld, the desire to "accompany Jesus," to hold every neighbor in love and in the friendship that Christ demonstrated, was the friendship Charles himself experienced in being nursed back to health by the people of Tamanrasset. It was not some Christian *noblesse oblige* but rather a humble, even humiliating experience of receiving from the poor, learning love from their love, that Charles himself knew and then struggled to communicate, both in his writings and life. Our author, himself having been a little brother for years, admits that something was lost or rather, not completely understood in the efforts of the communities to follow the model of their creator, Brother Charles.

We all, one day or another, realise that the "life of Nazareth" was already there, before the arrival of our Fraternity. We probably contribute the image which is a little like Nazareth and then the chapel and our faith, but Jesus is also hidden in the hearts that surround us.

Brother Charles's desire was **to see Jesus in every person** and that is not a utopian ideal, it is the fruit of faith in the mystery of the hidden life of Jesus.

All that Jesus **is** and **does** is both in time and of all times. Jesus, in secret, was already a little like the "only model" of Adam and Eve pardoned. Without being aware of it, they imitated the laborious life of their Saviour and future descendent.

Perhaps it would be better to say that it is He who, in the depths of their hearts, worked and also suffered and died with them.

The communities of little brothers and sisters of Jesus, along with several related groups, had to find their own way in living out the example first of Jesus in Nazareth and then of Brother Charles. Rather than becoming a recognized "school" of spirituality as well as ecclesiastically and canonically recognized communities (this in time did happen) those following Brother Charles had to see themselves living this hidden life not only officially in the church but more importantly with the "little ones," the working poor. And their goal was neither that of professional social work or of poverty-eradication programs.

In the world of today, Jesus is totally hidden and also active, in all people of good will, even those who do not know him. The last words of the Gospel of Matthew say that Jesus is with us **always.** Jesus is there, in several ways, but Jesus is **hidden.** The Nazareth of 2000 years ago and the "Nazareths of everywhere" are now the place of faith, without support, without proof. There is nothing to see. No sign, no marvelous teaching. There is only the ordinariness of the life of the people. People of goodwill, in silence, in the secret of their hearts shelter Jesus and resemble him, as brothers resemble one another. That is the hidden life of Jesus that continues . . .

It is in silence and hidden that God is with each person and accompanies each person. Faith in the secret work of God makes the erroneous boundaries, in which our poor heads have enclosed the Church of Jesus, disappear. For a long time we have not been able to understand "no salvation outside the Church." However, all the Holy Scriptures tell us that God wants the salvation of all. Our poor faith appeals to his infinite Mercy at the moment of death, in order to imagine, even so, salvation without baptism.

Our brother observes how the insights of Charles de Foucauld have been extended in fidelity to their original vision. The simplicity of Brother Charles's view cuts through the historical divisions—among the churches, amid clergy and laity, between those inside and outside Christianity—and offers a beautiful realization, namely, that the divisions and differences mean nothing to Christ. Thus these distinctions should not be important and certainly not divisive for us.

Vatican Council II taught us the invisible belonging to the Church. Abbé Journet, helped by our Jacques, had this very simple and luminous formula: "the boundary of the most holy Church passes through our hearts." All at once, as René Page never ceased repeating, the baptised are like everyone else. Knowing a little of the mysteries of the Kingdom is surely a great joy but one which also demands that we "live in hell and do not despair" (the Russian Orthodox monk and elder Silouan of Mt. Athos).

What the Council teaches, Brother Charles, thanks to his "vocation of Nazareth," discovered little by little and, in particular, practiced. He encouraged Moussa to be a good Muslim. He saw Jesus in Moussa as in all the poor (whatever you do to the least of these little ones . . .).

And then in the Gospel there is the overwhelming episode where Mary comes to seek Jesus who is no longer eating . . . "All those who do the will of God are my brothers, sisters, my mother." In this affirmation by Jesus, the Mystery of Nazareth and the Mystery of the Church are united.

At Nazareth, the Church of Jesus was like a seed, gathered and in silence. Now we know in faith that the visible tip of the Church, the Church of the baptized, is only the part that is out of the water, or rather, out of the ocean of silence in which the Kingdom is growing. The hidden part, as with icebergs, is immense! The kingdom journeys on earth in the sun of the Church and of faith and the sacraments of faith; it also journeys hidden in the poor hearts of people of all religions (the silent Church of the mystery of Nazareth?). And then the Kingdom arrives, reaches the goal through the mystery of the Cross (the second baptism of Jesus which he feared . . . and that of all his brothers and sisters?).

The communities, the little brothers and sisters and related groups, despite what we might think, are only the means to another end, our brother says. These communities did not exist when Charles de Foucauld died. They took years to appear, starting out small in size, remaining small to this day. All of Charles's own idiosyncrasies and weaknesses have been found again, over the years, in the brothers and sisters who follow his vision. Just as the church is described by Vatican II as the "sacrament of the mystery of salvation," so too the communities are the sacrament of the mystery of Nazareth. As sacrament, the little brothers and sisters have the reality of Jesus present within them. The communities are the words, the mysteries made visible, embodied—in water, bread, wine, oil, gestures. The communities show what people of faith can be today: women and men praying, working, reaching out in love. Yet these little brothers and sisters do not exhaust the reality they seek to communicate.

[Y]es, the Mystery of Nazareth places its imprint on everything that we do. Limping along, with the poor, daily life is not brilliant, nor is our prayer, but we continue . . .

The little brother who wrote this reflection speaks with the theological discernment that comes from prayer, careful observation, and most of all having lived a hidden life among the people of God and the poor in particular. This brother, in the spirit of Charles de Foucauld, breaks through the boundaries of the church, seeing many more united to each other by their love of God and neighbor. Of course, we are more taken by the heroic faith and actions of Mother Teresa, John Paul II, and other high-profile holy people. But as the little brother, and behind him, Brother Charles, insists, there is a hidden dimension in which all of us, women and men, poor and wealthy, gifted or most ordinary, can ourselves live the mystery of Nazareth, the hidden holiness of Jesus, his mother, and Joseph.

CHAPTER SEVEN
Differences

SAINTS WHO ARE DIFFERENT

Naturally speaking, people are filled with repulsion at the idea of holiness . . . After the last war, everyone was talking about the lost generation. After this war [World War II] thank God, they are talking more about saints . . . Archbishop Robichaud, in his book *Holiness for All,* emphasizes the fact that the choice is not between good and evil for Christians—that it is not in this way that one proves one's love . . . but between good and better. In other words, we must give up over and over again even the good things of this world, to choose God . . . It is so tremendous an idea that it is hard for people to see its implications . . . We have not begun to live as good Jews, let alone as good Christians. We do not tithe ourselves, there is no year of jubilee, we do not keep the Sabbath, we have lost the concept of hospitality . . . We devour each other in love and in hate; we are cannibals. There are, of course, the lives of the saints, but they are too often written as though they were not in this world. We have seldom been given the saints as they really were, as they affected the lives of their times—unless it is in their own writings. But instead of that strong meat we are too generally given the pap of hagiography. Too little has been stressed the idea that all

155

are called. Too little attention has been placed on the idea of mass conversions. We have sinned against the virtue of hope. There have been in
these days mass conversions to Nazism, Fascism, Communism. Where
are our saints to call the masses to God? Personalists first, we must put
the question to ourselves. Communitarians, we will find Christ in our
brothers and sisters.[1]

Always radical, Dorothy Day put those lines into her column in *The
Catholic Worker* in May 1948, and they ring with her passionate impatience.
As someone who converted to socialism and then to the Gospel, who wrote
and worked for the wretched masses, she knew of what she spoke. She knew
in her lifetime the fearsome power of mass movements, of the sway ide-
ology could have over millions of ordinary people. She knew how the des-
peration of poor wages, or during the Depression no work or money at all,
converted many against the "American Dream," how it revealed to them
the disparities that exist even in the best of times. Perhaps her unrepen-
tant social and political radicalism, something she found in the Gospel,
in Christ's very actions, will keep her case for canonization in slow motion
for a long time. Her granddaughter and others echo the line she herself
used quite often. "Don't call me a saint; I don't want to be dismissed that
easily."[2]

Michael Harrington, a social and political radical himself, worried
that despite her social and political radicalism an eventual canonization
would "use" her, as such official actions do, showcasing her theologically
(and culturally) conservative side, her obedience, in the end, to the hierarchy. Perhaps all the details of her own life—an abortion, a common law
relationship and a child born from it, numerous arrests (and jail time)
for protest activities both early and late in life—could be scrubbed clean
and buried by her later authentic piety and devotion to the church. But
along with Merton and the very real imperfections of his life—an illegiti-
mate child, a late-in-life love affair with a nurse, Dorothy does make sanctity accessible, as Jim Forest points out and as her recently published diaries, edited by Robert Ellseberg, powerfully affirm.[3] During WWII, in a
time of uncertainty about what *The Catholic Worker* was accomplishing,
she wrote:

We can do nothing today without saints; big ones and little ones. The only weapons we will develop will be those of prayer and penance. And the world will leave us alone, saying—after all, they are not doing anything. Just a bunch of smug fools praying. (July 19, 1943)

Dorothy's diary is less the literary document than say, Thomas Merton's is. Yet in documenting almost a half century of her life and the entire history, to that point, of the Catholic Worker Movement, her entries are not just chronicles of Catholic radical witness during the Great Depression, WWII, and the cold war period, but are very much the map of her personal pilgrimage. Most days are indicated not just by date but by the saint or the feast commemorated. Virtually every entry mentions praying the psalms and reading the scripture lesson, that is, Dorothy's commitment to the daily prayer of the church, the divine office. And most days she also is at Mass, receiving communion. Hers was very much a liturgical or ecclesial existence. But it was not just prayer that filled her days, and her life was anything but peaceful. We read of her constant guilt and concern for Tamar, her daughter, often left in others' care while Dorothy did Catholic Worker business. Later came Tamar's difficult marriage and financial worries. There are numerous clashes with the institutional church over pacifism; over her participation in actions of civil disobedience and protest against the nuclear build-up and the agriculture industry's treatment of migrant workers; over her engagement in the civil rights movement. Dan and Phil Berrigan are regular visitors to the Catholic Worker houses of hospitality. Thomas Merton's social criticism fills the pages of *The Catholic Worker* newspaper. There are photos of Dorothy with Cesar Chavez and Coretta Scott King at the funeral of Dr. Martin Luther King Jr. In time, what had been a "hidden life" of serving the poor became a much more visible prophetic witness. The entries contain both Dorothy's struggle with others in the movement as well as her efforts to speak out in many social and political issues with the vision of the Gospel.

She could get greatly incensed at priests unable or unwilling to live out their vocations.[4] Often the sheer volume of suffering people overcame her, as it did Mother Maria Skobtsova in the rue de Lourmel house of hospitality.

Our house will hold just so many, we can feed just so many, and after that we must say no. It makes us realize how little we can do. It is a constant grief, and a humbling of our pride. One woman said to me, "If I knew how sensitive you were, I would not have told you my troubles." So we cannot show how we suffer with them either. We make them feel we are adding to the sum total of suffering. (January 13, 1952)

It is one thing to have far-off and rapturous vision of reality. It is another to live in this world of corruption, deformity, vice, disease. (September 18, 1952)

Given her own complicated and wild life, she nevertheless found it hard to comprehend the massive cultural changes in the 1960s, in particular the sexual freedom and experimentation with drugs. Yet, after recalling the power of love in many forms, including lesbian relationships, she concludes:

All love is a reflection of the love of God, just as all sin is a perversion, a turning from God and a turning to creatures. All love must be respected. But evil is very close. (jail diary, 1959)

Ruminating on one of her favorite writers, Dostoevsky, Dorothy notes:

"The world will be saved by beauty". . . What is more beautiful than love? . . . For those who do not believe in God—they believe in love. (April 27, 1960)

Her sense of the goodness, the beauty, the pleasure of sex participation on God's own nature and work was tempered by an equal awareness of the ease with which it is misused and persons abused (January 18, 1967). Yet for all the struggle and conflict she endured, there was a strong conviction of the inherent goodness of God, present in all of creation.

All the more reason for me to keep on writing this most rambling account which is the only way one can write in a busy life. I am an occupied person, and my life is full indeed. I am a pilgrim in this world and a stranger. I hate the world and I love it, because God made it and

found it good, and He so loved it He gave His only begotten son. And
I love people because they are His and there is some reflection of Him
in all of them. (March 15, 1969)

Dorothy's complaint about saints and sainthood is the one sounded
here toward the beginning. Even though the heroics of the saints of the
past are admirable, the stories of their lives do badly in translation, in the
language of hagiography. We therefore are unable to see them as sisters and
brothers, as fellow human beings. They are indeed larger than life, graced
with far more stamina and will and courage than we ever could be. The
sufferings they endured, often freely taken on, are hard for us to imagine,
much less endure ourselves.

Simone Weil argued that in our time we need saints who are genius,
creative people, who show us new ways of connecting God to life and the
world. However, as we have also learned, such holy people must be human,
maybe for some of us entirely too human. Think of Etty Hillesum, Mother
Maria Skobtsova, Thomas Merton, or Dorothy Day. Each of the individuals
we have met and heard from surely could show us the range of humanity's
impressive and not so attractive sides. Though our time highly values
historical accuracy—"fact-checking" a crucial element of writing of any
kind today—it may be that we know too much of their personalities, their
issues, the details of their lives. And thus some of us cannot accept or for-
give them their rages, their sexuality, their doubts, or other presumed falls
from grace.

The very human (not all-too-human) personalities and lives of saints,
hidden or not, are also quite diverse. Through examples like the icons of
William Hart McNichols or the holy people gathered in Robert Ellsberg's
All Saints and the Bose ecumenical martyrology, we are coming to recognize no boundaries of nationality or language, of century or schism,
of gender or occupation or education, when it comes to God's friends, the
saints.[5] This may startle, puzzle, even offend some for whom there has
been a steady procession of saints to venerate. But as the World Council
of Churches consultation puts it, in Bose memorandum II:

The boundaries of the cloud [of witnesses] are always moving as God
adds to our number those whom he is calling. New faces emerge from

the cloud as different historical and cultural circumstances lead us to find new significance in witnesses previously unacknowledged. As the cloud grows, we invite the churches to explore together the criteria for identifying witnesses and martyrs for our time. This work undertaken in dialogue together can also help in healing the wounds of the past as we discover in the lives of our own heroes of the faith a common determination to reflect the image of Christ. Repentance and forgiveness for past acts of inter-confessional violence emerge more readily when we reflect together on those who in dying forgave their persecutors.

Some names raise few protests and even these are fading with time. Franz Jägerstätter, a married man and parent, the Austrian martyr for conscience, was beatified October 26, 2007, and Charles de Foucauld on November 13, 2005. The *aggiornamento* "good pope" John XXIII (Angelo Roncalli) was beatified earlier. The stigmatic Padre Pio has been canonized, but not yet Marthe Robin. Other holy people wait, such as the activist bishop and scholar Bartolomeo de las Casas and the Salvadoran martyrs Archbishop Oscar Romero, Rutilo Grande, Ignacio Ellacuría, Maryknoll sisters Maura Clarke and Ita Ford, Ursuline sister Dorothy Kazel, and lay missioner Jean Donovan. It is hard to say whether the Russian church will ever glorify the priest and martyr Alexander Men. Not well known at all outside his own church but exemplary is Metropolitan Leonty Turkevich, who until 1964 led the church body that became the Orthodox Church in America.[6] The film *Schindler's List* introduced us to Oskar Schindler, an otherwise not-so-virtuous businessman who saved many Jewish people by claiming them as necessary employees in his factories. Less known is the Japanese diplomat Chiume Sugihara, who also saved many Jews, as did Swedish diplomat Raoul Wallenberg. Through his journal, we have become familiar with the hidden holiness of Dag Hammarskjöld.[7] There is the Lutheran nurse and deaconess, Sister Elisabeth Fedde. Perhaps Alexander Schmemann and John Meyendorff will one day be recognized as saints, despite being rejected by some of their Orthodox brethren as heretical because of their ecumenism, their desire for liturgical reform and renewal, and their insistence that genuine tradition must be one that is living. Perhaps more deadly are their contemporaries who dismiss them as not scholarly enough, not organizationally savvy enough, too much the intellectuals and dreamers.

Official ecclesiastical process does take money and time, but there has been a renaissance of saint-making in our days and not just under Pope John Paul II. Even in those communities who do not create saints for their liturgical calendars, persons of faith are being recognized. Didier Rance has been gathering names and making their stories known.[8] The Greek Catholic Church in Ukraine has seen a number of recent martyrs and confessors beatified, and they have been commemorated in icons by Ivanka Kripiakevych-Dymyd.[9]

Dorothy Day, Thomas Merton, Martin Luther King Jr., and Elisabeth Behr-Sigel, for all the controversy they evoke, are quickly trumped when one thinks of other, more outsider figures included in martyrologies and iconography, from social radicals like Sojourner Truth, Malcolm X, Gandhi, and Cesar Chavez to writers William Blake, Fyodor Dostoevsky, and Emily Dickinson, musicians John Coltrane and Ella Fitzgerald, chief justice Thurgood Marshall, and anthropologist Margaret Mead. These are among possibly the most diverse collection of saints ever, gathered in depiction by iconographer Mark Dukes. There are almost 100 depicted in a two story fresco by him in St. Gregory of Nyssa Episcopal Church in San Francisco. Led by the "Lord of the Dance," the Risen Christ himself, these men and women, dancing in procession around the fresco, include many outside the ordinary boundaries of Christianity: the poet-mystic Rumi and martyr-mystic al-Hallaj, rabbi and scholar Abraham Joshua Heschel, Eleanor Roosevelt, and naturalist John Muir. It also includes many familiar holy ones: Seraphim of Sarov (with his bear), Maria Skobtsova, Thomas Aquinas, Mary Magdalene, and Patrick, even Pope John XXIII—probably the only Anglican church with a recent pope so memorialized. There is even a figure to represent all the nameless, anonymous saints, those of a "hidden holiness," such as an Alexandrian woman praying ceaselessly at her work, similarly to the physician who did the same, as noted by the desert fathers and mothers, making his work of healing prayer and prayer his work of healing. One of the priests and cofounders of St. Gregory of Nyssa parish, Rick Fabian, produced a commentary on the fresco, its development and meaning. This is essentially a very discerning theology of saints, in which Fabian argues for both a more ancient and expansive understanding of holiness. He also summarizes unwittingly a great deal of what has been said here in this book.

The identities of the saints portrayed will surprise some; but for years St. Gregory's church has fostered a broad idea of "sainthood," in place of the commonplace notion of rarified moral purity. Our Easter procession litany invites saints to "come rejoice with us," mixing famous saints with other departed folks the congregation nominate each year; and many combinations draw laughter: Lucille Ball and Charlie Chaplin, for example . . .

Our idea of sainthood comes from both the Bible and Gregory [of Nyssa's] books. The Hebrew concept of holiness originally had no moral content, but simply meant having God's stamp on you, like a branded steer: marked and set apart as God's own. Slowly the idea grew, that this mark implied a Godlike inner character and active life, or ought to. Hence St. Paul appealed to the Corinthian Christians: now you are saints, so clean up your act! As the Bible sees it, saints and sinners are the same people. We celebrate those whose lives show God at work, building a deep character to match the godlike image which stamps them as God's own from the start.

Of course God works with more than Christians, and more than Christians are saints. Gregory Nyssen held that every human can progress toward God—indeed, to stop our progress is already to move the other way. All humanity shares God's image, and shows it to the universe, so the whole can live and move toward God together. That is the job all people are made for, our natural function. Where God's image is obscured by sin, and nature's harmony is broken, Christ rediscovers this image for us, and teaches us to mend conflict and restore harmony so that all can move toward God once again. Every aspect of human nature—our minds, our bodies, our virtues, our desires, our sexuality, even our mortality—God has made for this purpose. And so every human progressing toward goodness plays a part in the salvation of the world. This universal view made Gregory an extraordinary theologian in his day—extraordinarily like the Biblical writers, in fact—and draws fresh interest today, as people of many world faiths find more and more they share.

For an icon portraying St. Gregory's vision, the dancers must
be diverse, and exemplify traits that Gregory's teaching emphasizes
and our congregation's life upholds . . . Christian or not, these men
and women and children each show us some of God's image, as Christ
makes that image fully plain to us. Our list includes people who crossed
boundaries in ways that unified humanity, often at their own cost.
Some proved lifelong models of virtue; others changed direction dramatically from evil to good, even near the end of life. Like Gregory
himself, some were on the frontier of Christian thought and living,
and had gifts that were unrecognized or disparaged in their time;
yet their gifts matter for what we do today. Others have been long
revered throughout the world's churches. Some overcame difficult
circumstances; others moved toward God despite the distractions of
worldly comfort and power. Many were mystics like Gregory, seeing
God in all creation. Some taught and still teach; all learned to pursue
goodness, even into the darkness where people must choose without
seeing.[10]

The list is challenging even to the most ecumenically open reader as
well may also be Fabian's theology of holiness. Yet aside from the distinct
vision and mission of his parish, the claims here are both biblical and liturgical as well as eschatologically faithful. Alongside the particularity of the
chosen people, Israel, God's universal creation and care break forth repeatedly. Especially in visions of the end of time, the glorious reign of God,
the prophet Isaiah sees room for everyone on God's holy mountain.

For look, I am going to create new heavens and a new earth . . . I am
coming to gather every nation and every language. They will come
to witness my glory . . . and from all nations they will bring all your
brothers as an offering to Yahweh . . . [A]ll humanity will come and
bow in my presence, Yahweh says. (Is 65:17–66:24)

Likewise, at the very close of the New Testament, in the book of Revelation,
all is revealed, the veil is drawn back on the Lord drawing all to himself,
filling all things. The seer John shares his vision of the fulfillment of all
things and the gathering of all in the New Jerusalem, where the Bride, the

church, and her Bridegroom, Christ, are united. (This scene is the subject of the fresco behind the presider's chair at St. Gregory of Nyssa church.)

> The Spirit and the Bride say, "Come!" Let everyone who listens answer, "Come!" . . . Amen. Come, Lord Jesus. (Rv 22:17, 20)

In this heavenly city, with the water of life flowing through glittering golden doorways and fruit trees, there is no day or night, no need for lamps because the Lamb of God is the light of the world (Rv 19–22). The same cosmic and inclusive sense is there in the liturgy when at the start of the eucharistic prayer everything in heaven and on earth, the angels and all people, are seen as singing together with the gathered assembly: "Holy, holy, holy, Lord God of hosts, heaven and earth are full of your glory, hosanna in the highest. Blessed is he who comes in the name of the Lord." The last book of the New Testament shows the martyrs robed in white calling out from under the heavenly altar, as well as the robed elders seated round the heavenly throne, the hosts of angels and archangels, cherubim and seraphim, many of the images coming from the visions of the prophets Daniel and Ezekiel. The saints are God's friends, those who have received him as gift and then become his witnesses in their lives.

What we learn from these holy people is that God knows no boundaries or barriers to his outpouring of his love and his life, his *kenosis*, his self-emptying. Gender, race, ethnicity, state in life, community of faith, political position—none make any difference when it comes to the gift and enactment of holiness. Holiness is God's very being and his gift to each, a sharing in his life, but it is also the task of revealing that to others, to the world, to be living icons of God. This brings us once more, at the end, to exactly the question with which we started. We are all called to be saints—wrinkles, warts, eccentricities, sins, and all. But . . .

CAN HIDDEN, ORDINARY SAINTS MAKE A DIFFERENCE?

Enzo Bianchi, while not well known here in America, is among Europe's leading religious authors. He writes a weekly column in *La Stampa*, a major paper in Milan, and now has a long list of books, translated into several languages. Originally trained in economics, Bianchi was inspired by the movement of renewal encouraged by Vatican II, and he sought to return to a simple, more basic, ancient form of monastic life that was also ecumenical, incorporating Christians from different churches in the same community. Brother Enzo's latest book, already a best seller, is titled *La differenza cristiana,* which I think might be best translated as a question: *Does Christianity Make a Difference?*[11] He argues that in his context—a Europe that is increasingly diverse, secular, and often relativistic—it seems an immense challenge for Christians or people of any faith to make a difference, to be seen or heard. Other than being the creators of monuments of great beauty and historical significance—one has to think not only of the Sistine Chapel and St. Peter's but of so many churches, monasteries, and other works of beauty—of what real use are believers?

In the eyes of Richard Dawkins or Christopher Hitchens, among others, religious traditions and their adherents are problematic, more than that, irreparably destructive to human life and society. They have caused great suffering in past centuries, imprisoned believers in fear and hostility toward those outside their boundaries, and they continue to do so. One need not make an exhaustive list, only consider the hatreds fueled by radical Islam, by evangelical Christianity, by triumphant and aggressive Russian orthodoxy. Lest anyone cry foul, the list could go on, from both liberal as well as conservative perspectives. Scarcely a day passes when we do not hear of some outrageous position based on religious belief or claims of oppression perpetrated by believers. Religious reporting from Europe suggests that the issue of Muslim women wearing veils or more extensive covering seems to be an obsession of religious as well as secular folk, from political leaders to educators and the clergy. Very negative public judgments from the Moscow patriarchate on issues from religious freedom to democracy and the legitimacy of religious monopoly are no better. The recent bungling of the text of Pope Benedict XVI's lecture on Islam set off riots and threats to exterminate him and all other "crusaders." One could well conclude that religion is causing more problems than it is solving.

The prior of Bose monastery, however, suggests that believers offer some very important contributions to life in the society and culture in which they find themselves. No fan of aggressive and intolerant faith, Enzo Bianchi does not see Christians as particularly oppressed, even by recent efforts to produce a constitution for the European Union that does not refer to God. The role that Christians have is one of witness, a prophetic and eschatological presence. They stand for hope in a global climate of despair, whether over Darfur or the growing threat of militant Islam or the specter of global warming. Christians stand up, despite political pull in opposite directions, for love and acceptance of the stranger, for peace over against conflict, for sharing their affluence and knowledge with so much of the world that lives on the margins. Christians make a difference *because* they tend to think and act differently—not always better, not necessarily heroically, but differently.

I would say that even when the "Christian difference" is not easily recognized or seen or heard, it nevertheless is there. And the Christian makes a difference. This is the hidden eschatological difference that pops up now and again in the gospels. The wheat harvested with the weeds. The treasure hidden in the field. The yeast kneaded into the loaf. The woman's coins left somewhere in her home. The guest at the wedding feast who solved the problem of the wine running out. The cup of cold water given to the thirsty person, the meal provided to the hungry one, the clothes for the underdressed, and so on.

The wave of interest in saints seems to lead to an impasse for the argument I have tried to raise here, one I found in Paul Evdokimov as well as other writers. The saints who appear to really make a difference are the ones who light up the sky with their courageous teaching or witness, with the force of their extraordinary, heroic actions as well as their words. At the outset I mentioned those who first came to mind—Pope John Paul II, Mother Teresa of Calcutta, Padre Pio of Pietriclina. Every time I offer a course of holy people of our time at my school, I end up assigning biographies of "celebrity" figures, whether canonized or not, for example, Merton and Reinhold Niebuhr, Day and Mother Maria, in addition to others. To head to the library or use a search engine for a writing project in this course by definition will mean finding persons of faith about whom articles and books have been written, whose faces are visible in photos or icons.

Whether in Bose's *Il libro dei testimoni*, Elizabeth Johnson's *Friends of God*, Robert Ellsberg's *All Saints*, or the dancing saints in St. Gregory of Nyssa Church, it is either the case of encountering more deeply names one has already heard or discovering ones previously obscure. So much, it would seem, for the everyday, simple, and hence invisible saintliness of nobodies, Evdokimov's "hidden holiness." A friend whose opinion I very much appreciate offered this as a very basic question to and criticism of the project of this book. The litanies and lists we have of saints presume that we know of whom we speak, of whose intercession we ask, whose lives we seek to imitate. Of course, from the beginning of the Christian tradition, inherited from the Judaism in which it appeared, there was the very personal, very intimate, and local attachment to holy ones in the community. We know that martyrs or witnesses either of the "red" or, after the era of persecution, of the "white," the confessing kinds were greatly beloved, their burial places and "heavenly birthdays" remembered. The very lists we still use are called "martyrologies." Many feasts stem from the annual commemorations and celebrations, both liturgical and familial.

Yet the rest, whose lives did not demonstrate such heroism, nonetheless were *agioi, sancti*, the holy people of God, the flock of the Shepherd, "God's friends." And so it is for the vast majority of us today. Whether in icons or stained glass, on pedestals or in the stirring accounts of their time of testimony, we look up to the saints who are named and remembered in the community. And yet as the assembly surrounds the altar week after week, there is that great throng, the cloud of witnesses without names, noted in the Book of the Apocalypse.

Elisabeth Behr-Sigel, Olga Michael, Joanna Reitlinger, Paul Anderson — as well as others we have heard about — are hardly household names for most. They stand here as examples of the everyday humanity that shines forth as boldly as miracles or unusual actions in the lives of other saints. So many others could be mentioned, names that mean much to me but not to most readers. There is Jane Penny, who typed and filed and listened so quietly and so well in the church office staff of the parish I first served. Or there is Elvira Erickson, the ninety-year-old whose arthritis kept her homebound and whose joy in the face of a life of much suffering always made me think she was the one paying an encouraging visit to me, a young pastor.

There is a retired cleric, who despite being forgotten by his denomination, nonetheless persists, despite disappointments, gathering people for study, fellowship, prayer both in person and online. There is Father Albert Daly, a Carmelite teacher of mine in minor seminary and later in the novitiate, whose earlier rising career track seemed to end in flames in alcoholism. Books will not be written about him, though some might have if he had climbed to the rank of Prior Provincial of the Order, a post for which he was being groomed. Rather, he returned from his addiction, never to be a superior or administrator but a beloved counselor, even after his retirement, serving as informal chaplain in a skilled-care facility. There was also the Carmelite Fr. Vincent McDonald, a seasoned parish priest and chaplain, who stopped me in my tracks one day. As a young, overly sensitive seminarian I lamented, in confession, that I was unhappy, that the cold, dark days in western Massachusetts, and the monotonous schedule of prayers, classes, work, and more prayers was boring and depressing. Did I get my ears cleaned! "HAPPY? HAPPY?" (I can still hear his loud, squealing, high-pitched New York accent.) "Who do you think is always happy? A mother up all night with a sick child? A man working overtime when he's exhausted, to support his family? And YOU, you want to be happy all the time?" What an epiphany those words produced for me, in my relationship to others, to work, to myself—so vivid his wide grin and those lilting words that whenever I recall them, I am again the naive, idealistic, eighteen-year-old seminarian who heard them and held on to them. And no matter my experience or age, Fr. Vincent still echoes that I should know better than to expect life to make me happy! There is a brilliant academic, whose humility, despite his enormous gifts, always astonishes me. He gave up a stable civil-service career to help reconstruct higher learning in Eastern Europe. Also surprising is his ingenuity in creating opportunities for students and many others to grow and learn, beyond the confines that years of Soviet oppression imposed on them. But even more astonishing are his hope and tireless efforts to bring together divided and often suspicious and hostile Christians from many different churches. The ever-growing list of his scholarly publications will never reveal the hidden work, the real miracles he has brought to life in a country that is not his own. There is a priest who has never learned to say no to troubled, needy people and whose willingness to listen, to be there for and with them has created more joy and a community that amazes all who come to visit it. And I could go on to many other saints of hidden holiness I have known.

Since the days of Ronald Reagan, speech writers and preachers have employed the strategy of naming the nameless heroes and saints, whether in the military, emergency services, our schools, or simply in their own families and neighborhoods. Only when media reporters go digging can they tell the more complete story of such individuals whose lives get a sentence and a few seconds in a speech. But it may well be that rather than diluting the meaning of "hero," in the post 9/11 years, we have come to rediscover the vision of Aaron Copland, who during the Depression entitled a movement from his first symphony a "fanfare," a name usually reserved for dignitaries, but, in those hard days, one he used in a "Fanfare for the Common Man." The photography of Dorothea Lange similarly draws our gaze back toward the beauty of the worn clapboards of a farm house or small town church, back to the creased faces of Dust Bowl refugees and nameless others who would become victims of the financial disaster of the 1930s. And then there is the nameless Alexandrian housewife in the fresco of the dancing saints at St. Gregory of Nyssa in San Francisco.

I will add a nameless but very real saint to this list. There is Tracey, dental hygenist near to where I live who is patient with my phobia of dentists and their tools. And she speaks with spontaneous joy of her life, her work, her husband and children, and about her parish and priest too. Having searched far and wide for a church home, she is radiant and eager to tell me about the Episcopal parish her family has joined since last I was there for my check-up. (Her husband even comes occasionally, especially after hearing that at the St. Patrick's Day celebration there was not only corned beef and cabbage and green iced cake but beer!) Has she done anything extraordinary? It does not seem so. Her love and care for her children and spouse is witnessed by the bulletin board in the dental office, plastered with photos of family trips, birthdays, and other holidays. The smiling faces took my mind off the exam and cleaning, just as her cheerful, warm professionalism did. The priest and parish came up in conversation. She knows I am a priest too, calls me "Father Mike." She does not discuss theology or church gossip, but especially important is her children's insistence on finding a church when off on vacation, now that they are receiving communion. "We want the bread," she tells me is their demand. There was no mention of a sermon or anything else liturgical, and I am not sure the name of Christ was mentioned. But there Christ surely was, in her joy, in her face, in her care for me and her other patients.

Paul Evdokimov must have recognized saints among the people in the hostels he headed. Mother Maria too, though sometimes exhausted by their sorrows and needs, saw saints in the faces of the unemployed, homeless, and discouraged in her hostels. She was able to call them, as we learned, "living icons," as they were censed by the deacon or priest at services. One wall of her chapel had a tapestry into which were stitched as well the names of all the departed mentioned by those in the hostel. All these ordinary women and men were precisely the invisible saints, those whose holiness was hidden because of its ordinary and diverse qualities. If anything, the examples of the extraordinary witnesses, the "prophets and friends of God" who look down on us from the walls of the church should encourage rather than discourage us in our living out the Gospel. They heard the same "good news" as we do, week after week, and were nourished with the same bread and cup, supported also by their communities as well as those who went before them. "Hidden holiness," in the end, is neither magical nor theoretical, but personal and interpersonal—an invitation to follow Christ where we are.

THE ALL TOO HUMAN FACTOR

After opening not only a food pantry at her own parish, one that fed 250 or more every Friday, and helping several other pantries to start up, Sara Miles encountered something new in her experience-rich life. To be sure, she had seen torture, destruction, death, and disease in her journalist days in Central America. She witnessed the urban underclass on both coasts and their lot—emotional illness, abandonment and abuse, hunger, lack of housing or medical care—as much degradation as anyone would want to inventory.

She had also encountered the living, risen Christ in the bread and cup offered freely to her the morning she drifted into St. Gregory. She had navigated her way through the details of ecclesiastical culture, confronting there some of the same things she knew well in politics: issues of gender and class prejudices and discrimination, obsession with rules and procedure. One of the priests noticed the polarization her plans for the food pantry were provoking in the beautiful, newly built church building where liturgy (as well as many other community gatherings) brought people together. As Sara herself describes it,

> [T]he food pantry itself takes place beneath the icon of the Dancing Saints. And around the altar . . . the theology of St. Gregory of Nyssa himself, and the example of the saints, informs everything we do at the food pantry. It is no accident that the sacrament of the brother and sister exerted such urgency on me . . . [I]t was already expressed in the worship and in the iconography, and the company of the saints includes every thief and whore and foreigner who comes to get food.

But when she tried to extend the food pantry—to her a logical extension of the Lord's table—to another day, Sunday, the Lord's day, in the afternoon, she hit a new wall of human messiness.

> I tried to argue that a Sunday pantry would bring in new people to volunteer and to get food, and some of them might join the church and change it in exciting and wonderful ways. "Why do we need to grow?" a longtime member challenged me. "We're fine just as we are." Things heated up. "What am I supposed to do if we have people coming to the door for the pantry and we're still having church?" Carol demanded of me one afternoon when I was lobbying a group of members about my proposal. "And what am I supposed to do if they start talking to me in Chinese or Russian?"[12]

Of course, she had directly encountered much of the nastiness of human nature many times before in her work. The head chef of one of the restaurants in which she worked had a standard and unprintable description for "the public," beginning with the word "mother." But now it seemed as if the dream of open communion and community in imitation of the Jesus who welcomed sinners and ate with them (as inscribed on the St. Gregory altar table) was being put aside because of inconvenience, messiness, and prejudice.

> A former Jesuit who sang in the choir took me aside, pointing out that I was hardly the first person to get excited about Jesus, then disappointed in his church. "Get over yourself," he said, not unkindly. "Welcome to Christianity. This is just the beginning."[13]

I hear echoes of my Carmelite Fr. Vincent in what the former Jesuit said to Sara. We may be looking for the kingdom of heaven and even trying to plant it here, where there is so much injustice and suffering. But it first has to be planted, and by suffering, in ourselves. Most of the best teachers in the Christian tradition make the explicit point, from Ambrose of Milan and Augustine to Martin Luther and his namesake, Martin Luther King Jr., and so many others, that we are at one and the same time sinners and redeemed, *simul justus et peccator*. The line demarcating good and evil, Sergius Bulgakov used to say, does not run outside but right through every one of us. The little brother of Jesus echoed this, but about the boundary of the church: it is within us. Hence the confessional, the sacrament of reconciliation and absolution and all the prayers before and during the liturgy in which we acknowledge ourselves to be sinful. The Eastern Church funeral liturgy affirms that "no one is without sin" except Christ.

The opposite of evil is not virtue, Evdokimov says many times, not just life according to rules but a life of seeking goodness, the Godness implanted in us. However one wants to put it, whether our being created in God's image and likeness, the indwelling or "seal" of the Spirit in us in baptism and confirmation/chrismation, the eating of the body and drinking the blood of the Lord in communion—no theological litany will be able to do away with the reality of sin, of human weakness, selfishness, deceit, delusion, hatred, and ugliness. What often appeared as ugly to Sara Miles was not only the long-term effects of evil and not even personal evil but the consequences of poverty, lack of care and education, the effects of all sorts of illness.

There are rules in many of the churches, about who can preside, usually only the ordained. There are also all kinds of rules about who may and may not receive, about the kind of bread and wine, even about what happens when these are spilled or regurgitated or go bad. There are many other prohibitions, obstacles, and contradictions built into church culture and religious life, and it can very well seem as though most are working against the very point of it all: communion with God and with each other. Which is really another way of describing holiness. But to quote Sara Miles once more, about a family meal and a lunch for volunteers and the Eucharist: "We're eating together. The door opens. It is never over."

GROWING UP IN AND GROWING OUT OF FAITH . . . AND FINDING GOD EVERYWHERE

I am lucky if I can believe in the resurrection ten minutes a month. I have doubt. But I have faith as well. My doubt fuels my faith. To me doubt connects to the mystery of God much more than certainty. The finite cannot contain the infinite. Once, a New York cab driver told me he was a former Muslim who now subscribes to no organized religion. "Religions are not directly from God," he said animatedly from the front seat. "Religion is finite. God is not finite, but infinite."

[On Easter, Rev.] Banks comes down out of the pulpit. *You need to be sure, Dearly Beloved, absolutely sure, Christ died for you. Hello somebody! Are you positive, absolutely positive?*

I slip from my pew and walk out of the church. On the sidewalk I think: Jesus himself was a doubter. He questioned the validity of the established religious order. He doubted his ability to do what he was asked to do and, on the cross, he doubted the loyalty of God.

Rather than certainty, I try to cultivate a sense of sacredness. Life is brutal, full of horror and violence. Life is beautiful, full of passion and joy. Both things are true at the same time. The paradox extends to my own being. I think of the words of Slovenian philosopher Slavoj Žižek, who calls Christianity the religion of Love and Comedy, à la Charlie Chaplin: "The point is not that, due to the limitations of his mortal sinful nature, man cannot ever become fully divine, but that due to the divine spark in him, man cannot become fully man."[14]

Even when it has had a bad start, even when it has turned toxic and one has had to walk away from it, the life of holiness, life in and with God, can be rediscovered. It is possible to return to faith once more and experience it, warts, wrinkles, ugliness, and all, to know that despite all these, as Dostoevsky said, that beauty does save. The daughter of a Lutheran pastor, writer Darcey Steinke's first few novels—*Up Through the Water, Jesus Saves, Suicide Blonde,* and *Milk*—would hardly suggest her as a person of spirit except in a rather extended, some might say twisted, way. In the novels there is a child abduction and torture, some very confused, depressed, and wild people, a lot of sex and drugs—not what most would consider spiritual searching. A PK (pastor's kid), hers was an explosive life after she left behind the mainstream Lutheran piety of her childhood—a sometimes very painful childhood and adolescence, living on the edge financially, her parents' marriage slowly dying. In her honest and most beautiful memoir, she guides us through her own adult journey—the struggle to make it as a writer, marriage, parenthood, and divorce, among other things. Possessed of her mother's good looks, a gifted writer dubbed a hipster-rocker-"it"-girl writer by reviewers, she now has a pre-teen daughter, plays in a band, loves to eat her way through New York's paradise of restaurants, and is in a good relationship. On her website and the cover of *Easter Everywhere* Darcey sports a mean tattoo—of the Sacred Heart no less. She now teaches at the New School.

But her memoir is no facile confession of the miseries that too much Jesus and church caused her—and her family. Her life was far more complicated than that, the experiences more bittersweet and forceful. Rather than shatter, her pilgrimage empowered and deepened her. For all of his inadequacies as a parent and a pastor, she is forgiving and generous to her father. There is a great deal of compassion for the one who suffered far more in their family, her mother. Skeptical about institutional religion, given her childhood immersion in it, and critical of literary genres, not the least of which would be the memoir, her story—and its meaning—are not easy to summarize. Her stories of being a PK in upstate New York and in parish and other professional stints in Connecticut, Kentucky, Pennsylvania, Virgina, and then New York City in the 1970s and '80s are at once hilarious and poignant. Like many in recent decades, she saw her parents' marriage disintegrate. Her father's vocation as a pastor, despite coming from a family full of Lutheran clergy, seems over time to have worn thin. He eventually earned credentials as a counselor and now is the head chaplain at a New York hospital. After divorce, he bounced through bad times in relationships, failing in one marriage to an Episcopal priest but eventually landing in a happy one with a woman Baptist pastor.

Darcey also rocked through life, professionally and personally. She worked as a reporter for *Spin* magazine, interviewing Kurt Cobain and Courtney Love and covering the David Koresh/Branch Davidian conflagration in Waco. Later the novels start coming, to wonderful reviews. She receives a writer's fellowship, confronts the end of her marriage, struggles with depression, financial uncertainty, with life as a single parent. Recent years bring her even more enthusiastic reviews of her writing. She is on the lecture circuit and is solicited for reviews of other leading writers in major venues. She does interviews, edits, and is featured in articles in the *New York Times* and elsewhere. Lest her memoir be thought of as a gloss on "Amazing Grace"—"I once was lost, but now am found"—Steinke's is an ambivalent journey with God. She both moves away from and toward the sacred. She knows way too much about religion. She has been part of a neighborhood evangelical church and also has become close to the Episcopal Community of the Holy Spirit and one Sister Leslie in particular.

> "Jesus is a drama queen," I say. "Every time I see a crucifix I feel like shouting, 'Get down off that cross, you big faker.'" Sister Leslie sits across from me smiling. She sees my agitation and seems amused by it. Her face is serene, though the eyes behind her glasses sparkle. I know she won't yell at me, but I'm pretty sure she won't agree with my assessment of Jesus.
>
> "This is a very good thing," she says, leaning forward. "You're finally feeling it. You're uncomfortable because you're up there pinned with Christ to the cross."

"Do you think God loves the rest of us as much as he loves Jesus?"
I ask. It's idiotic, I know, but my soul is tightly fisted around this concern. She leaves her chair and comes to me with a box of Kleenex, her
voice low and confident. "Absolutely," she says.[15]

Darcey Steinke has had a very interesting life, far more so than most,
mine for sure. And her voice is important here not because in her memoir
there was a "happy ending" when it comes to faith. I am not myself a PK,
but because I have had many years inside institutional religion, including
monastic life, seminary, and ordained ministry in more than one church
tradition, much of her experience rings clear and true. For all the damage
institutional religion can do to marriages, families, and a young person
growing up—this I have seen—there remains much that is good, true,
and beautiful, real, that still draws, pulls a person to God. I can't remember which of all those Carmelites in my past said it, but I hear it and have
clung to it: "Mostly they teach what to do. But you had better learn what
NOT to do. It is far more important."

It is not only the intellectual challenge and elegance of theological
texts, not just the beauty of liturgy, the marking of time passing by feasts
and fasts, the cavalcade of saints and their lives, that beckons. There is also
much left in the wake of "bad religion": discouragement, disillusionment,
doubt. The abuse of young people by clergy, the denial of wrongs, and the
concealment and protection of clerics has shaken the faith of many and
not just in the Roman Catholic Church. So too the fanatic condemna-
tion of others for holding the wrong position in the "culture wars" issues of
abortion, the rights of gay and homosexual persons, end of and quality of
life ethical issues, not to mention racism, war, and patriotism. Read Chris
Hedges and Gary Wills on these matters.[16] Faith can be creative, nurtur-
ing, beautiful, but many elements of its institutional apparatus and or-
ganization, its life and activity, can be destructive. To even put it this way,
for those who know, is quite an understatement.

Darcey Steinke captures and then holds out for us both the terrifying
textures and ineffable beauty of the life of holiness and of faith. A rousing
Easter sermon at her Brooklyn church provoked the doubt expressed in the
passage cited above. She spent time in class with parish members, following

Rick Warren's "purpose driven" way, shared lots of suppers, saw both the arrogance religion fosters as well as the quiet graciousness. But what she has to give us is exquisitely captured in what follows.

> I am not able to break with Christianity, no matter how uncomfortable I am with many of its current manifestations. Biblical imagery and Christ's message of forgiveness continue to haunt me, and I know my own redemption lies in Christian tenets, not in others' religious beliefs. Still, I can interpret the Bible in my own way. I can choose from the creeds that have been passed down, I can make my relationship to God my own, not one that is defined by church doctrine. And I can pray. Of all the gifts Sister Leslie has given me, her Aunt Birdie's Book of Common Prayer has been the most valuable. Thin colored ribbons stick out the bottom. I read Morning Prayer and sometimes Compline. The Compline antiphon is my favorite: *Guide us waking, oh Lord and guard us sleeping, that awake we may watch with Christ and asleep we may rest in peace.*
>
> Since I was a teenager I've lived in a world mostly devoid of divinity. But now I see the sacred includes not just churches but hospitals, highways, costume jewelry, garbage dumps, libraries, the cruising area of public parks. Also pet stores, subway platforms, Ferris wheels and rain storms.
>
> [M]y conflict, I see now, has not been with any individual church, but with church life in general, a life that began at my baptism in my father's shabby cottage [church] in Sylvan Beach. The idea of church still has a grip on my imagination, but I realize that what I thought was held only inside those walls—grace and divinity—are actually located directly and authentically inside myself. Church is not a set of rules or a specific building but a way of life.[17]

Darcey's pilgrimage, if one can call it that—and I think she would not balk at the description—is much more believable than the stereotypic religious "happy ending." It does not matter whether she and her daughter and her partner are in church every Sunday, whether she can affirm every line of the Apostles' or the Nicene Creed or the Small Catechism she surely studied for Lutheran confirmation. Like a lot of those whose voices we have listened to here, her holiness does not fit the profile sketched in Christian educational texts. I wonder the reaction to her Sacred Heart tattoo if she were to join us at our parish picnic—no, I don't wonder, actually I know what the reaction would be, and she as a PK would too! But she'd love the beer and sausages grilling, the sweetness of the people chowing down in the "liturgy after the liturgy," the ongoing feast of food and humanity among people of faith you find really nowhere else these days.

Darcey reminds us, with great honesty, that the search for God as an adventure should never end or grow stale. She assures us that we can be broken by religion but not irreparably, and that in the end it is possible to see the holy in so very many faces, and places . . . everywhere

A Saint in Darkness

Aside from Dr. Martin Luther King Jr. and possibly Pope John Paul II, there would seem to be no more universally recognized saint in our time than Mother Teresa of Calcutta. Moreso than the other two, in her own lifetime many called her a "living saint," and even the winning of the Nobel Peace Prize was a secular confirmation of her extraordinary work on behalf of the poorest of the poor and the dying, not only in India but, as her order spread, internationally. However, in 2007 the publication of her letters through the years to her spiritual directors caused a storm of controversy because of their contents. She appeared to have felt distant from God, even abandoned by him, unable to feel towards God any of the love she demonstrated for the suffering. Some even took statements from the letters to indicate that she had ceased believing in God! How could a "saint" feel this way?

In 1956 she wrote to her confessor: "The more I want him [God]— the less I am wanted." In a collection of letters to various spiritual fathers she also writes

> Such deep longing for God—and . . . repulsed—empty—no faith— no love—no zeal.—[The saving of] Souls holds no attraction—

Heaven means nothing—pray for me please that I keep smiling at Him in spite of everything . . . What do I labour for? If there be no God—there can be no soul—if there is no Soul then Jesus—You also are not true . . . I utter words of Community prayers—and try my utmost to get out of every word the sweetness it has to give—But my prayer of union is not there any longer—I no longer pray.[18]

Even the notices of the publication of these letters, known of for years, evoked a storm of comment, pro and con, and all kinds of musings on whether Mother Teresa's years of "spiritual dryness," as she called them, might disqualify her from canonization, that is, official recognition by the Catholic church as a saint. Some felt the use of St. John of the Cross's concept of *la noche oscura,* the "dark night of the soul," did not accurately describe what Mother Teresa recorded in numerous letters from virtually the start of her religious community's ministry to the sick, dying, and homeless in 1948. Previously, her experiences were of the sort that would appear to guarantee canonization. After nearly twenty years of teaching as a Sister of Loreto, she had a kind of mystical experience, on a vacation trip to Darjeeling, in which she heard Christ telling her to leave her comfortable life in an Irish religious community working with middle class children in order to serve the poorest and especially the outcasts of Indian society, sharing their own poverty, wearing the traditional *sari* rather than the Western habit. These messages were accompanied by an intense intimacy in prayer with Christ and culminated in a vision of him on the cross and conversation with the crucified Lord.

The letters, however, also show Mother Teresa to be a most enterprising mystic. Her arguments for the founding of a new community to minister to the poor are ingenious as well as incessant. We would say she pushed the envelope very hard, a rarity in the Roman Catholic Church, especially for a woman religious, in the late 1940s. But she succeeded not only with her local ordinary, Archbishop Périer, but with all the other ecclesiastical levels.

Yet it seemed that no sooner than she had obtained all the necessary permissions from ecclesiastical superiors and her order, having pleaded her case relentlessly, she experienced a radical loss of religious fervor and felt instead the sense only of God's absence. God abandons her, to remain for most of the rest of her life silent, absent. And her reaction was hardly indifference or stoic acceptance but, as these collected letters reveal, enormous pain, self-doubt, and self-loathing. She lost the ability to feel anything about God or her community or the work for which she gathered them, supposedly at Christ's direct command, with the church's blessing. Nevertheless she persisted in her work, grew the community over the decades, expanded its houses and work far beyond India. She became, in time, an unofficial voice of the Catholic Church, offering condemnations of legalized abortion, of cultural decadence and social unrest. She explicitly identified the source of modernity's ills, on many occasions, as a lack of faith and thus a lack of participation in worship, prayer, and good works.

To her bishop she wrote in March 1953: "Please pray specially for me that I may not spoil His work and that Our Lord may show Himself—for there is such terrible darkness within me, as if everything was dead. It has been like this more or less from the time I started 'the work.'"[19] One of her confessors—and these tried many strategies with her—suggested she address a letter to the same Christ who had told her to leave her old community and embark on the new one, with its work for the very poor:

> Lord, my God, who am I that You should forsake me? The Child of your Love—and now become as the most hated one—the one—You have thrown away as unwanted—unloved. I call, I cling, I want—and there is no One to answer—no One on Whom I can cling—no, No One.—Alone . . . Where is my Faith—even deep down right in there is nothing, but emptiness & darkness—My God—how painful is this unknown pain—I have no Faith—I dare not utter the words & thoughts that crowd in my heart—& make me suffer untold agony.
>
> So many unanswered questions live within me afraid to uncover them—because of the blasphemy—If there be God—please forgive me—When I try to raise my thoughts to Heaven—there is such convicting emptiness that those very thoughts return like sharp knives & hurt my very soul.—I am told God loves me—and yet the reality of darkness & coldness & emptiness is so great that nothing touches my soul. Did I make a mistake in surrendering blindly to the Call of the Sacred Heart?[20]

Only on a few occasions in the letters does she approach what could be called a loss of belief in God. Rather the portrait of her that the letters create is of a tormented soul, and in this, as commentators, including James Martin, have noted, she is in good company with quite a few of the saints, most notably the widely revered Thérèse of Lisieux.[21] An unsigned editorial in the *New York Times* calls her a "saint of darkness," and connects her with the American writer often thought of as an uncanonized saint, Flannery O'Connor.[22] Some of her critics, most notably Christopher Hitchens, jumped on these undoubtedly tortured letters of real emotion, set in the pious Catholic jargon of another era, writings Mother Teresa preferred to have destroyed because they were indications of her emotional illness, of the contradiction between her own spiritual suffering and the ruthless discipline and obduracy with which she governed the Missionary Sisters of Charity she founded. Yet the letters are a very powerful reminder of the *humanity* of holy women and men. Feeling close to God, even believing to hear his voice with a mission, does not spare one from the loss of such strong communion. It does not immunize a person to doubt, discouragement, perhaps even failure. Despite the Nobel Prize and her face on many publications, international recognition perhaps topped only by the pope, Mother Teresa suffered another very different, hidden path of holiness, and in so doing, like many others we have heard and met here, she gives us courage. Even without inner confidence and consolation, it is possible to love.

Holiness: In the End

Alexander Schmemann was known during his lifetime primarily as a specialist in liturgical theology, a reorientation of theological thinking he was largely responsible for shaping. Yet many knew him as a pastor, a confessor, a counselor with both a great mind and an immense heart. The publication of a selection of entries from his journals revealed even more—a man who himself struggled with church, with liturgy, with the hierarchy, with faith itself, as we heard earlier. These same entries also reveal him as one who loved good food and company and conversation and knew these were liturgy and contained the sacred—without having to define them as such.

Thus some of what he wrote in this entry from Good Friday, April 16, 1982, a year and a half before he died, is a startling revelation that he did not, could not, conform himself to traditional definitions and practices of piety. But in the simple questions with which he concludes, he sketches not only what was essential for himself in living a holy life but really what Evdokimov and all the rest tried to point out.

Yesterday, the Twelve Gospels [read at matins of Good Friday]. Before that, the Liturgy of the Mystical (Last) Supper [celebrated on Holy Thursday]—"I will not speak of Thy mystery to Thine enemies." Today, the Burial service and the immersion into "This is the Blessed Sabbath . . ." How many times in my life? Always in these days memory resurrects that time, that moment? that year? I do not know when it was all revealed in my life, when it became so beloved, so "absolutely desirable," and even though hidden in my heart, so decisive an event: rue Daru, the Cathedral of Alexander Nevsky in Paris, spring, home, youth, happiness. Then the key to everything was given me. As priest, as theologian, as author, as lecturer, I essentially witness only to "that." I almost never pray in the conventional sense; my spiritual life—as heroic feat, rule, spiritual guidelines—is zero, and if it exists, it does so as a constant consciousness, a subconscious feeling that all is elsewhere. On the other hand, deep down, I live only by it, or rather it lives in me.

Simple questions:

What does God want from us?

That we would love Him, accept Him as the source, the meaning, the goal of life: "the heart of my heart and my King . . ."

How can one come to love God? Where is the locus of this love?

In His self-revelation to us in the world and in life.

The summit and the fulfillment of this self-revelation is Christ.

Everything relates to Him. The Incarnation, the entrance into the world of nature, of time, of history is for Him.

It follows that love for God is Christ.

Joy in Him.

Love for Him.

The reference of everything to Him.

The gathering of everything in Him.

Life in Him, by the knowledge of Him in everything through the Holy Spirit.

The Church: the possibility and the gift of this love and life. Amen.[23]

I don't know if Fr. Schmemann and some of the others we have listened to would get along. I wonder what drinks or a dinner with them all would produce—a little taste of paradise or the all too human inability to play nicely together? Maybe because of his openness to the world and people around him on the train into New York City or on its streets, Schmemann would connect immediately with Darcey Steinke, with Sara Miles and Thomas Merton, not because they wrote spiritually interesting books, but because they were immensely gifted and interesting human beings, people who were alive in every way. Intuitively, I believe he would have respected Rowan Williams's efforts to keep speaking the Gospel, even when journalists are looking for a tantalizing sound bite about sex or Islam or the dark side of some cleric. And Rowan Williams's love for poetry and literature would be a joy they shared. Schmemann would surely have resonated with the honest questions raised by Kathleen Norris or Etty Hillesum. He enjoyed a great steak, a good bottle of wine, a quality film or novel, and, most of all, people who were passionate, who had something to say. Merton raved about Schmemann's first book published here. Schmemann must have known Mother Maria Skobtsova and Paul Evdokimov from many mutual acquaintances in the Russian Paris. He certainly met and knew Dorothy Day from Helen Iswolsky's Third Hour group, which met in New York City.

Despite some generational and cultural differences (I keep thinking of Darcey Steinke's tattoo and her years in the music scene) there is great kinship in vision, a camraderie in the experience and vision of these people I have brought together here. I do fantasize about an evening with them all together, of course, with good things to eat and plenty of wine. It would be a feast that you'd wish would just go on, the candles never burning out or the bottles running empty—without end. Can you imagine it? Thomas Merton and Alexander Schmemann, Dorothy Day, Elisabeth Behr-Sigel and Sara Miles, Simone Weil, Etty Hillesum and Alexander Men, Mother Maria Skobtsova and Darcey Steinke, Rowan Williams, Kathleen Norris and Paul Anderson. What a gathering, what conversations. But at the risk of this beginning to look like a writers' Chautauqua, a conference of spiritual literati and gliteratti, there would be room indeed for the quieter, simpler souls, such as Olga Michael, Joanna Reitlinger, Mother Teresa, or Charles de Foucauld. There would be room for us all. There are so many points of contact among accounts that could be cited here: the ruthless honesty of Schmemann's journal entries about religious fanatics, Etty Hillesum's many diary entries on the simple joy of being with God, even of sheltering him, or Merton's surgically precise critiques of piety and his eloquent reflections on searching for the true self. Perhaps some earthier scenes from Sara Miles's memoir in which the food she's preparing is fragrant or the hungry people coming to the food pantry are cursing and fighting. Or the kaleidoscope of faces and emotions, childhood to adulthood, in Darcey Steinke's memoir, with a little depression, anxiety, sex, and drugs, but also the joy of seeing one's child grow up—all mixed together. Darcey is quite right—Easter is everywhere, "God was calling my name," she wrote, "in restaurant bathrooms, on the Q train, from the water that streamed from the showerhead, and on the sidewalk along Flatbush Avenue."[24]

Holiness—the presence and pull of the Other, of God—does not behave according to the prim and proper rules of middle class life, much less the requirements of all too churchy and pious folk. Yet God is no stranger to the misery and messiness of war or the destructive grinding of poverty on body and mind. If all these persons of faith are to be believed, God remains present when marriages fall apart and as relationships emerge. The life of holiness can be lived in all these and countless other circumstances, when everything's like a wedding party or when the incessant friction of personalities rubbing turn people against each other. Many who write about the spiritual life or saints love to cite Merton's words:

It is true to say that for me sanctity consists in being myself and for you sanctity consists in being *your* self and that, in the last analysis, your sanctity will never be mine and mine will never be yours, except in the communism of charity and grace. For me to be a saint means to be myself. Therefore the problem of sanctity and salvation is in fact the problem of finding out who I am and of discovering my true self.[25]

But Merton goes on to say that our real identity is to be found in God. To find him, or better to be found by God, is to find who we really are.

Father Alexander Schmemann's journal entry, reproduced above, is a good way to end this look at holiness, holy lives lived in most ordinary and diverse ways. Holiness enables us to find God anywhere, everywhere, no matter who we are and what has happened to us—as Darcey Steinke and so many others have told us. As Darcey's church friend Pat says to Sister Leslie: "God communicates with us . . . in every form and pattern."[26] And in looking for God, in finding him, we find ourselves. And we find that everything and everyone is gathered in, referred back to him. Here is joy and peace.

Notes

Introduction

1. Martin Buber, *For the Sake of Heaven* (New York: Simon and Schuster, 1972), 24.

2. I will have more to say about Evdokimov throughout the book, but cf. Paula Huston, *By Way of Grace: Moving from Faithfulness to Holiness* (2003) and *The Holy Way: Practices for a Simple Life* (2007, both published Chicago: Loyola Press).

3. See my *Living Icons: Persons of Faith in the Eastern Church and Holiness in Our Time* (Notre Dame, IN: University of Notre Dame Press, 2002) and *Tradition Alive: On the Church and Christian Life in Our Time; Readings from the Eastern Church* (New York: Rowman & Littlefield, 2003).

4. Personal communication, October 16, 2007.

5. Paul Evdokimov, *Ages of the Spiritual Life,* revised trans. Michael Plekon and Alexis Vinogradov, (Crestwood, NY: St. Vladimir's Seminary Press, 1998). This is really a classic text on holiness in our time, but also see his essays collected in *In the World, of the Church: A Paul Evdokimov Reader,* eds. and trans. Michael Plekon and Alexis Vinogradov (Crestwood, NY: St. Vladimir's Seminary Press, 2001).

6. While one can cite some publications, a great deal of the information about the "emerging/emergent church" is to be found online. See, for example, the web site of Emergent Village, http://www.emergentvillage.com/. Scot McKnight provides an overview both of the literature as well as the principal figures in the

movement, such as Brian McLaren and Doug Pagitt, in his article "Five Streams of the Emerging Church," *Christianity Today* (February 2007), available online at http://www.christianitytoday.com/ct/2007/february/11.35.html. The most recent statement is Brian D. McLaren, *Everything Must Change: Jesus, Global Crises and a Revolution of Hope* (Nashville, TN: Thomas Nelson, 2007). Difficult to describe or define because of its diversity, the emerging/emergent movement does take seriously the profound differences in practice needed to be church in postmodern society and culture, such as turning worship to fellowship, and social outreach and communication. While remarkably minimalist in structure, its orientation to the Christian faith is traditional yet flexible.

7. Alexander Schmemann, *For the Life of the World: Sacraments and Orthodoxy* (1973), *Liturgy and Tradition* (1990), and *The Eucharist: Sacrament of the Kingdom* (1988, all published Crestwood, NY: St. Vladimir's Seminary Press). David Faberberg, *Theologia Prima: What Is Liturgical Theology?* (Chicago: Hillenbrand, 2004).

CHAPTER 1   Holiness and Holy People

1. Evdokimov, "Holiness in the Tradition of the Orthodox Church," in *In the World, of the Church,* 95–153.

2. *In the World, of the Church,* 149.

CHAPTER 2   Celebrities as Saints

1. Susan Ashbrook Harvey, "Holy Women, Silent Lives," *St. Vladimir's Theological Quarterly* 42, nos. 3 and 4 (1998): 403.

2. Keith Woodward, *Making Saints: How the Catholic Church Determines Who Becomes a Saint, Who Doesn't, and Why* (New York: Simon & Schuster, 1990).

3. Lawrence Cunningham, *A Brief History of Saints* (Oxford: Blackwell, 2004).

4. Michael Higgins, *Stalking the Holy: The Pursuit of Saint Making* (Toronto: House of Anansi, 2006).

5. Elizabeth Johnson, *Friends of God and Prophets: A Feminist Reading of the Communion of Saints* (New York: Crossroad, 1999).

6. Robert Ellsberg, *All Saints: Daily Reflections on Saints, Prophets, and Witnesses for Our Time* (New York: Crossroad, 1997), *The Saints' Guide to Happiness*

(New York: North Point Press, 2003), and *Blessed Among Women* (New York: Cross-road, 2005). Ellsberg has also edited several of the volumes in the Orbis Books series *Modern Spiritual Masters* and has been involved in choosing figures for this series.

7. Communità di Bose, *Il libro dei testimonio: Martirologio ecumenico* (Milan: Edizioni San Paolo, 2002).

8. Madonna Sophia Compton, with Maria Compton Hernandez and Patricia Campbell, *Women Saints: 365 Daily Devotions and Prayers* (New York: Cross-road, 2006).

9. Paul Elie, *The Life You Save May Be Your Own: An American Pilgrimage* (New York: Farrar, Straus & Giroux, 2003).

10. Carol Lee Flinders, *Enduring Grace: Living Portraits of Seven Women Mystics* (New York: HarperCollins, 1993), and *Enduring Lives: Portraits of Women and Faith in Action* (New York: Tarcher/Penguin, 2006).

11. James Martin, *My Life with the Saints* (Chicago: Loyola Press, 2005), and *Becoming Who You Are* (New York: Hidden Spring, 2006).

12. For a review of *100 Saints You Should Know,* see Ben Brantley, "Seeking Spiritual Bonds and Earthly Ones, Too," *New York Times,* September 19, 2007, available at http://theater2.nytimes.com/2007/09/19/theater/reviews/19saints.html.

13. See Gianna Baretta Molla, *Love Letters to My Husband* (Boston: Pauline Books & Media, 2002), and Giuliana Pelucchi, *Saint Gianna Baretta Molla: A Woman's Life, 1922–1962* (Boston: Pauline Books & Media, 2002).

14. Philip Zaleski, "The Saints of John Paul II," *First Things* 161 (March 2006): 28–32.

15. George P. Fedotov, *The Russian Religious Mind* (Belmont, MA: Nordland, 1975), 1:94–131.

16. Evdokimov, *Ages of the Spiritual Life,* 113–31.

17. On George Fedotov and the Paris Russian émigré scene see Antoine Arjakovsky, *La génération des penseurs religiuex de l'émigration russe* (Kiev: L'Ésprit et la Lettre, 2002). Also see George P. Fedotov, *The Collected Works of George P. Fedotov* (Belmont, MA: Nordland, 1960–75), and Paul Evdokimov, *Ages of the Spiritual Life* and "Holiness in the Tradition of the Orthodox Church."

18. Jim Forest, *Living with Wisdom* (Maryknoll, NY: Orbis, 1991); Michael Mott, *The Seven Mountains of Thomas Merton,* 2nd ed. (Boston: Houghton Mifflin,1993); Nadia Gorodetsky, *Saint Tikhon of Zadonsk* (Crestwood, NY: St. Vladimir's Seminary Press, 1976); Gillian Crow, *"This Holy Man": Impressions of Metropolitan Anthony* (Crestwood, NY: St. Vladimir's Seminary Press, 2005); Elisabeth Behr-Sigel, *Un moine de l'église d'orient: le père Lev Gillet* (Paris: Cerf, 1993); and

Olga Lossky, *Vers le jour sans déclin: une vie d'Élisabeth Behr-Sigel, 1907–2005* (Paris: Cerf, 2007).

19. For example, see Crow, *"This Holy Man,"* 241.

20. Thomas Craughwell, *Saints Behaving Badly* (New York: Doubleday, 2006).

21. Jonathan Wright, *God's Soldiers: Adventure, Politics, Intrigue, and Power; A History of the Jesuits* (New York: Doubleday, 2005), and Raymond A. Schroth, *The American Jesuits: A History* (New York: New York University Press, 2007).

22. John L. Allen Jr., "Torture Taints Spanish Martyr's Beatification," *All Things Catholic*, vol. 7, no. 6, October 12, 2007; see his web column at http://ncrcafe.org. In the case of Olaso, Allen uses the historical research of John N. Schumacher, *Revolutionary Clergy* (Quezon City: Ateneo de Manila University Press, 1981), and William Henry Scott, *Cracks in the Parchment Curtain* (Quezon City: New Day Publishers, 1982).

23. See the article on the Voice of Russia web site at http://www.ruvr.ru/main.php?lng=eng&q=12374&cid=115&p=01.06.2007.

24. See Vassily Maruschack, *The Blesssed Surgeon: The Life of St. Luke, Archbishop of Simferopol,* trans. Ann Vassilyeva and Nicholas Palis (Point Reyes, CA: Divine Ascent Press, 2002).

25. See the article on suite101.com, http://modern-war.suite101.com/article.cfm/evgeniy_rodionov_soldier_martyr.

26. See http://www.ruvr.ru/main.php?lng=eng&q=10744&cid=115&p=11.05.2007.

27. Klaas A. D. Smelik, ed., *Etty: The Letters and Diaries of Etty Hillesum* (Grand Rapids, MI: Eerdmans, 2002), 488–89.

28. Ibid., 586.

29. Ibid., 547.

30. See Alexandra Pleshoyano, "Etty Hillesum: For God and with God," *The Way* 44 (January 2005): 7–20, and Heather Walton, "Sex in the War: An Aestethics of Resistance in the Diaries of Etty Hillseum," *Theology and Sexuality* 12, no. 1 (2005): 51–61.

31. Rowan Williams, "Religious Lives," the Romanes Lecture, delivered at Oxford, November 18, 2004; the text can be found through the web site http://www.archbishopofcanterbury.org.

32. Etty Hillesum's diaries extend from March 8, 1941 through October 13, 1942, her letters adding to the written record.

33. Williams, "Religious Lives."

34. In a manner very similar to that of Etty Hillesum, the Ukranian Greek Catholic priest Emilian Kowcz, as the "pastor of Majdanek" camp, cared for all im-

prisoned with him, regardless of their religious or ethnic belonging. See Oleh Turij, ed., *Church of the Martyrs* (Lviv: Svichado, 2004).

35. Williams, "Religious Lives."

36. See the article "El Salvador Remembers Its Slain Prelate," on the Zenit web site, at http://zenit.org/article-22118?l=english.

37. Thomas Rosica, "Is There Room for God in Our World Today?" on the Zenit web site, at http://www.zenit.org/article-21438?l=english.

CHAPTER 3   God's Humanity and Humanity's Becoming Godly

1. Sergius Bulgakov, *The Bride of the Lamb,* trans. Boris Jakim (Grand Rapids, MI: Eerdmans, 2002), 479–80.

2. On the path of Bulgakov's theological career see Paul Valliere, *Modern Russian Theology: Bukharev, Soloviev, Bulgakov* (Grand Rapids, MI: Eerdmans, 2000). Also Antoine Arjakovsky, *Le géneration des penseurs religieux.*

3. A number of the essays in this collection are translated and gathered in Plekon, *Tradition Alive.*

4. Although this essay, "On the Question of the Apocatastasis of the Fallen Spirits," was an excursus in *The Bride of the Lamb,* it does not appear in Boris Jakim's translation. See Sergius Bulgakov, *Apocatastasis and Transfiguration,* trans. Boris Jakim (New Haven, CT: The Variable Press, 1995).

5. Alexander Schmemann, "Trois images," *Le messager orthodoxe* 57 (1972): 2–20.

6. Plekon, *Living Icons,* 19.

7. Henry Bettenson, ed., *Documents of the Christian Church,* 2nd ed. (Oxford: Oxford University Press, 1967), 51.

8. See Paul Valliere, *Modern Russian Theology.* Also see Vladimir Soloviev, *Lectures on Divine Humanity,* rev. trans. Boris Jakim (Hudson, NY: Lindisfarne Press, 1995). Although the term is often literally translated as "Godmanhood," Valliere makes a compelling case for the clearer, more idiomatic translation "the humanity of God." See *Modern Russian Theology,* 11–15.

9. Here and throughout, see Nicolas Afanasiev, *The Church of the Holy Spirit,* trans. Vitaly Permiakov, ed. Michael Plekon (Notre Dame, IN: University of Notre Dame Press, 2007).

10. Aidan Nichols, *Theology in the Russian Diaspora: Church, Fathers, Eucharist in Nikolai Afanas'ev (1893–1966)* (Cambridge: Cambridge University Press, 1989).

11. See Afanasiev, *The Church of the Holy Spirit,* 273–74.

12. *Service Book of the Holy Orthodox Catholic Apostolic Church,* trans. Isabel Florence (Hapgood, NY: Association Press, 1922), 314, 318, 331.

13. See the summary in French of Nicolas Ozoline's contribution at the October 13, 2007, conference on Afanasiev at St. Sergius Theological Institute in Paris: http://www.saint-serge.net/article.php3?id_article=145.

14. Afanasiev, *The Church of the Holy Spirit,* 14–15.

15. Paul Evdokimov, *Le Christ dans le pensée russe* (Paris: Cerf, 1986).

16. Thomas Merton. *The Collected Poems of Thomas Merton* (New York: New Directions, 1977), 363.

17. Ibid., 368.

18. Thomas Merton, *Seeds of Contemplation* (New York: New Directions, 1949), 10.

19. This icon is now at the Merton Center at Bellarmine University, in Louisville, Kentucky.

20. Thomas Merton, *The Sign of Jonas* (New York: Doubleday Image, 1956), 351–52.

21. Michael Mott, *The Seven Mountains of Thomas Merton* (Boston: Houghton Mifflin, 1984); Monica Furlong, *Merton: A Biography,* new rev. ed. (London: SPCK, 1995); William H. Shannon, *Thomas Merton: An Introduction* (Cincinnati: St. Anthony Messenger Press and Franciscan Communications, 2005); and Lawrence Cunningham, *Thomas Merton and the Monastic Vision* (Grand Rapids, MI: Eerdmans, 1999).

22. Sara Miles, *Take This Bread: A Radical Conversion* (New York: Ballantine, 2007).

23. Ibid., 151, 185–91, 211–16, 250–66.

CHAPTER 4   A Call to All, But Can There Be Models?

1. Richard J. Mouw, "Communion with the Saints," *The Christian Century,* "Faith Matters," May 15, 2007.

2. Michael Oleksa, *Orthodox Alaska: A Theology of Mission* (Crestwood, NY: St. Vladimir's Seminary Press, 1992), 205.

3. George Gray and Jan V. Bear, eds., *Portraits of American Saints* (Diocesan Council and Department of Missions, Diocese of the West, OCA, 1994). I have drawn on John Shimchick's portrait of Olga Michael, 84–90, for my discussion and for the quotations in this chapter.

4. The anonymous remembrance from which these words have been taken can be found on the web site OHoly.net; see http://oholy.net/stolga/mo_olga.html.

5. See the similar features in the lives of Saints Paraskeva and Euphemia in Compton, *Women Saints*, 298, 421–22.

6. Elizabeth (Michael) Rupert, "The Beauty of My Grandmother," available online at http://oholy.net/stolga/beauty.html.

7. The biographical account relies on Sister Joanna's own autobiographical sketch at http://www.crookedstane.com/sjp/autobiog.htm. See also Elizabeth Robert's work at http://www.crookedstane.com/sjp/biog.htm and her forthcoming translation of the correspondence between Joanna Reitlinger and Fr. Alexander Men, *The Wise Sky*; see her "The Wise Sky: The Letters between Father Alexander Men (1935–1990) and Sister Joanna (Julia) Reitlinger (1898–1988)," *Theandros* 1 (2003), available at: www.theandros.com/wisesky.html. Also see the album of Sister Joanna's work assembled by Nikita Struve (who wrote the biographical essay, with Bronislava Popova, who did an essay on Sister Joanna's artistic context). See http://www.crookedstane.com/sjp/context.htm, and the volume, *РЕЙТЛИНГЕР Ю.Н. Художественное наследие* (Paris: YMCA Press, 2006).

8. Riassophor is the traditional descriptor for the first level of monastic life, simply, "one who wears the monastic habit."

9. See "The Final Days of Father Sergius Bulgakov, a Memoir by Sister Joanna Reitlinger" in Bulgakov, *Apocatastasis and Transfiguration*, 32–53.

10. Elizabeth Roberts is documenting this in her translation of the letters exchanged between Sister Joanna and Fr. Alexander.

11. I use here Mike Whitton's translations of Ella Layevskaya's and Dmitri Baranov's memoirs, graciously provided by Brother Christopher Mark of the Anglican monastic community the Servants of the Will of God in Crawley Down. Also see *Le messager orthodoxe* 136 (2001), which contains a French version of Sister Joanna's autobiographical sketch as well as a memoir of her from Nadine Fuchs and some excerpts from Sister Joanna's letters.

12. A number of these later icons are reproduced in the previously cited YMCA Press album of her works.

13. Elisabeth Behr-Sigel, "Orthodox Theological Formation in the Twenty-first Century: The Tasks Involved," in *Discerning the Signs of the Times: The Vision of Elisabeth Behr-Sigel*, ed. Michael Plekon and Sarah Hinlicky (Crestwood, NY: St Vladimir's Seminary Press, 2001), 13–14, 18–19.

14. Elisabeth Behr-Sigel, *Lev Gillet: The Monk of the Eastern Church*, trans. Helen Wright (Oxford: Fellowship of St. Alban and St. Sergius, 1999).

15. Elisabeth Behr-Sigel, *Alexandre Boukharev: un théologien de l'église orthodoxe russe en dialogue avec le monde moderne* (Paris: Beauchesne, 1977). Also see Plekon and Hinlicky, *Discerning the Signs,* 41–80.

16. See the introduction to Elisabeth Behr-Sigel, *The Ministry of Women in the Church,* trans. Steven Bigham (Crestwood, NY: Oakwood/SVS Press, 1991; 2nd ed., 2004), 1–24.

17. We included it in the anthology, *Discerning the Signs of the Times,* 5–11 as well as Lyn Breck's biographical essay, "Nearly a Century of Life," 125–36.

18. See http://christophe.levalois.free.fr/fichier/Ent_Olga_Lossky.pdf. Also see Lossky, *Vers le jour sans déclin.*

19. Plekon and Hinlicky, *Discerning the Signs,* xi.

20. The vision and support of Metropolitan Evlogy for so many key figures— Frs. Sergius Bulgakov, George Florovsky, Lev Gillet, Basil Zenkovsky, and Nicolas Afanasiev and St. Mother Maria Skobtsova, among others—is not so startling given his earlier influential role in the years leading up to and culminating in the important reforming Moscow Council of 1917–18. See his memoirs, *Le chemin de ma vie,* trans. Pierre Tschnesakoff (Paris: Presses Saint Serge, 2005); also see the recent, masterful study by Hyacinthe Destivelle, *Le concile de Moscou (1917–1918)* (Paris: Cerf, 2006).

21. Brandon Gallaher, "Catholic Action: Ecclesiology, the Eucharist and the Question of Intercommunion in the Ecumenism of Sergii Bulgakov" (MDiv thesis, St Vladimir's Theological Seminary, 2003). Also see his "Bulgakov's Ecumenical Thought [Part I]," *Sobornost* 24, no. 1 (2002): 24–55, and "Bulgakov and Intercommunion [Part II]," *Sobornost* 24, no. 2 (2002): 9–28.

22. Elisabeth Behr-Sigel, "La sophiologie du Père Serge Boulgakoff," *Revue d'histoire et de philosophie religieuses* 19, no. 2 (1939): 130–48, republished in *Le messager orthodoxe* 57, no. 1, (1972): 21–48.

23. Elisabeth Behr-Sigel, *Prière et sainteté dans l'Église russe* (Paris: Cerf, 1950; rev. ed. Bégrolles: Bellefontaine, 1982).

24. Elisabeth Behr-Sigel, "Notes sur l'idée russe de la sainteté d'après les saints canonisés de l'Église russe," *Revue d'histoire et de philosophie religieuses* 13 (1933): 537–54; "Études d'hagiographie russe," *Irénikon* 12 (1935): 242–54; 13 (1936): 25–37; 14 (1937): 363–77. See in addition Fedotov, *Collected Works.* Also in this vein see two Evdokimovs close to Elisabeth Behr-Sigel: Paul Evdokimov, *Le Christ dans le pensée russe* (Paris: Cerf, 1986); and Michel Evdokimov, *Le Christ dans la tradition et la littérature russe* (Paris: Desclée, 1996), *La prière des chrétiens de Russie* (Chambray: C.L.D., 1988), and *Pèlerins russes et vagabonds mystiques* (Paris: Cerf, 2004).

25. Le Carmel de Saint-Rémy/Stânceni, ed. *Toi, suis-moi: Mélanges offerts en hommage à Élisabeth Behr-Sigel par la Fraternité Saint-Élie* (Iafli: Editura Trinitas, 2003), 25–44. The bibliography, which extends only to 2003, includes seven books, over one hundred articles, and another two hundred essays and reviews.

26. Elisabeth Behr-Sigel, *The Place of the Heart*, trans. Stephen Bigham (Crestwood, NY: Oakwood/St Vladimir's Seminary Press, 1992).

27. Behr-Sigel, *The Ministry of Women in the Church*.

28. Elisabeth Behr-Sigel and Kallistos Ware, *The Ordination of Women in the Orthodox Church* (Geneva: World Council of Churches, 2000).

29. Lossky, *Vers le jour san déclin*, 99–262.

30. Elisabeth Behr-Sigel, "The Ordination of Women: A Point of Contention in Ecumenical Dialogue," *St Vladimir's Theological Quarterly* 48, no. 1 (2004): 49–66.

31. Jim Forest's set of photos is available at http://www.flickr.com/photos/jimforest/sets/164907/; the photo of Elisabeth is at http://www.flickr.com/photos/jimforest/67912043/in/set-164907.

32. I have a last letter from her from the UK dated November 12, 2005, just two weeks before her death. In it typically she laments a number of things including not being able to present the lecture in Oxford, as well as her diminishing energy and age ("I am a tired old woman"). But she also discussed, as usual, various publishing projects, as well as unfortunate situations in the churches.

33. Plekon and Hinlicky, *Discerning the Signs*, 76–77. Also see Valliere, *Modern Russian Theology*.

34. Plekon and Hinlicky, *Discerning the Signs*, 92–93.

35. "The Ordination of Women: Also a Question for the Orthodox Churches," in Behr-Sigel and Ware, *The Ordination of Women in the Orthodox Church*, 43.

36. Behr-Sigel, *Lev Gillet*, 129.

37. Plekon and Hinlicky, *Discerning the Signs*, 12–14.

38. Sarah Hinlicky Wilson, "Woman, Women, and the Priesthood in the Thought of Elisabeth Behr-Sigel" (PhD dissertation, Princeton Theological Seminary, 2007).

39. Paul B. Anderson, *No East or West* (Paris: YMCA Press, 1983), 1.

40. Ibid., 3.

41. Ibid., 14–23.

42. Ibid., 27–35.

43. Ibid., 58–65.

44. Ibid., 43–55. Also see Arjakovsky, *La géneration des penseurs religieux*, 109–65, 221–38.

45. Anderson, *No East or West*, 58–59, 73–78.
46. Ibid. 56.
47. Ibid., 48–55.
48. Ibid., 95–100, 137–38, 148.
49. Ibid., 101–5.
50. Ibid., 151–57
51. Ibid., 157.

CHAPTER 5   Equipment for Holiness: Liturgy in Life, as Life

1. Anthony Bloom, *Beginning to Pray* (Mahwah, NJ: Paulist Press, 1982), *Living Prayer* (Springfield, IL: Templegate, 1989), and *Meditations on a Theme: A Spiritual Journey* (New York: Continuum, 2004).

2. Communità di Bose, *Il libro dei testimoni.*

3. See for example *Evangelical Lutheran Worship,* Leader's Desk Edition (Minneapolis, MN: Augsburg-Fortress, 2006), 57–59. Also see a Catholic website that includes holy women and men from other traditions: http://www.santiebeati.it/index.html.

4. "By Jacob's Well," originally published in 1930 in Russian, and available in English in the *Journal of the Fellowship of St. Alban and St. Sergius* (1933), is contained in Plekon, *Tradition Alive*, 51–66.

5. See Gordon W. Lathrop, *Holy Things: A Liturgical Theology* (1995) and *Holy People: A Liturgical Ecclesiology* (2006; both published Minneapolis, MN: Augsburg-Fortress).

6. On icons in the Eastern Church, their relationship to the feasts, liturgy, and their veneration, see Leonid Ouspensky and Vladimir Lossky, *The Meaning of Icons* (1983); also the catechetical volumes, Catherine Aslanoff, ed., *The Incarnate God,* 2 vols. (1995), and *The Living God,* 2 vols. (1996; all published Crestwood, NY: St. Vladimir's Seminary Press).

7. Maria Skobtsova, *Mother Maria Skobtsova: Essential Writings,* trans. Richard Pevear and Larissa Volokhonsky (Maryknoll, NY: Orbis, 2003), 81.

8. Ibid., 80–81.

9. Alexander Schmemann, *Introduction to Liturgical Theology* (1996), *For the Life of the World: Sacraments and Orthodoxy* (1973), *Of Water and the Spirit* (1974), *Liturgy and Life* (1974), *The Eucharist Sacrament of the Kingdom* (1988), and *Liturgy and Tradition* (1990; all published Crestwood, NY: St. Vladimir's Semi-

nary Press). Also see Aidan Kavanagh, *On Liturgical Theology* (Collegeville, MN: Pueblo/Liturgical Press, 1984), and David W. Fagerberg, *Theologia Prima.*

10. Jim Forest, *Silent as a Stone* (Crestwood, NY: St. Vladimir's Seminary Press, 2007).

11. Skobtsova, *Essential Writings,* 81–83.

12. Natalie Ermolaev, "Motherhood, Mariology, and Modernism: Maria Skobstova and Russian Poetry and Theology" (PhD diss., Columbia University, 2008).

13. Paul Evdokimov, "God's Absurd Love and the Mystery of His Silence," in *In the World, of the Church,* 175–94.

14. Skobtsova, *Essential Writings,* 70–71.

15. Aidan Kavanagh, *Confirmation: Origins and Reform* (Collegeville, MN: Pueblo/Liturgical Press, 1992).

16. Skobtsova, *Essential Writings,* 161.

17. Ibid., 185.

18. As quoted from John Chrysostom (Homily 20, 3 on 2 Cor 10:5), in J.-M.-R. Tillard, *Flesh of the Church, Flesh of Christ: At the Source of the Ecclesiology of Communion,* trans. Madeline Beaumont (Collegeville, MN: Pueblo/Liturgical Press, 2001).

19. Afanasiev, *The Church of the Holy Spirit;* John Zizioulas, *Being as Communion* (Crestwood, NY: St. Vladimir's Seminary Press, 1985), and *Communion and Otherness* (New York: T&T Clark/Continuum, 2006).

20. Robert Farrar Capon, *An Offering of Uncles: The Priesthood of Adam and the Shape of the World* (New York: Sheed & Ward, 1967), and *The Supper of the Lamb: A Culinary Reflection* (New York: Doubleday, 1969).

21. Sara Miles, *Take This Bread,* xiii.

22. Ibid., xiv–xv.

23. Alexander Schmemann, *Church, World, Mission* (Crestwood, NY: St. Vladimir's Seminary Press, 1979), 216. A completely different approach to Schmemann, that of his pastoral theology, is taken by William C. Mills, *Church, World, Kingdom: The Sacramental Foundations of Alexander Schmemann's Pastoral Theology* (Chicago: Hillenbrand Press, 2008).

24. Alexander Schmemann, *The Journals of Father Alexander Schmemann, 1973–1983,* ed. and trans. Juliana Schmemann (Crestwood, NY: St. Vladimir's Seminary Press, 2000), 284–85. This is only a selection of journal entries, unfortunately edited by family members, with many very powerful ones omitted. We still wait for a more open, thorough account of both Schmemann's life and thinking.

25. Ibid., 294–95.

26. Ibid., 295.

27. Ibid., 315.

28. Ibid., 316–17.

29. Ibid., 321.

30. For New Skete, see Monks of New Skete, *In the Spirit of Happiness* (New York: Little, Brown, 1999); and for Bose, see Mario Torcivia, *Il segno di Bose* (Casale Monferrato: Piemme, 2003). Also see Charles Cummings, OCSO, *Monastic Practices* (1986), and Patrick Hart, ed., *A Monastic Vision for the Twenty-first Century* (2006, both published Kalamazoo, MI: Cistercian Publications/Liturgical Press).

31. Alexander Schmemann, *The Mission of Orthodoxy* (Ben Lomond, CA: Conciliar Press, 1994), 21–23.

32. Valliere, *Modern Russian Theology.*

33. Over half the essays of this 1937 anthology appear in translation in Plekon, *Tradition Alive.*

34. See their web sites: http://www.newskete.com/ and http://www-1 .monasterodibose.it.

35. Among his many publications, see Enzo Bianchi, *Il corvo di Elia: introduzione all preghiera* (1972), *Pregare la Parola: introduzione all lectio divina* (1974), *Amici del Signore* (1990), *Il radicalismo cristiano* (1980; all published Milan: Gribaudi), *Le parole della spiritualità* (Milan: Rizzoli, 1999), and *Altrimenti: Credere e narrare il Dio dei cristiani* (Casale Monferrato: Piemme, 1995).

36. See Piorangelo Sequeri, "'Beata solitudo'? Monachesimo cristiano e città postmoderna," in *Un monastero alle porte della città,* 63–75 (Milan: Vita e pensiero, 1999). Enzo Bianchi's words are from "Monasticism, the Heritage of the Past and the Overture to the Future," presented at a conference held for the prior of Bose at Congrès d'études monastiques du Pontificio Ateneo Sant'Anselmo à Rome on June 1, 2002, trans. Matthias Wirz. Also see. E. Bianchi, "Le monachisme au seuil de l'an 2000," *Collectanea cisterciensia* 61 (1999): 3–21, and "Quelle spiritualité les moines offrent-ils à l'Église?" in *Si tu savais le don de Dieu: La vie religieuse dans l'Église,* 238–81 (Brussels: Lessius, 2001).

37. For a fuller expression of the vision of New Skete, see Monks of New Skete, *In the Spirit of Happiness.*

38. Monks of New Skete, *Monastic Typikon* (Cambridge, NY: New Skete, 1988), 2

39. Ibid., 4–5, 10.

40. André Louf, *The Cistercian Way* (1984), *Tuning in to Grace* (1992), *Grace Can Do More* (2002), *The Way of Humility* (2007; all published Collegeville, MN: Cistercian Publications), and *Teach Us to Pray* (Boston: Cowley, 1992).

CHAPTER 6   Holiness, Hidden, Ordinary, Yet New

1. Simone Weil, *Waiting for God,* trans. Emma Craufurd (New York: Harper Colophon, 1973), 98–99.

2. Simone Pétrement, *Simone Weil: A Life* (New York: Schocken, 1988), and Francine du Plessix Gray, *Simone Weil,* Penguin Lives (New York: Lipper, 2001).

3. Among Simone Weil's writings see: *On Science, Necessity and the Love of God,* ed. Richard Rees, (Oxford: Oxford University Press, 1968), *Gravity and Grace,* ed. Gustave Thibon, trans. Emma Craufurd (New York: Putnam, 1952), and *The Need for Roots* (London: Routledge, 1995).

4. Gustave Thibon and Jean-Marie Perrin, *Simone Weil as We Knew Her* (London: Routledge, 2004).

5. Jillian Becker, "Simone Weil: A Saint for Our Time?" *New Criterion* 21 (March 2002): 15–23.

6. Weil, *Waiting for God,* 71.

7. Eberhard Bethge, *Dietrich Bonhoeffer* (New York: Harper & Row, 1977), 555–59.

8. Weil, *Waiting for God,* 47–48.

9. Ibid., 97.

10. Oliver Clément, *Orient-Occident: deux Passeurs, Vladimir Lossky, Paul Evdokimov* (Geneva: Labor et fides, 1985).

11. Evdokimov, *Ages of the Spiritual Life,* 241–42.

12. Thomas Merton, *Asian Journal,* ed. Naomi Burton, Patrick Hurt, and James Laughlin (New York: New Directions, 1975), 338

13. Thomas Merton, *Day of a Stranger* (Salt Lake City: Gibbs M. Smith, 1981), 41.

14. Thomas Merton, *Conjectures of a Guilty Bystander* (New York: Doubleday-Image, 1968), 156–58.

15. See the original journal entry in *A Search for Solitude,* The Journals of Thomas Merton, vol. 3, ed. Lawrence S. Cunningham (San Francisco: HarperSan Francisco, 1996), 181–82. Also see the discussion in Michael Mott, *The Seven Mountains of Thomas Merton* (Boston: Houghton-Mifflin, 1984), 310–13.

16. Thomas Merton, *The Springs of Contemplation: A Retreat at the Abbey of Gethsemani* (Notre Dame, IN: Ave Maria Press, 1992), 37.

17. Lev Gillet, *In Thy Presence* (Crestwood, NY: St. Vladimir's Seminary Press, 1977). See also Elisabeth Behr-Sigel, *Lev Gillet.*

18. Kathleen Norris, *Dakota: A Spiritual Geography* (New York: Houghton Mifflin, 1993), *The Cloister Walk* (New York: Riverhead, 1997), *The Quotidian*

Mysteries (Mahwah, NJ: Paulist Press, 1998), *Amazing Grace* (New York: Riverhead, 1999), and *The Virgin of Bennington* (New York: Putnam, 2001).

19. These excerpts are from Kathleen Norris's talk, "Holy Realism Living Life as It Matters," from the April 28–29, 2003, Trinity Institute conference, "Shaping Holy Lives." The text is at http://www.explorefaith.org/holiness/life1.html.

20. Anthony the Great, in *The Desert Christian: The Sayings of the Desert Fathers,* trans. Benedicta Ward (New York: Macmillan, 1975), 6. The *Trisagion* is an ancient prayer found in both the Eastern and Western churches: "Holy God, Holy Mighty, Holy Immortal, have mercy on us."

21. Anonymous, *The Diveyevo Chronicles,* trans. Ann Shukman, forthcoming.

22. Evdokimov, *In the World, of the Church,* 129–39.

23. Paul Evdokimov, *The Sacrament of Love,* trans. Anthony P. Gythiel and Vicoria Steadman (Crestwood, NY: St. Vladimir's Seminary Press, 1995), 92.

24. In addition to Dietrich Bonhoeffer, *Letters and Papers from Prison* (New York: Macmillan, 1971), also see *The Cost of Discipleship* (New York: Collier/Macmillan, 1963), *No Rusty Swords* (New York: Harper & Row, 1965), *The Way to Freedom* (New York: Harper & Row, 1966), *Ethics* (New York: Macmillan, 1965), *Life Together* (New York: Harper & Row, 1954), as well as *Dietrich Bonhoeffer: Works,* 16 vols. (Minneapolis, MN: Augsburg-Fortress, 1998–2007).

25. Bonheoffer, *Letters and Papers from Prison,* 369.

26. Rowan Williams, sermon delivered February 5, 2006, at the Dietrich Bonhoeffer centenary service, St. Matthaus Church, Berlin; the text can be found through the web site http://www.archbishopofcanterbury.org.

27. Noah Feldman, "Orthodox Paradox," *New York Times Sunday Magazine,* July 22, 2007, 40–45.

28. Williams, sermon of February 5, 2006.

29. Sophie Koulomzin, *Our Church and Our Children* (1975), and *Many Worlds: A Russian Life* (1980; both published Crestwood, NY: St. Vladimir's Seminary Press).

30. Even among voices that are sometimes cynical and quite critical, such as those in the "Almost Holy" thread on the equally irreverent but serious Busted Halo website, are concerned with issues of holiness. See http://www.bustedhalo.com.

31. See Charles de Foucauld, *Charles De Foucauld: Writings,* Modern Spiritual Masters, ed. Robert Ellsberg (Maryknoll, NY: Orbis Books, 1999); Jean-Jacques Antier, *Charles De Foucauld,* trans. Julia Shirek Smith (San Francisco: Ignatius Press, 1999); Jean-François Six, *The Spiritual Autobiography of Charles De Foucauld* (Ijamsville, MD: Word Among Us Press, 2003).

32. Personal correspondence, August 2007. This essay is the source of the subsequent quotations concerning Charles and the little brothers and sisters.

33. "Nazareth" for Charles de Foucauld meant the hidden life of Jesus, in his family, work, and religious life of the synagogue, throughout the thirty years before his public ministry.

34. Jean-Jacques Pérennès, *A Life Poured Out* (Maryknoll, NY: Orbis, 2007).

CHAPTER 7 Differences

1. Dorothy Day, *Dorothy Day: Selected Writings,* ed. Robert Ellsberg (Maryknoll, NY: Orbis Books, 1992), 215–16. Also see Jim Forest, *Love Is the Measure: A Biography of Dorothy Day* (Maryknoll, NY: Orbis Books, 1994), and her autobiography, *The Long Loneliness* (New York: Harper & Row, 1952).

2. Rosalie G. Riegle, ed., *Dorothy Day: Portraits by Those Who Knew Her* (Maryknoll, NY: Orbis Books, 2003), 193 ff.

3. Riegle, *Portraits,* 196; Dorothy Day, *The Duty of Delight: The Diaries of Dorothy Day,* ed. Robert Ellsberg (Marquette, WI : Marquette University Press, 2008).

4. Day, *The Duty of Delight,* 164.

5. See William Hart McNichols's icons reproduced in Megan McKenna, *Mary, Mother of All Nations* (2000), Daniel Berrigan, *The Bride: Images of the Church* (2000), and John Dear, *You Will Be My Witnesses: Saints, Prophets, and Martyrs* (2006; all published Maryknoll, NY: Orbis Books).

6. C. J. Tarasar, ed., *Orthodox America, 1794–1976: Development of the Orthodox Church in America* (Syosett, NY: Orthodox Church in America, Department of History and Archives, 1975), 228–33.

7. Dag Hammarskjöld, *Markings,* trans. Leif Sjöberg and W. H. Auden (New York: Knopf, 1964).

8. Didier Rance, *Prier 15 jours avec les martyrs chrétiens du XXe siècle* (Montrouge: Nouvelle cité, 2003), *Un siècle de témoins: les martyrs du XXe siècle* (Paris: Sarment, 2000), and *Chrétiens du Moyen-Orient: témoins de la croix* (Mareil-Marly: Bibliothèque AED, 1990).

9. For the icons of Ivanka Kripiakevych-Dymyd, see the web site of Ukrainian Catholic University, specifically in the background of pictures found at http://www.ucu.edu.ua/ukr/current/chronicles/slideshow/exposition_d_icones/.

10. Richard Fabian, "Who Are These Like Stars Appearing," *God's Friends* 8, no. 2 (1997) available online at http://godsfriends.org. In the same volume, see

Donald Schell, "The Dancing Saints," for a list and very brief biographies of most of the individuals depicted in the fresco.

11. Enzo Bianchi, *La differenza cristiana* (Torino: Giulio Einaudi, 2006). Also see his *Una vita differente* (Milano: Cinisello Balsamo, 2005).

12. Miles, *Take This Bread*, 253.

13. Ibid., 254.

14. Darcey Steinke, *Easter Everywhere: A Memoir* (New York: Bloomsbury, 2007), 218–19.

15. Ibid., 192.

16. Gary Wills, *Head and Heart: American Christianities* (New York: Penguin, 2007); Chris Hedges, *War Is a Force That Gives Us Meaning* (New York: Public Affairs, 2002), *American Fascists: The Christian Right and the War on America* (New York: Free Press, 2007), and *I Don't Believe in Atheists* (New York: Free Press, 2008).

17. Steinke, *Easter Everywhere*, 220.

18. Mother Teresa, *Mother Teresa: Come Be My Light; The Private Writings of the "Saint of Calcutta,"* ed. Brian Kolodiejchuk (New York: Doubleday, 2007).

19. Ibid., 149.

20. Ibid., 186.

21. James Martin, "A Saint's Dark Night," *New York Times,* August 29, 2007.

22. Editorial, "A Saint of Darkness," *New York Times,* September 5, 2007.

23. Schmemann, *Journals of Father Alexander Schmemann*, 324.

24. Steinke, *Easter Everywhere*, 178.

25. Merton, *Seeds of Contemplation,* 10; or Thomas Merton, *New Seeds of Contemplation* (New York: New Directions, 1961), 31.

26. Steinke, *Easter Everywhere*, 222.

Index

Michael Plekon

is a professor in the department of sociology/anthropology
and the Program in Religion and Culture at Baruch College,
City University of New York. He is also an ordained priest
in the Orthodox Church in America.